THE GUINNESS BOOK OF
AIR FORCE BLUNDERS

GEOFFREY REGAN

GUINNESS PUBLISHING

Design: Cathy Shilling

The Work Copyright © 1996 Geoffrey Regan

The right of Geoffrey Regan to be identified as the Author of this Work has been asserted in accordance with the Copyright, Design and Patents Act 1988.

First published in 1996 by Guinness Publishing Ltd.
Reprint 10 9 8 7 6 5 4 3 2 1 0

This Publication Copyright © 1996 Guinness Publishing Ltd.
33 London Road, Enfield, Middlesex

This book is also published as *The Guinness Book of Flying Blunders*

'GUINNESS' is a registered trademark of Guinness Publishing Ltd.

Printed and bound in Great Britain by The Bath Press, Bath.

A catalogue record for this book is available from the British Library.

ISBN 0-85112-607-3

Dedicated to the memory of my father
Captain G.A.Regan, M.B.E.
(R.F.C. 1914–1918
A.T.A. 1940–1945)

CONTENTS

INTRODUCTION

It is ironic that aerial warfare, the most recent development in the area of human conflict, has in such a short time become not only the most destructive of all 'killing fields' but has actually come to challenge man's very existence on this planet. Its very seriousness has set alarm bells ringing for myself, as a chronicler of military blunders. Any author setting out to examine the blunders of aerial warfare faces a dilemma. How do you present such information in an entertaining and sometimes humorous way without trivializing it? The approach that I have adopted is to 'tell it straight' with as little embellishment as possible. Where I have encountered eccentrics I have allowed their eccentricity to rule my pen. Where I have met strange designs for planes I have tried to do justice to their strangeness and rejoice in their variety. But where I have met incompetence in all its stark simplicity, I have not attempted to embroider nor to qualify it. My research has revealed that aviation blunders have tended to have the most dreadful consequences for humanity. In an era of 'total war', aircraft may have made enormous strides from the simplicity of the reconnaissance scout plane and the hand-held bomb, to the nuclear deterrent and the smart weapons of American Stealth bombers, yet those who make the decisions in air warfare and have now a far greater responsibility than any military or naval planners have ever had before, are no more immune to blundering. Aerial warfare has removed the walls and moats with which mankind has protected itself from armies and navies throughout history. Civilians can no longer be considered 'non-combatants'. Every man, woman and child in Britain – or Germany – during the Second World War was as much in the front line as any soldier, sailor or airman. Even a 'moat' as large as the English Channel was successfully crossed by the Zeppelin airships of 1914. And it was the fear of a repetition of this German bomber threat in the late 1930s – on a vastly magnified scale – that drove the British government of Neville Chamberlain to panic in 1939. Fear of the bomber and the effect that it would have on the urban centres of Britain conditioned the way that His Majesty's Government pursued its policies and yet neither made them abjure war nor commit themselves to civilian defence against air attack. Instead, in Britain, the politicians – having committed their people to war against Germany – simply told the millions of ordinary folk that large numbers of them were doomed and would be killed by overwhelming aerial attacks from bombers that could not be stopped. No more enormously disruptive – and ultimately ridiculous – advice has ever been given by any democratically-elected government. Its effect on British morale was more damaging than the reality of the Blitz was ever to be.

Yet public attitudes towards military aircraft have not always been like that. At one stage, at the turn of the century, the art of making planes – beloved of every schoolboy or origamist – involved the sort of imaginative challenge that attracted the more eccentric inventor. From Igor Sikorski's flying 'tramcar bomber', named after a hero of Russian myth to Mr W.G. Tarrant of Byfleet with his mighty 'Tabor', the first 20 years of the century witnessed a riotous flourishing of strange shapes that took to the air with the enthusiasm of Daedalus and fell to the ground with the finality of Icarus. Aviation was the preserve of the amateur and during the First World War it offered an opportunity for chivalry and 'derring-do' to those with the 'cavalry mentality' who were denied their chances on the ground by trenches, barbed wire and machine-guns.

But the onward march of professionalism was relentless. The introduction of the synchronized gear on fighter planes made aerial warfare as ruthless and anonymous as ever it was on the ground. Some British pilots – notably one Puggy Shone - continued to enjoy themselves, dive-bombing German soldiers relaxing on a beach in Belgium and pelting them with oranges or dropping bogus bombs (painted footballs with attached streamers) onto German airfields, just to see the panic, but their life expectancy was now measured in hours rather than weeks. The pitifully vulnerable planes with which the pioneer aviators had taken to the air in 1914 were soon replaced by technically efficient killing machines and so the youthful innocence of the early days was gone. Sikorski's mad marvels opened the way to the German 'R' bombers and the huge Handley-Page bombers that Britain produced. Both of these were designed to bomb civilians. In view of the outrage that ensued from Bomber Command's 'area bombing' in the Second World War, it is interesting to note the ease with which British and German commanders bombed civilians in London and Berlin in 1917-18; there were no bruised consciences here.

Much of this book, inevitably, deals with the Second World War. As a result, it would be quite wrong to isolate the aircraft from its natural prey – civilians. For the first time in history non-combatants suffered on the same scale – if one believes Soviet figures, on a much greater scale – as military combatants. Once civilian morale had become a justifiable war aim, it was just a short step to Dresden, Hiroshima and Nagasaki. As a result, I have devoted space to 'civilian blunders' that were a product of air attack. The blunders I describe in the section on the 'Phoney War' are not designed to sneer at people who had no way of knowing better, but to criticize those in authority who had every means of knowing better and should have provided appropriate leadership. It was the social upheaval that they instigated in 1939 through the 'fear' of the aircraft rather than its actuality that imposed more hardship on British civilians than the Germans achieved at any time during the First World War. Fear is not in itself a blunder, particularly for civilians. But unfounded fear, of an unreal threat, may so effect morale that the war effort is diminished. Work in aircraft and munitions factories may suffer and divisions in society – apparent in London between the unsheltered and heavily-bombed 'Eastenders' and the more lightly-bombed and better sheltered 'Westenders' – may create civil unrest, as was often close to being the case in London during the Blitz.

It would be impossible to deal with aviation blunders and not cover two of the most dramatic events of the Second World War, the Battle of Britain and the London Blitz. In any aerial battle lasting for months mistakes will be made by both sides. However, from the German point of view the battle should never have taken place because the Luftwaffe had nothing to gain and, as we shall see, everything to lose. Contrary to the British 'myth' of the battle – which is rather selective in the facts it employs – the Germans had little chance of winning. After all, their aircraft were intended mainly for ground support and were ill-equipped to fight a 'purpose-built' defensive air force. Fighter Command always had the upper hand and rarely came near to losing it. The Blitz, of course, is the 'fear' of the bomber made fact. And, terrible though it was, casualties and destruction never came near to the levels predicted during the 'Phoney War'. Nevertheless, blunders were made by those responsible for defending against the bomber, and I have included four of these in this book. But these blunders are dark ones, providing salutary lessons, where those of the 'Phoney War' provide some light entertainment. This was 'war to the knife', in the words of the Spanish guerrillas during their struggle against Napoleon. If one occasionally glimpses humour it is because that was a weapon of the British and a way of maintaining morale. I am fully aware of the ease of being 'wise after the event'. However, the British government had claimed to be wise 'before the event' in 1939. Having prepared people for a holocaust, how was it that when the bombers eventually did arrive – twelve months later – there were still no deep shelters in the East End, no national fire service and no legally-enforcable scheme for fire watching? This smacks of incompetence.

My approach has necessarily been chronological. Less than a century of air warfare to choose from has made a thematic approach unworkable. Nevertheless, if a theme is needed, it should be that aerial blunders have been more truly damaging than any other type I have considered. Even in the post-war world, aviation blunders are present. In fact, they seem to have grown apace, having played a significant part in all of the wars fought since 1945. I have questioned the use of defoliants in Vietnam and wondered how the Task Force that regained the Falklands in 1982 managed without a system of early warning of enemy planes. With regard to the recent conflict in the Gulf, I have queried the use of the word 'smart' to describe weapons that kill your own soldiers, or women and children in a bomb shelter or target baby milk factories.

In the introduction to the *Guinness Book of More Military Blunders* I quoted Ben Jonson's phrase about 'sporting with human follies not with crimes'. This time I cannot do so, as I am only too aware of the numerous crimes of which I have had to write. It is the aircraft that is the weapon of 'total war'. No longer can warfare be left to the soldiers, for there is not a square mile of inhabited land on this planet that cannot be reached by missile or bomb – a disturbing thought.

The German Armada

Some people regard the loss of Singapore as Britain's lowest point in the Second World War. They are wrong. The lowest point occurred much nearer home than the Far East. And it involved rather more than the loss of face suffered by Britain's colonial élite vis-à-vis their Asian subjects. It came about as a result of Britain's failure to pre-empt a brazen and astonishing act of cheek on the part of the German Navy. It happened in the Straits of Dover, of all places, and it must have made generations of mariners from the Drakes and Raleighs of Elizabethan England to men like Nelson and Collingwood, Jellicoe and Beatty, turn in their graves. And it occurred because an Austrian ex-corporal understood that the psychology of appeasement ran deeper in Britain than was generally realized. Just as in 1940 Hitler had rightly surmised that those who led France's army were pale imitations of the great men who had built up the reputation of French military might, so in 1942 he instinctively felt that the men who led Britain's war services would not react with the 'Nelson touch'.

Swordfish torpedo-bombers of Coastal Command. Six of these planes were all that were available for use in 'Operation Fuller' against the German battle-cruisers Scharnhorst *and* Gneisenau, *during their 1942 'Channel dash'.*

They were either frail old men, who were afraid of their responsibilities, or arrogant and smug place-seekers whose reputation had grown thanks to the innate courage of their men. Where his own commanders were afraid of the ghosts of Britain's great past, Hitler saw only the weakness of her present. If he pushed hard enough Britain's commanders would panic.

During the spring of 1941 the RAF had been making numerous attempts to sink the German battlecruisers *Scharnhorst* and *Gneisenau* which lay in dock at the French port of Brest. These massively armoured vessels resisted the best the British bombers could throw at them, but they sustained damage that kept them from actively threatening British shipping in the Atlantic. Moreover, the ease with which Bomber Command was able to strike soon convinced Hitler that it would be safer to move the ships to German waters, where they would be protected by an umbrella of Luftwaffe fighters. In Britain it was believed that the Germans must eventually try to withdraw their ships from what had turned into a trap. This meant that they would have to return to Germany either round the coast of Ireland and Scotland and into the North Sea, or – surely unthinkable –

by travelling up the English Channel and through the Straits of Dover. Although the British thought the latter most unlikely – even suicidal – Coastal Command ordered three dawn-to-dusk radar patrols outside Brest, while Fighter Command organized daylight sweeps of the Channel under the code-name 'Jim Crow'. If the Germans came the British would be ready for them. Or so it seemed, particularly when, on 29 April 1941, the Air Ministry warned all service commanders that the Germans might attempt a 'Channel dash' at any moment. It was supposed that they would try to pass through the Straits of Dover under cover of darkness.

Constant news of RAF's damaging raids on the *Scharnhorst* and *Gneisenau*, was proving too much for Hitler's patience. He was not interested in having such prestigious weapons of war sitting uselessly so far away and achieving nothing. He told his admirals that unless they returned to Germany he would have their main armaments removed and used as shore batteries. It was a measured insult to the German Navy and forced the admirals' hands. Better to go down fighting the enemy, they decided, than be dismantled by French workmen.

However, as the Germans pondered the unthinkable – to pass through the English Channel under the eyes of the RAF and the Royal Navy – the British were making a series of highly dubious decisions that suggested that, even after two years of war, they were still not taking things seriously. The seven submarines that had been patrolling outside the harbour at Brest were suddenly reduced to just one, even though a German 'escape dash' was now very possible.

The German naval commanders were weighed down by the burden of British maritime superiority. They could not believe that the nation that had ruled the waves for centuries would be so careless as to let such prizes as two German capital ships just sail past them in their own home waters. The recent destruction of the *Bismarck* by the British Home Fleet was surely evidence if any was needed of the risks *Scharnhorst* and *Gneisenau* would take in sailing down the Channel. But the Führer had demanded it and so they must go, but they would demand the strongest possible air cover for the journey. And in the person of Colonel Galland, the fighter ace, the Germans had a man of courage and efficiency to organize the air umbrella. Galland was Germany's not-so-secret weapon. While the RAF could count many men as courageous as the German, none of their commanders in the operation ahead came anywhere near him for intelligence and organizational ability.

The Germans planned their 'dash' for the night of 11/12 February, 1942. They would maintain a cruising speed of 28 knots and aim to pass through the Straits of Dover in daylight – the opposite of what the British might expect and plan for. It was a daring and dangerous decision. To cover the fleet in the Channel the Luftwaffe would provide 280 fighters, rotating so that there were never fewer than 30 overhead at any one time. If the RAF broke through the Luftwaffe's umbrella, as might be expected occasionally, the heavy ships were supported by destroyers and E-boats (fast torpedo-boats) which would put up such a defensive fire that no British planes would survive. The greatest danger, apart from mines, would come from the torpedo planes which had contributed to the loss of the *Bismarck*.

While the Germans prepared themselves meticulously, the British evaluated their options and decided that – harebrained as it might seem – the Germans might well opt for a Channel dash, as their ships had recently been damaged and would prefer the shorter journey to the longer northern route round the

British Isles. Unknown to the Germans, however, the British were not entirely confident about stopping them. The Germans would present quite a threat: two battlecruisers and the heavy cruiser *Prinz Eugen*, probably ten destroyers (five of which were better and bigger than any British destroyer), a swarm of powerful E-boats, and a strong air umbrella supplied mainly by the Messerschmitt Me-109s. Stopping them would presumably require the efforts of the Royal Navy and the Royal Air Force, not to mention Coastal Command. Not so. First Sea Lord Sir Dudley Pound declared, 'On no account will heavy ships be brought south where they will be exposed to enemy air-attack, torpedo-boat attack and risk being damaged by our own and enemy mine-fields.' The Admiralty, still shaken by the loss of the *Repulse* and the *Prince of Wales* off Malaya simply did not want to know about the English Channel; it was too close to Luftwaffe airfields. If the Germans did the decent thing and came up to Scotland for a naval duel in the best traditions of the service, then the British would oblige by sending them to Davy Jones's Locker. But if they skulked near the coast with a mass of air cover, the Navy was happy to rely on the RAF to sink the blighters.

At Dover, meanwhile, the German ships would encounter six British torpedo-boats (MTBs), but no destroyers with torpedo capability. Coastal Command would come into the equation, with their Swordfish torpedo bombers, but at the time they could muster perhaps nine of them, perhaps fewer. The fears of the German admirals were groundless. The British were so stretched on the peripheries of the war that at home they were virtually helpless. Certainly the RAF would fill the skies with planes, but the record of bombers against well-defended, fast-moving warships was not good. Dive-bombers or torpedo-bombers would be better equipped, but not the four-engined heavies. There was little chance of a Stirling hitting a battleship from four miles up. However, Coastal Command seemed to hold the trump cards, not the RAF. Sir Philip Joubert had under his control Beaufort torpedo-bombers and it was within his power to locate these planes at Dover where they could be brought into action should the German battlecruisers dare to come out. Incredibly, he did nothing of the sort, leaving one squadron on duty in Scotland and another in Cornwall. Moreover, although his staff had studied the likelihood of a German break-out and prepared contingency plans, they were all designated 'top-secret' and locked away. The entire plan was called 'Operation Fuller' and the codename 'Fuller' was to be used as soon as it became apparent that the German ships had come out. It was imperative, therefore, that everybody knew the significance of 'Fuller' and what they were to do if they heard the codeword. In fact, hardly anyone knew what 'Fuller' meant. It was an intelligence 'cock-up' of the most staggering kind that was to have grave repercussions later on.

The Admiralty made merely token gestures by calling up six MTBs and six old destroyers to block the German battle fleet. One would have to scour hard in the annals of British history to find a single occasion since the thirteenth century when the Straits of Dover had been so thinly defended against an enemy fleet. On the evidence of this one wonders what difficulties Hitler would have had in implementing 'Operation Sealion' (the planned German invasion of Britain) in September 1940. Would the toothless lion that Britain had become have been capable of defending its own cage or would it have relied instead on its roar to mislead the world as to its real strength? The defences at Dover, notably the six Swordfish planes – capable of just 90 m.p.h. and widely referred to as 'Stringbags' – were being placed on 'suicide alert' if they were thrown into action against the Germans. Brave men's lives would be squandered in an attempt to make up for the shocking mismanagement of Britain's armed forces. Pound later described the Admiralty's efforts thus: 'We have scraped together all that is at present available.'

The use of the Swordfish and, perhaps, the Beauforts, was actually based on a misreading of the situation. On the assumption that the Germans would not dare to pass through the Straits of Dover in daylight, it was thought possible to use the (very slow) biplanes under cover of darkness. Had the Germans chosen to go through in daylight – as they did – the Swordfish would be easy meat for the swarms of German fighters. The only chance the Swordfish had of succeeding was in darkness, or under a massive umbrella of British fighters. In the event, the six Swordfish would be sent into action without either, for which the RAF must bear the blame.

Why, one is inclined to ask, were six old biplanes the best that was available? For which the answer is that they were there and nothing else was. Of three squadrons of Beauforts, one (of fourteen planes) was stationed at Leuchars in Fife. In view of the apparent imminence of the German break-out from Brest, Joubert ordered this squadron south to Coltishall in Norfolk. However, heavy snow prevented the Beauforts leaving Scotland until later. The other two squadrons (nineteen aircraft) were covering a breakout from Brest by the German battlecruisers, but one designed to take them cruising into the Atlantic. As a result, they were placed in Cornwall, too far from the action, as we shall see. To recap: the German battlefleet would meet at Dover six Swordfish aircraft, nine MTBs (each inferior to the dozens of E-boats which accompanied the German fleet) and six 20-year-old destroyers, which would sail round from Harwich if they were needed.

THE EYES OF COASTAL COMMAND

During the evening of 11 February 1942, RAF Wellington bombers staged a raid on the German ships in harbour at Brest. They created some panic in the town, and an awful lot of smoke, but no damage to the ships. They then took photographs and flew away. Unfortunately for the British, the photographs showed the three heavy ships in their normal positions. They were clearly not coming out that night. But they were. Their engines were churning all the way through the raid and as the Wellingtons flew away, the German battlefleet began to leave Brest under cover of smoke from the British bombs. The first threat to the Germans was that they would be spotted by Coastal Command's three Hudson reconnaissance planes. But luck was with the Germans that night.

The first Hudson patrol, known as 'Stopper', covered the French coastline around Brest. It was a very black night, which made visual identification impossible. As a result, the Hudson was entirely dependent on its radar. After a close encounter with a German nightfighter, the crew of the Hudson hastily switched off its radar only to find that when they tried to operate it again later it had broken down. The crew failed to make it work again and so the pilot returned to base. Engineers back at St Eval airbase, in Cornwall, were unable to get the radar working again. It turned out to be nothing more than a blown fuse. The pilot of the Hudson was offered another plane to resume his patrol, but found that that would not start either. Engineers now set about repairing this second Hudson. An hour passed – during which the German fleet sailed peacefully through the patrol area – before the engineers identified the problem with the plane: a damp plug. A third Hudson eventually took over but by now it was too late.

The Germans now passed into a second patrol area known as 'Line SE', which covered the rest of the Brittany coast. In this area, the pilot of another Hudson had to report a broken radar set. He continued to patrol in darkness for 90 minutes but his crew could not repair the equipment and he too returned to base having seen nothing. This plane was not replaced on patrol and the Germans calmly continued their westward progress unseen by the British. By the time the battlecruisers were approaching Le Havre they were in the third patrol area for the Hudsons, codenamed 'Habo', which covered the coastline as far as Boulogne. In this part of the Channel the mist was so thick that the commander of the Thorney Island air base told the Hudson pilot to make just a couple of circuits and then land before the fog set in. As a result he missed the opportunity to detect the German fleet. The pilot's report was: 'Duty performed. Nothing sighted.'

'JIM CROW' FAILS AS WELL

As dawn came the Germans could hardly believe their luck. They were still steaming towards the Straits of Dover and as yet they had not even been spotted by the British. Were they asleep? Or were the British planning a trap in the narrows between Dover and Calais? Only time would tell.

Where Coastal Command had failed, surely the RAF 'Jim Crow' sweep would succeed. The Germans were approaching Dieppe when two Spitfires took off on reconnaissance missions. What might have been put down to bad luck so far now took on the appearance of disgraceful mismanagement. In the first place, nobody had informed the pilots on 'Jim Crow' duty what the word 'Fuller' meant. The code had been kept so secret that even the air controllers at Number XI Group at Uxbridge, who would be required to scramble hundreds of fighters across Southern England, did not know what 'Fuller' meant.

The two 'Jim Crow' Spitfires missed the German fleet in heavy cloud, but by the time they returned to base to report 'All clear', radar blips were indicating swarms of German planes possibly covering something bigger. A radar station on Beachy Head had already advised the RAF that heavy shipping movements as well as swarms of enemy planes had been detected. The RAF's interest waned as soon as ships were mentioned. That was not their responsibility. When the same station radioed Naval HQ at Newhaven, a harassed young Wren informed them that the Navy was not interested in planes. Why did the radar station not ring the RAF? Sadly, this was typical of the lack of coordination between the services that day. As one of the officers aboard the German fleet observed, 'This could well be an instruction trip for quartermasters.' It could also have been a 'how not to do it' exercise in combined operations on the British side. At 0900 hours, the Beauforts that Joubert had ordered to fly from Leuchars to Coltishall finally took off, four days after they had received the order. Bad weather had been partly to blame but so were 'administrative difficulties'.

At last the radar stations were picking up a convoy of unknown ships, travelling at 25 knots – far too fast a speed for them to be merchant vessels. The penny finally dropped - perhaps they were the *Scharnhorst* and *Gneisenau*. An officer from Biggin Hill rang Uxbridge, Group XI's HQ, and urgently said, 'Fuller, I think.' 'Afraid not, old chap. Wrong number,' came the reply. 'No, it's Fuller,' the officer insisted. But nobody at Uxbridge knew who 'Fuller' was or what was his significance. Squadron-Leader Bill Igoe from Biggin Hill gave up in disgust and decided to send up a plane to check for himself. There now followed a series of errors so ridiculous that they might have supplied a sub-plot for one of Shakespeare's less successful comedies. Igoe rang the airfield at Hawkinge and asked Squadron Leader Oxspring to go out and check the radar traces of German planes and possibly ships as well. Oxspring took another pilot, Sergeant Beaumont, with him.

WHO OR WHAT IS 'FULLER'?

Meanwhile, the radar controller at Swingate, Flight Lieutenant Gerald Kidd, reached the conclusion that the radar blips were the German heavy ships that had been expected to approach in darkness. Instead they were coming in daylight and they had got this far undetected. He therefore got on to Dover Castle to warn them that the *Scharnhorst* and *Gneisenau* could be expected shortly in the Straits of Dover. The line was defective. He next tried a scrambler line, but that did not work either. (When the GPO later investigated the fault it was found that both the GPO line and the top secret scrambler were plugged into the same line by mistake. As a result, anyone in the Dover area had been able to listen in to secret RAF radar reports.)

It was as if everyone was simultaneously waking from a long sleep. Group Captain Beamish at Kenley aerodrome in Surrey decided that as it was a quiet day he might as well take a Spitfire up for a spin, and he took Wing Commander Finlay Boyd with him for a bit of company. Their aerial 'constitutional' merely added to the confusion. Four Spitfires, two from Hawkinge and two from Kenley, were now wandering the skies, but otherwise no other planes were following the German ships. Nevertheless, three senior officers were aloft and presumably once they had reported that the German ships were at sea they would be believed. Perhaps Britain's moribund defence system might even spring into action to challenge the threat to Britain's naval heritage. Unhappily not. Although Beamish and Boyd sighted the German ships and identified them they followed regulations insisting on radio silence. Beamish should have broken every regulation in the book to get his vital message through to Dover. Instead, he waved to Boyd to follow him and both set off back to base to carry the message verbally. The two Spitfires from Hawkinge put on a better show in that they at least had a sense of urgency. Oxspring decided that radio silence was quite inappropriate and radioed Biggin Hill to tell them what he had seen. Unaware of the significance of the word 'Fuller', Oxspring did not use the codeword and so his report was not believed. Even though four pilots had identified the German ships no action was taken by the British defences for a whole hour. Intercepting Oxspring's message on his own radio, the German aerial commander, Colonel Galland in his Me-109 allowed himself a grim smile. He doubted if the British air controllers would act on a single report, and he was right.

It took Oxspring and Beaumont just eight minutes to reach base at Hawkinge. Beaumont had once seen *Scharnhorst* at a naval review and was convinced about the sighting. An intelligence officer sent a man to fetch a book of German ship silhouettes. The man went by bicycle and stopped off at the NAAFI on the way back for a cup of tea, wasting a further fifteen minutes. Beaumont's story – coming from a sergeant as it did – was doubted by everyone except Oxspring and Bill Igoe, who had ordered the sweep in the first place. Igoe and Oxspring now encountered a dead hand more heavy even than that of a bureaucrat, namely that of an aide protecting his lord and master from contact with the real world. They tried to speak personally to the commander of Group XI, Air Vice Marshal Trafford Leigh-Mallory. They might have found it easier to speak to God. Leigh-Mallory, it appeared, was visiting Belgian air units at Northolt and was handing out 'gongs' (medals). When Oxspring explained that he had personally identified German battlecruisers approaching Dover, he was told by someone at HQ in Uxbridge, 'You saw fishing boats.' It is astonishing that a man who had risen to the rank of Squadron-Leader in the Royal Air Force was thought to be unable to tell the difference between two 32,000-ton battlecruisers, surrounded by a heavy cruiser and ten destroyers, and a fleet of fishing boats. This helpful type at Uxbridge concluded, 'We are not going to bother the AOC over this.'

In desperation, Igoe and Oxspring asked for a message to be passed to Leigh-Mallory. No, they were told, he was on parade. He'll be livid when he finds out, they replied. No he won't, they were assured. Nor, apparently, was he. While Igoe and Oxspring were besieging Uxbridge, Beamish and Boyd were sedately returning to Kenley, with their radios off and their lips tightly sealed. When he landed, Beamish tried to ring Leigh-Mallory, only to encounter the same rebuff. Beamish, however, now contacted Biggin Hill and confirmed that it was the *Scharnhorst* that had been sighted. There could no longer be any doubt. At last, nearly twelve hours after they set sail from Brest, the German fleet had been spotted at sea. Fortunately, Flight-Lieutenant Kidd had by this time managed to inform Dover – via Portsmouth – that the whole German fleet was about to force the Straits of Dover and that they had better organize something to stop it. At Manston, the six Swordfish bombers under Lieutenant-Commander Esmonde were placed in readiness for their 'dice with death'.

After 30 minutes of trying Beamish succeeded in getting Leigh-Mallory to come to the phone. His Majesty was not amused to be summoned by a mere Group Captain, but when he heard what Beamish had to say he realized that he had no excuse any more for inaction. He must utter the word 'Fuller' and watch to see what would happen. Dover Command had already heard the word and was girding its loins. The Cabinet Office was also informed and Winston Churchill was baying for blood. Britain was gathering herself for action, but very slowly. It had been so long since a foreign power attempted to pass through the Straits of Dover in wartime.

But what exactly was 'Operation Fuller'? Did anyone know? There was a 'flap on' and throughout southern England the search began for the plans. Who had them? At Biggin Hill, hub of Britain's fighter defences, it was discovered that the plans were in a locked safe and the man with the key was away on leave. In a dozen airfields fighter pilots waited for the order to scramble, while the pilots who were to escort the Swordfish torpedo-bombers rushed about asking everyone who passed what they were supposed to do and what was the target? Some people said it was the *Scharnhorst*, while others said it was a German convoy. Nobody seemed to know the truth.

THEY'RE THROWING MOTHBALLS AT US

Like prisoners in the Tower of London awaiting execution, Esmonde and the seventeen air crew of the Swordfish waited for what was to be their death warrant. The job of stopping this powerful German fleet had been given to them alone. In World War One – famously – the lions had saved the donkeys. But this time there were so few lions and so many donkeys.

Esmonde led his Swordfish patrol out to rendezvous with the Spitfires which were to guard him while he took on the Germans. At least they would have nothing to fear from Galland's Me-109s: five Spitfire squadrons would keep the Germans busy. As the Swordfish circled near Ramsgate there were no Spitfires in sight, when there should have been 60. Ten minutes after the agreed rendezvous, with the German ships pulling away all the time, just ten fighters arrived. The other four squadrons never made the rendezvous at all. At the fighter stations nobody seemed to know what all the fuss was about. Here and there some people had heard about 'a small naval scuffle' or 'a fight between German E-boats and British MTBs'. No one mentioned battleships.

Denied even an aerial umbrella, the six Swordfish set off for their version of the 'Charge of the Light Brigade'. This time it was left to the German admiral to sum up the futile courage of the British at war. The flak was probably the most formidable ever put up by a fleet until the Americans used multiple AA guns in the later stages of the Pacific War. On the *Prinz Eugen* the gunnery officer called out that it was a suicide attack. He can be forgiven this misassumption. While German fighters pounced on the Swordfish, knocking sections off

The German battlecruiser Gneisenau, *pictured at sea in June 1941. The* Gneisenau *and her sistership* Scharnhorst *exposed the inadequacy of Britain's air defences in the Channel during their voyage from the French port of Brest to German waters in February 1942.*

their fabric fuselages, the ship's tracer cut holes in the wings until it seemed nothing was holding the old biplanes up, just feet above the waves. Esmonde held on to the bitter end, getting his torpedo away just as his plane crashed into the sea. It was as well that he did not live to see the *Prinz Eugen* steer easily around it. On the bridge of the *Scharnhorst* even as dull a man as Admiral Ciliax was stirred to memorable utterance: 'The English are now throwing their mothballs at us.' He later recorded Esmonde's attack in his log: 'The mothball attack of a handful of ancient planes, piloted by men whose bravery surpasses any other action by either side that day.' The British public would have loved it. Esmonde's sacrifice contained just enough magnificent futility to become memorable. He had snatched enough meaning from a day of disgraceful blundering to add to the myth of Britain's unconquerable spirit in wartime. The award of a posthumous Victoria Cross sanctified his sacrifice in a noble cause. Meanwhile, Leigh-Mallory strutted and paraded, and reminded people of how important he was.

All six Swordfish were destroyed and fifteen of the eighteen crew were killed. No hits were scored by their torpedoes. The efforts of their pilots seemed to find more appreciation from their enemies than from their own side. Some of the Spitfires which were supposed to have covered them began to appear on the scene soon after the last of the Swordfish had been destroyed. Their pilots were not to blame. They had never been briefed on what was their task and what the Swordfish were being sent to torpedo.

The German ships were almost past the danger point when the RAF at last stirred itself. From all over southern and eastern Britain some 700 bombers and fighters were going into action. Moreover, the Beauforts were coming. Modern torpedo-bombers were on their way. But where were they when Esmonde's Swordfish had suffered martyrdom? The story of the Beauforts is a story of blunders almost without parallel.

At midday seven Beauforts from Thorney Island, in Sussex, tried to enter the action. An officer rang Uxbridge asking them there to arrange a fighter escort to rendezvous with the torpedo-bombers over Manston, in Kent, 90 minutes later. Thorney Island were told that all available fighters were scheduled to escort the Swordfish, but they would do what they could. The Beauforts were ordered to take off. Before they could do so several more 'cock-ups' occurred. Two of the seven were found to have been armed with bombs instead of torpedoes, while a third developed a technical fault. Instead of launching the other four into the attack, the whole half squadron was made to wait 60 minutes while all were made ready. Eventually, the four 'fit' machines took off – just five minutes before they were due to rendezvous with their escorts at Manston, 120 miles away. The Beaufort pilots may appear to have lacked urgency, but they had been told that they would merely be operating against a German convoy. Moreover, nobody at Manston was warned that the Beauforts would be late. Unlike the escorts that did not arrive when Esmonde and his Swordfish needed them, the Spitfires arrived punctually to escort the Beauforts and began circling the airfield wondering where their bombers were. Manston then contacted Hornchurch, where the Spitfires had come from, and asked 'Why are your fighters circling over here? Are they waiting for something?' Eventually someone thought fit to ring Thorney Island to ask where the Beauforts had got to, receiving the answer that they had taken off just five minutes before. The decision was reached that the Spitfires would rendezvous with the Beauforts at sea, in the vicinity of the German ships. But by now madness of the kind that only bureaucratic ineptitude can create ruled the skies above the Home Counties. While the Spitfires headed out to sea, Thorney Island's four Beauforts arrived over Manston to find that their escorts had gone. Manston tried to signal the Beauforts to follow the Spitfires, but someone had forgotten to inform Manston that the Beauforts had recently changed from Morse signals to radio telephone and could not receive Manston's Morse signals. The Beauforts now began circling Manston airfield, waiting for orders and waiting for their escorts, while Manston kept signalling them to follow the Spitfires that were heading out to sea on a trip to nowhere. Eventually, frustration overcoming orders, the Beaufort pilots headed off on their own to hunt for a German convoy that did not exist. They scrupulously searched an area of sea now 50 miles behind the German fleet but drew a blank. Later two more Beauforts arrived from Thorney Island and also took up the circling, wondering where everyone had gone. When nobody turned up the pilots landed and stormed into the control room to ask what was going on. 'We were told to rendezvous with some fighters over here and follow them to our target. Where are the fighters? And what is the target?' The station commander at Manston was astounded that anyone in southern England still did not know that German battlecruisers had broken through the Straits of Dover. Eagerly, the two Beauforts refuelled and roared off looking for a slice of the action. Incredibly, after such a delay, they actually caught up with the German fleet, dived to sea level, faced the flak, fired their torpedoes - and missed. But at least they lived to tell the tale.

THE MISSING TORPEDOES

Meanwhile, the Beauforts ordered down from Leuchars in Scotland had at last arrived at Coltishall. Unfortunately, the bizarre cloud of secrecy surrounding 'Fuller' had not yet lifted and so the newly arrived aircrews were not told about their mission, only that they would soon be in action. But 'soon' was a flexible word on this day. Three of the Beauforts had arrived without torpedoes, but Coltishall being a fighter station, there were no torpedoes to be had anywhere nearer than North Coates, close to Grimsby, which was 150 miles away. A call to North Coates set in motion the 'Mobile Torpedo Servicing Unit' (MTSU). The police were alerted to have siren-cars and motorcycles escorts ready to speed the torpedoes down to Norfolk, while all the time the Germans were getting ever closer to German waters. The MTSU had not been used since the start of the war; now their great moment had come at last. Everything had to be done properly, down to the last possible item. The Unit could have reached Coltishall in three hours, but that would have involved cutting corners. Instead, a whole column of lorries left North Coates, travelling steadily because of the ice, and slowly wound its way south. The Germans were in port, in the bar and halfway to insensibility by the time the 'Immobile Unit', as it was unkindly called, was even halfway to its destination.

Meanwhile, back at Coltishall, it had been decided that seven 'armed' planes should wait for the torpedo-less ones to be fitted with their weapons, so that the squadron could achieve maximum impact when it did finally take off. For two-and-a-half hours the Beauforts waited patiently, until a decision was made to send in the 'armed' planes without the others. The Beauforts arrived over

Manston at nearly three o'clock, to find the skies there full of circling Hudson bombers and Spitfires. Chaos, not for the first or last time that day, now took over. Following their orders the Beauforts, as last arrivals, formed up behind the Hudsons and prepared for the Spitfires to lead them towards the enemy. However, the Hudsons broke formation and – presumably acting on orders of their own or with a due sense of deference to the new arrivals – formed up behind the Beauforts. The Beauforts were clearly baffled. Their orders had been to fly behind the Hudsons, which is what they now proceeded to do. The Hudsons, unable to communicate with Manston – they were experiencing the same problems the Beauforts had of having recently changed over from Morse to radio telephones – had received no orders at all. Disobeying orders, but in an effort to retain his sanity, the Beaufort leader set off on his own to try to find a 'German convoy'. Happily the Hudsons gave up circling and followed the Beauforts, though what they would find when they got wherever they were going was anybody's guess.

The Germans had chosen their date to break out – 11/12 February – with rare good fortune. Bomber Command was temporarily leaderless. Their new commander, Arthur Harris - not due to take over until 22 February - was in America, while their old one, Sir Richard Peirse, had left office two weeks before, on 8 January. As a result, there was a temporary hiatus. For the previous ten days 300 bombers had been on a two-hour standby for a possible breakout by the *Scharnhorst*, but now that number had been reduced to just 100, with the others merely stood by in case they might be needed. As a result, when the news came through that 'Fuller' was in operation, no bombers were able to take off to intercept the German ships for some three hours.

While the air defences of Great Britain were grinding into action, three more Beauforts had arrived over the German fleet, flying in from Thorney Island. They attacked the German ships with exemplary courage, fired their torpedoes and missed before flying back to base. One of them, damaged by the flak, tried to fly to Manston – and, to add insult to injury – was engaged by British guns, further damaged and was forced to crash land at Horsham St Faith in Norfolk.

The heavyweight planes of Bomber Command were drawing a blank in most instances. Of the great armada that set off, just 39 sighted the enemy and dropped their bombs. All missed. Fifteen of them were shot down or were lost when they flew into the sea. Altogether 675 British planes took part in the action against the *Scharnhorst* and *Gneisenau*, made up of 242 bombers, 398 fighters and 35 Coastal Command Hudsons and Beauforts.

WHERE WAS THE NAVY?

It had been a massive operation and, lacking a single guiding hand, it could hardly have been more chaotic and less effective. The German air commander, Colonel Galland, commenting favourably on the heroism of the British flyers, added that 'they were sent into action with insufficient planning, without a clear concept of the attack, without a centre of gravity and without systematic tactics'. Galland was right, of course, but in such a situation the air crews had every right to enquire, 'Where was the Navy?'

In fact, the Navy, or what there was of it, had been in action as well. But, of their wounds, many had been inflicted by their own side. One wonderful

example of the 'fog of war' involved the destroyer *Walpole*. Two British
Wellington bombers suddenly emerged from the clouds above the destroyer
and tried to bomb her. As their bombs exploded nearby they were suddenly
attacked and driven off by a formation of German Me-109s, which promptly
took station above the British destroyer and continued to escort her for some
way before they discovered their mistake and flew off in embarrassment.
Nearby, Hampden bombers were attacking the British destroyers *Mackay* and
Worcester. The destroyers were enjoying a thoroughly rotten day, being alter-
nately attacked by British and German planes. Swarms of bombers, German
alongside British, kept making low-level attacks on the six old British destroyers, while not far away two German battlecruisers were cruising by like swans
watching a group of moorhens squabbling over bread pellets thrown into the
water. The destroyer *Worcester*, carrying the reputation of the Navy on its tiny
shoulders, engaged both the *Prinz Eugen* and the *Gneisenau* and was shattered by
heavy gunfire. In her plight she was then attacked by Beauforts newly arriving
from heaven knows where, which fired torpedoes at her. Happily the torpedoes
missed but the attack forced the destroyer's captain to curtail an operation to
rescue men in the icy water.

The Germans were by now home and dry. After avoiding everything the
RAF and Coastal Command had thrown at them it was perhaps fitting that just
before reaching safety the *Scharnhorst* should hit a mine and suffer serious, but
not fatal, damage. To the Germans the whole operation had been a vindication
of Hitler's shrewd assessment of how the British would react: with a kind of
slow-motion panic like an old man looking for his glasses. If courage can be
measured in terms of the Germans cautiously pushing open a door only to find
that it falls off its hinges, then fortune certainly favoured the brave. No fortune
accompanied the sublimely courageous crews of the Swordfish, whose massacre
was certainly the bitterest moment of the whole disaster. On this subject the
RAF and Coastal Command would be at daggers drawn for a long time. The
destruction of Esmonde's command might have happened anyway. But to have
ordered these old planes to take on the sins of the rickety RAF defence system
was faintly blasphemous. The Navy was also particularly bitter at the loss of
Esmonde and his men. Without adequate fighter cover they should not have
been sent in. In the aftermath of what had become a fiasco the search for scapegoats began. There were many who performed below an acceptable level, from
Leigh-Mallory down to the bored Wren who refused to take one of the initial
sightings seriously. When Dudley Pound finally told Churchill that the
Germans had escaped, the prime minister uttered one word, 'Why?' and
slammed down the phone.

'Why?' might have been a useful question if there had been a similarly useful
reply available. Dudley Pound would not have known 'Why'. He was in poor
health and his misjudgments were soon to inflict several naval disasters on the
nation. Churchill should have replaced him with a younger and more active
man. But Pound was no more to blame than Leigh-Mallory, who was smugly
living on his 'good show' during the Battle of Britain. The man once called a
'pompous, ambitious fuddy-duddy', would continue to occupy high office and
perpetrate other blunders, for instance his part in Operation 'Cobra' (see p.155).
Below them, dozens of RAF personnel were basking on the achievements of
the 'few' in 1940. Real incompetence does not seem to have prevented the
head of Coastal Command, Sir Philip Joubert, from reaching the top and bang-

ing his head on the ceiling. The performance of the Hudson patrols had been frighteningly inept and the movement of the main anti-warship force available to Britain – the Beauforts rather than the Swordfish – had been shamefully clumsy. But probably the greatest problem had been the secrecy that had accompanied the whole operation. Few pilots, either Coastal Command or RAF, knew what they were looking for. The fighter pilots thought they were in a general 'dust-up' with the Luftwaffe, the torpedo-bombers that they were intervening in a battle between rival MTBs and Bomber Command that they were attacking a German convoy. Those who reached the action were astonished to find two German battlecruisers sailing off Dover. On this sort of showing one wonders if Britain could have risen to the challenge of a second Battle of Britain in 1942. But the British were soon laughing again, however inappropriate their choice of jokes. A radar operator, noticing large blips on his screen travelling west, remarked, 'It's those buggers coming back again.'

What follows disasters of this kind is usually a government whitewash, and so it proved. When the Committee of Inquiry issued their report it had reached the astonishing conclusion that, 'The general findings do not reveal that there were any serious deficiencies either in foresight, cooperation or organization.' While Esmonde and his men were being sacrificed, 24 Swordfish aircraft were resting unused at Lee-on-Solent. Why were they not in action with the others? Because there were no trained pilots available to fly them. Coastal Command's state of unreadiness is illustrated by the fact that several of the crews flying the Beauforts had never before had any experience of firing a torpedo.

Operation Fuller was everything that has already been said about it. It pitched six old biplanes against overwhelming German naval and aerial superiority not somewhere in the Baltic, off the coast of Germany, but in the Straits of Dover, an area of vital British strategic importance. All the Navy could offer to help was the 20-year old destroyer, *Worcester*, which had to take on a battlecruiser and a heavy cruiser single-handed, not to mention a hybrid air force of German and British bombers trying to sink her.

At any other time the prime minister would have resigned. To preside over a war effort that could manage no more than this was to make Chamberlain's Narvik blunders seem very slight. Too many men at the top were grossly incompetent and should have been removed before they could inflict further damage on the country. While the Germans had achieved the 'impossible' through careful preparation the British had reacted as they usually do, offering botched planning cemented together with the blood of the ordinary British serviceman. The British love of improvisation was merely a front for an incapacity to act professionally. The RAF was still smug after its victories in 1940–41 and felt that it merely needed to turn up for the enemy to curl up its toes. The great air battle over Dieppe showed it the error of its ways (see p.101).

PART ONE:
IN THE BEGINNING

Man approached the problem of flight in a number of distinct ways, which resulted in simultaneous experiments with balloons, airships, helicopters and man-powered and machine-powered aircraft. The pioneers in each field were concerned first and foremost with the problem of keeping airborne, and few – except philosophers or strategists – looked forward to ways in which the newly-acquired skills could be put to use. Those who did frequently allowed military considerations to form part of their justification, though few thought further than to see their 'aircraft' as aids to military reconnaissance rather than as aerial weapons. Leonardo da Vinci, for example, experimented in a number of different fields, including man-powered flight and the ornithopter (helicopter).

LEONARDO IN A FLAP

The Renaissance was a period not only of rebirth of interest in the Classical world, but of great and forward-looking scientific investigation. In terms of military science there was a revolution in tactics, as well as the development and use of new weapons. Science and war often moved

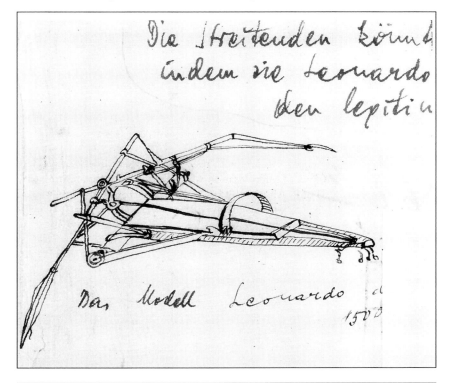

A sketch by Leonardo da Vinci of a man-powered flying-machine. As far as is known Leonardo produced no working models of his designs and was, in any case, mistaken in his view of how birds fly.

'hand in hand' as military advantage became a fertile field for applied science. But as yet aerial warfare was still limited to the use of missiles - arrows and crossbow bolts - as well as stone balls fired from a bewildering variety of primitive cannons. Flying, where it was thought of at all, was the realm of lunatic fanatics (who jumped from high towers and flapped the wings that they had attached to their arms). The imitatation of Chinese kites never gained much popularity in Europe for, while it may have frightened Chinese peasant soldiers, it was useless against the hardened professional troops of sixteenth-century Europe.

As an application of scientific principles, military aviation was of interest to some Renaissance scholars, of whom Leonardo da Vinci was by far the most famous. Patronage - in the arts or sciences - was still the vital route to fame and fortune, and so any machine which might add to the military strength of a great noble or, even better, a monarch like Francis I of France, would be an invaluable discovery or development. To a man like Leonardo, science was its own justification. There was no moral issue involved in designing novel ways of killing one's fellow-men and so had his design for a machine-gun proved workable, there is no doubt that the French would have been scything down their adversaries with such a weapon by the mid-sixteenth-century and Leonardo's fame might have rested on the smile of a French monarch, rather than on that of an obscure Italian merchant's wife.

Throughout his life Leonardo was intrigued by the subject of flight and its potential applications. However, he never solved the secret of how birds fly and actually blundered - if one dare suggest it - in trying to find similarities between the swimming style of a fish and the style of a bird in flight. Had he succeeded in building a working model we might have discovered that his 'bird craft' tried to row through the skies, with a downward and backward motion. However, birds do not displace air in that fashion and are not able to beat their wings in a backward motion. Leonardo's human-powered craft could not have maintained itself in the air because of the sheer impossibility of lifting the weight of the body. Leonardo was better in the field of parachutes, gliders and ornithopters (helicopters). His screw helicopter was in itself a recognition that at that stage man-powered flight was impossible. Unfortunately, Leonardo had no natural successor and it was several centuries before pioneers took up his ideas and tried to take them further - also without success.

THE BALLOONATICS

Opposite:
The ascent of the Montgolfier balloon in 1783. This was the first occasion on which men became truly airborne. The Montgolfier brothers hoped to use their balloons to lift French troops up the Rock of Gibraltar, held by the British.

Until the present century balloons offered mankind the only vaguely reliable means of travelling above the surface of the earth for any length of time. Furthermore, it did not take him long to devise ways in which the balloon could assist him in warfare. Although experiments in ballooning had been tried in earlier times, they were doomed to failure until the development of lighter-than-air substances during the eighteenth century, as a result of Cavendish and Lavoisier's work on phlogiston – or hydrogen. Building on the theories of the English chemist Joseph Priestley, Joseph Michael Montgolfier worked on using hydrogen as a lifting agent and managed to 'float' a small, silken balloon by heating the hydrogen. After this there was no stopping him and, on 21 November 1783, with the help of his brother, Jacques Étienne, he prepared a balloon for the first aerial ascent by man - or in

The Battle of Fleurus in 1794 was the first known occasion when balloons were used in warfare. Unfortunately for the French, Napoleon later abolished the balloon corps, failing to appreciate the enormous advantages it could have given him, notably at the battle of Waterloo in 1815.

this case, two volunteer men, the Marquis d'Arlandes and Jean-François Philâtre de Rozier. The Montgolfier brothers already had a military purpose in mind for their balloon, nothing less than a plan to help the French to capture the British garrison at Gibraltar. They planned to build a whole fleet of balloons and lift thousands of French soldiers to the top of the Rock of Gibraltar. The idea looked good on paper but, fortunately for a large number of unnamed French soldiers, the Montgolfiers were prevailed upon to move more slowly. Balloons therefore began their military career in reconnaissance work, rather than military transport.

BALLOONATICS AT WAR

The successful flights of the Montgolfière hot-air balloons in the 1780s inspired the world's generals to seek ways to exploit their military potential, but progress was slow and not without its setbacks. The French successfully used a reconnaissance balloon named *L'Entreprenant* to observe troop movements at the battle of Fleurus in 1794 and their subsequent victory over the Austrians owed much to the heroism of France's new élite balloon unit – the aeronauts or aérostiers. The Austrian troops had panicked at the sight of the balloon, supposing it to be supernatural and a product of Republican France's known pact with the 'Evil One'. (The less imaginative British troops simply shot down the balloon that was used against them by the French at the Battle of Aboukir Bay four years later.) Nevertheless, by 1798, preeminence in air warfare rested with the French, who by then had two 'balloon companies' attached to the Republican Army. And, moreover, the potential of the new weapon was apparently limitless. But one man put an end to military ballooning even more completely than the British guns - Napoleon Bonaparte. The problem was that the gallant French aeronauts were regarded as the 'glamour boys' of the French army and were idolized as the heroes of the hour, notably by the fairer sex. As a result, the French hot-air balloons were used less and less for military purposes and more for amorous ones. When not on duty the 'daring young men in their floating machines' took their girlfriends to heaven and back. Mere earthbound mortals could only gloomily speculate as to what was going on aloft. Bottles of champagne and hampers of food – not to mention rugs – were more associated with the aeronauts at this stage than military hardware or even telescopes. When one French aeronaut, Lieutenant Beauchamp, was hauled down to the ground with his female companion, he could only stammer out an apology to his commander and express a willingness to marry the young lady. In 1799, Napoleon suppressed his aerial corps on the grounds that it was unnecessary in view of his own extraordinary military powers and because its reputation – among the fairer sex at least – was in danger of exceeding his own. History can only reflect on what would have happened at the battle of Waterloo in 1815 had Napoleon possessed a balloon which could have peered over the Mont St Jean Ridge and seen Wellington's troop dispositions.

DEATH IN VENICE

Slow as the Austrians had been to come to terms with the new aerial phenomenon at the Battle of Fleurus, by 1849 they were ready to try a 'first' of their own - the aerial bombing of civilians. During the siege of Venice in June 1849, the Austrian commanders ordered the construction of 200 small unmanned Montgolfière balloons. Each was fitted with a 30-pound bomb which would be released by a time fuse. The idea was simple: the balloons would be floated over the city and would release their deadly cargo when a certain time had elapsed. However, even the simplest Austrian recruit could have told his commander that the wind could be a disobliging ally. And the worst happened. The balloons were launched with a favourable wind, but no sooner had they reached the city walls than the wind capriciously turned about and blew them back over Austrian lines. Pandemonium erupted. The Austrian troops now were forced to open fire on their own balloons as they flew over their camp. Although some were shot down, many others released their bombs proving that - as Daedalus had discovered - human ingenuity was no match for the powers of nature. A century later the Japanese were to learn the same lesson (see p.78)

THE WINDS OF WAR

Balloons played a significant role in reconnaissance operations during the American Civil War, though mishaps were frequent. One of the strangest setbacks was suffered by a Confederate officer, Captain John Randolph Bryan, during General Joseph Johnston's campaign in the Yorktown Peninsula in 1862. Bryan's balloon was short of lifting power and was equipped with just one restraining cable. Unfortunately, when Bryan went aloft for the first time, he found that the balloon continually rotated about this single axis, until he was so dizzy that he fell to the floor of his basket and had to be hauled down and revived. His second attempt to ascend was even more disastrous. It took place at night, in bright moonlight, near a wood at Yorktown. As the balloon first rose a nearby soldier got his foot caught in the restraining cable and was lifted upside down, held by one ankle. One of his comrades rushed forward and slashed through the rope to let him free, whereupon the long-suffering Captain Bryan and his balloon were cut free and drifted towards enemy lines. As he did so, the Union troops opened a withering fire on Bryan, so that he could only peep over the rim of his basket. Then the wind changed direction and to his relief he was blown back towards his own lines. But his relief was shortlived. Confederate troops, alarmed by the huge shape in the sky, took up the cry 'Yankee spies' and opened fire on the balloon. By now, the balloon – shot at by both sides – was drifting towards the York River, between the two armies. Bryan took his chance and climbed down the severed rope and, half-dragged and half-swimming in the river, he managed to attach the balloon to an apple tree. Only then did he notice that a sharp branch of the tree had ripped the balloon's fabric and with a hissing noise his erstwhile chariot collapsed in a heap.

PAR AVION

During the Franco-Prussian War of 1870, Paris was subjected to a close siege by the triumphant German troops. However, the citizens of the French capital made use of balloons to maintain communications with French armies in the south of the country. Their ingenuity revealed the potential of aerial warfare, though some of their efforts met with an unfortunate fate.

Until the abdication of the Emperor Napoleon III, War Minister Leboeuf was absolutely opposed to the use of balloons, but once the Third Empire had fallen more progressive policies were followed. For example, the French forces employed four balloons at the battle of Valenton on 17 September, 1870, though they were severely hampered by poor visibility. But it was not in reconnaissance alone that the balloons found their métier, but in communications and even in transport.

The provisional French government had left Paris before the Prussians tightened their siege and had established themselves at Tours. On 23 September, the professional aviator, Jules Durouf, decided to leave Paris by air and fly to the temporary capital. Taking with him over 200 pounds weight of mail, Durouf almost literally shot himself through the roof, releasing so much ballast than the balloon flew up like a bullet from a gun. This was, however, what Durouf intended as his balloon was old and leaky and, otherwise, might not have cleared Prussian lines. Cocking a Gallic snook at the Pickelhaubes below, Durouf sprinkled his visiting cards over the irate Germans, who could only shake their fists at the intrepid aviator above them, well beyond the range of their guns. His success inspired the women of Paris to flood into the great railway terminals and there, either at the Gare d'Orléans or the Gare du Nord, begin stitching at unprecedented speed. Soon, balloons of all sizes - bearing the names of French luminaries such as *Victor Hugo, George Sand, Daguerre, Lavoisier,* and *Montgolfier* – began taking shape on the Paris skyline. Crazy plans were suggested for methods to help the balloons over the Prussian lines. The best idea – and a truly Napoleonic one – was for a quartet of eagles to be harnessed to the balloons. Others suggested pigeons (not to pull the balloons) but to return from the provinces with messages. The Prussian 'spoilsports' used hawks to kill the pigeons. When the Parisians heard they decried this latest German 'atrocity'. The pigeons flew to and from Paris carrying microfilms wound round their legs containing thousands of letters: it was a veritable 'pigeon-post'. As well as the pigeons returning to Paris, trained dogs ran back with microfilms concealed in their collars.

Unfortunately, the Parisian balloon-service was experiencing problems. Once the balloons had passed the Prussian lines and survived bombardment by a Krupps vertical-firing gun, the first anti-aircraft gun in history, they were subject to the vagaries of the wind. And the wind could be quite capricious. One balloon, *La Ville d'Orléans*, took off for the south on 24 November 1870.

The French made substantial use of balloons during the Franco-Prussian War of 1870–1. During the Siege of Paris, the garrison was able to keep in touch with the rest of France through the numerous balloons that escaped from the city over German lines.

Hopes were high for a safe and swift passage. The flight was safe but anything but swift. The two passengers flew north not south, crossed the Baltic Sea and landed in Norway, having travelled over 2000 miles. Personification allows suns to smile. Does it allow winds to laugh? The wind that took the crew of the *Général Chanzy* all the way to Munich, where they were promptly imprisoned, had quite a sense of humour. Nevertheless, out of a total of 66 balloons that left Paris, 58 landed safely in friendly territory. One tried to cross the Atlantic and was last seen heading out to sea off the coast of Cornwall.

It was history's first recorded airlift and history's 'firsts' always require their victims.

AERIAL RECONNAISSANCE IN REVERSE

One of the most ridiculous examples of aerial blunders occurred during the battle of San Juan Hill on the island of Cuba, during the Spanish–American War of 1898. The whole campaign was going badly enough for the Americans without introducing a new and thoroughly unreliable factor into the operation - an observation balloon that was to accompany the troops as they approached the Spanish positions.

On 1 July, some 8000 American infantrymen were struggling along a congested jungle path towards Spanish entrenchments on San Juan Hill, which guarded the approaches to Santiago. Travelling with the troops, though a hundred feet or so above them, was an inflatable hot-air balloon, from which one Lieutenant-Colonel Darby made observations of the enemy positions. So thick was the jungle that from where he was, all that Darby could see below him was a thick blanket of green foliage. He could not see any more of the Spanish positions than he could see of his own men. Unfortunately, the same could not be said for the Spaniards. From their hilly positions they could not see the American infantry on the ground, but they knew exactly where they were because Darby's balloon was directly over the top of them, acting as a marker for their guns. As a result, a heavy barrage of fire rained down on the American soldiers, but where it came from nobody seemed to know. Colonel Wood, who was marching with his men through the jungle, wished Darby would be shot down as he considered that his aerial reconnaissance was 'one of the most ill-judged and idiotic acts' that he had ever seen. Unfortunately, Darby was the only man in the whole US army who had the faintest idea where they were and where they were going. Unfortunately, as he bellowed down the news that they would getting into range of the Spanish guns, the men on the ground found out for themselves by being rolled over in their dozens by enemy fire. Of all the Americans that day, Darby seemed to bear a charmed life, though he was wished dead by most of his own troops.

PART TWO:
WORLD WAR ONE

WHAT'S IN A NAME?

The problems of designing aircraft during the First World War were exaggerated by the lack of knowledge as to what exactly military aircraft should look like. Could one easily tell a plane's function from its name? Well, perhaps not. What does one expect from the Avro Spider? or the B.A.T. Baboon? or the Blackburn Kangaroo? (Presumably, a bumpy ride). And surely the Bristol Badger sounds subterranean rather than celestial. The De Havilland Okapi sounds fast, as does the Gazelle, but the Martinsyde Elephant? Is that a name for a plane? And surely Sopwith are pulling our legs with the 2.B.2 Hippo or the 3.F.2. Rhino. Now that's better – the Sopwith 8F.1 Snail – slow but steady. But at last we have it – the White and Thompson 'Bognor Bloater' – a name to strike fear into the Germans. From this bestiary it should be easy to visualize the shape of things to come.

BRING YOUR OWN PLANE!

How do you train a pilot when his teachers are still learning themselves? Answer: Carefully. Unfortunately, 'carefully' was not a word much in vogue with the sort of young men who wanted to fly during World War One. One might as well have screwed up the instruction manual or used it to pelt the Huns. Indeed, that is probably what many unarmed pilots used as the first weapon of aerial warfare, either that or a hunting rifle or blunderbuss.

Creating an air force in Britain in 1914 was no easy matter. For a start, the 'cavalry mentality' of most senior commanders tended to see the aircraft relegated in importance below the horse. There was nothing, apparently, that the aeroplane could do that the horse could not. Fly, one might suggest tentatively. But General Haig would not be listening. He had already spoken *ex cathedra* to a group of young officers: 'I hope none of you gentlemen is so foolish as to think that aeroplanes will be able to be usefully employed for reconnaissance in the air. There is only one way for a commander to get information by reconnaissance and that is by the use of cavalry.' There one has it, so to speak, 'from the horse's mouth'. It is instructive to realize that within eighteen months Haig would be in command of the largest army ever raised by Britain.

There were more progressive thinkers in Britain, yet those who wished to enrol men to train as pilots were still rooted in a class system that made the following advertisement unremarkable: 'Members of the RFC who own their own aeroplanes should be encouraged to bring them to the Central Flying school when they undergo their training there.' Candidates for training had to obtain an Aero Club certificate, which would cost them a fee of £75 – more than a year's wages for a manual worker. Moreover, it took a small fortune to own your own aircraft, when engines alone cost upwards of £700.

The War Office had decided to cease making any experiments with aeroplanes as the cost has proved too great . . . Aircraft are useless for army purposes as it was impossible for anybody moving at more than forty miles an hour to see anything at all.

WAR OFFICE MEMORANDUM TO LIEUTENANT J. W. DUNNE AND COLONEL S. F. CODY, 1909

Early military aviators faced ignorance and prejudice from traditionalists at the War Office.

One of the main qualifications for being able to fly was being able to ride a horse. It was supposed that equestrian skills were so transferable that a good rider would be able to fly after a mere two hours' tuition. In 1914 just 197 pilots went to France with the RFC – it was hardly surprising that the number was so few, for hundreds of lives had been lost in training accidents, making learning to fly as dangerous an activity as drinking in the German officers' mess or collecting litter in no-man's land.

It was left to the Canadians to demonstrate how to train pilots professionally. By 1916, with a quarter of all RFC pilots dying each month, there was a severe shortage of manpower. The Canadians, and to a lesser extent the Australians, made up the deficiency in numbers. From their own officer training school near Toronto they were, by 1918, sending 200 new pilots to Britain each month. Almost all the best flyers of the RFC were Canadian, compared to whose performances the British came distinctly second best. As for explaining this, the facts are irrefutable. The Canadians spent at least three times as much on training each recruit as was the case in Britain and, secondly, the Canadians did not allow class differences to encroach on their training methods. By the time the British public school eccentrics like Lanoe Hawker and Albert Ball had gone, it was time for the colonials to take over: men like Bishop, Collishaw, Barker, McClaren and McEvoy were scoring far more 'kills' than their British contemporaries. It was not a matter of 'blood' as some absurd British theorists believed, it was far more simply a matter of talent. One of the drawbacks of the British system based on class distinction was that the thoroughbred type with courage in his blood frequently ended by spreading his courage all over no-man's land while hard fighters like the Australian Albert Jacka did a hundred brave things before breakfast but still lived to boast about it over a pint in the evening.

The editor of the influential journal *Aeroplane* protested against the increasingly young and plebeian men who were joining the RFC. This tirade in June 1915 seems to a modern reader redolent of breeding foxhounds in a pre-industrial age. As Grey, the journal's editor, insisted, 'There is an idiotic theory that a man is too old at 30 if he wants to fly and that a howling little bounder of 20 is going to make a better officer aviator than a thoroughly sound sportsman of 32. The youngster, who may certainly fly more recklessly till his nerve breaks just as a mongrel dog will go yapping into a fight till he gets a damned good hiding, will never fly after a bad smash in the way the better class of man will do. Blood tells in a man as much as it does in a horse or dog.' Fortunately, the Canadians were not listening.

British methods of training pilots were about as progressive as those used to prepare troopers for service in the Peninsular War. The training depot's motto seemed to be, 'If your pupils are slack, give them drill and see that it is carried out thoroughly.' One later flyer recollected that several times he was confined to barracks for failing to polish the soles of his spare boots. After kit inspection came lashings of P.E., including marching at 140 steps a minute – a vital skill (along with flapping the arms like a bird) for the prospective British aviator, at least in the minds of those devising the training. While the British were square-bashing and polishing their boots, the French trainees, on the contrary, were at an aerodrome watching planes take off and land, and identifying faults.

After the serious side of the day's training, when the boots were bright and the body was purring with health, came the lectures – frequently ignored – leading to exams of the usual military sort which could hardly be said to be a test of mental prowess since the answers were circulated in advance so that gaps in knowledge could be concealed. In any case, neatness – particularly of dia-grams – was held in higher regard than knowledge or accuracy. One man who was unable to operate his Morse buzzer correctly was, nevertheless, passed as 'proficient in wireless' because his diagrams were so neatly copied.

Flying technique was often subordinated 'to moral fibre'. One test frequently used was for the instructor to deliberately stall the engines so that he could talk to the trainee as they fell towards the ground. As one instructor explained, 'This gives a useful indication of the state of the pupil's nerves. Those who are likely to prove unsuitable to single-seater flying generally cling to the side with an unintelligent expression instead of conversing fluently and with confidence.' In contrast, by this stage of his training the typical French trainee pilot was dis-mounting engines, stripping carburettors and learning that stalling was not a condition to be recommended for a plane.

So many British trainees were killed during training that it became a national scandal. Of 14,166 British pilots killed during the First World War, no fewer than 8000 of them were killed while training. This was Darwinism – the 'sur-vival of the fittest' – taken too far. When questions were asked in the House of Commons about this haemorrhaging of talent the Secretary of State replied, 'Discipline after all was not the pre-eminent quality of youth.' This was frankly a disgraceful judgement, since tens of thousands of young men had accepted the discipline of the Army and the Navy without question. And at the same time the German figures for trainee deaths were only a quarter as high as those of the British. It was not until Robert Smith-Barry introduced a sensible training sys-tem that things improved. Smith-Barry was a 'natural' teacher as well as a capa-ble flyer. Described in his Eton school report as 'an awful little boy, he has no aptitude whatsoever', he proved this wrong by learning seven languages fluent-ly and becoming the greatest of aviation instructors. The problem was that the subject of pilot training was not being taken seriously enough. It was being taught by incompetents. The planes used – Farmans – had a maximum speed of 40 mph and a stalling speed of 35 mph, providing no room whatsoever for pilot error. Instructors were often chosen from men taking a break from active ser-vice through injury or nervous exhaustion, who taught bad habits rather than good practice and encouraged trainees to try low-level stunting to demonstrate their control of the aircraft. When the trainee went solo this led to many of the fatal crashes. One pilot later reported that during training he had been given three different instructors in his first four hours and had gone solo for the first time while his instructors were at lunch.

Some instructors combined training with social flying. One Australian pilot remembers how he first went solo. His instructor took him over Worthing, 'did a few stunts' and landed on the wet sand. For twenty minutes he chatted to a girl on the beach, while a crowd stood gawping at the plane. Then they returned to base and he was told to go solo. He survived, but thousands did not. Another man was taught by his instructor in a single-seater. The instructor, with no seat and no controls, sat on the fuel tank behind the trainee's back and bellowed instructions in his ear. It apparently worked. After just fifteen hours of solo flying the trainee was considered good enough to start teaching others as an assistant-instructor. Many pilots in later years were astonished by the ignorance and incompetence of their instructors and wondered frankly how anyone had ever survived. Action over the Western Front came almost as a relief after the deadly risks of being taught to fly in Britain.

SCOUTING FOR BEGINNERS

The design of scout/fighters was limited by a functional problem. What was a fighter supposed to do? Initially, the role of military aircraft seemed to be a combination of reconnaissance and spotting for artillery. In that way an aircraft's job was to be an extension of the ground forces. It could virtually ignore enemy aircraft as neither it nor they carried any form of armament. However, it did not take long before the reconnaissance or scouting role was extended to include many other tasks, most of them exploiting the plane's advantage of height and manoeuvrability, and almost all involving the scout in direct conflict with either the enemy ground troops or enemy aircraft. The veritable 'Noah's Ark' of aircraft that started the war moved inexorably towards a Darwinian standardization: only the fittest survived. Some of those that did not survive made their mark in unfortunate ways before their demise, as we shall see.

The Blackburn White Falcon monoplane was designed as a scout in 1915 and contained an extraordinary arrangement for the pilot and observer. The pilot was placed in the rear seat while the observer, who was armed with a machine gun, sat in the front seat directly behind the numerous wires which supported the single wing, as well as the spinning propeller. In simple terms the observer could see nothing to his front and must have spent each journey twisted round in his seat trying to look over his shoulder, while in danger of shooting off his own wing supports each time he opened fire. The White Falcon was not in much demand after pilots had made their first exploratory flight.

The Martinsyde S.1. fighter was used by the Royal Flying Corps (RFC) in France during 1915. Unfortunately, its pilots reported that it was very unstable and had, moreover, so dangerous an arrangement for its Lewis gun, perched on top of the upper wing, that it nearly cost the lives of several of them. One incredible episode revealed the dangers of First World War flying. Captain L. A. Strange was flying his Martinsyde on 10 May 1915, and was in action against a German Aviatik two-seater. He had just fired off a drum of ammunition from the Lewis gun and therefore had to stand up in his seat, reach up to the wing and try to unjam the drum before reloading. But the screw was crossed and the drum would not loosen. While he was struggling with the gun, he was holding the joystick between his knees. Suddenly the plane was lifted by the wind and was sent into a spin. Strange lost hold of his stick and was thrown out of the plane, hanging on to the Lewis gun by his finger tips at 5000 feet. Then the plane turned over on its back with Strange hanging underneath. Incredibly he held on to the ammunition drum and was able to struggle back into his flying seat, and turn the plane upright. The Germans had flown off at the point when his plane turned over and he was flung out, counting him as lost. But Strange survived, although he was too exhausted to continue the battle with the Hun and happy enough to fly back to base in one piece. He survived the war and actually flew during the Second World War. Still, the placement of the Lewis gun on the Martinsyde – above the pilot's head on a wing, and four or five feet forward – could only have been devised by someone who has never tried aerial acrobatics. Unsurprisingly, the Martinsyde was not a popular plane to fly and was withdrawn in the summer of 1915.

The Nieuport Nighthawk was built under subcontract in England and was a high quality plane in performance, being faster and more manoeuvrable than

General Nicholson, the Chief of the Imperial General Staff, was of the opinion that aviation was a useless and expensive fad advocated by a few cranks.

MAJOR-GENERAL SIR FREDERICK SYKES, 1911

At a time when men like Sikorski in Russia were planning great bombers, and while the French were building the biggest air force in the world, British military aviation was still blocked by soldiers mired in a previous era.

virtually any plane in existence. Yet when it went into production for the RFC in 1918 it represented probably the worst blunder of the entire aerial war. The engine-maker, Granville Bradshaw, nearly put paid to the entire RFC with one optimistic design – the Dragonfly engine. Having already impressed the government with a smaller Wasp engine, Bradshaw claimed that his new Dragonfly would provide far more power for no more weight.

The Air Board thought they already had a good engine for the Nighthawk and had placed an order for the Bentley B.R.2 rotary engine. Then Bradshaw appeared on the scene with the Dragonfly. Its specification was far better than the Bentley yet the Air Board was cautious. There had been too many promising 'duds' before. They therefore asked Vickers to build the Dragonfly, while the order for the B.R.2 was fulfilled. But the Air Board's caution began to crumble as more and more impressive reports were received from Vickers. Eventually, 11,050 Dragonfly engines were ordered, intended to replace most of the engines in use by RFC fighter planes.

However, when the first engines were produced, they were very disappointing. Heavier and less powerful than specified, they vibrated so violently that mechanical failure followed after a few hours. The life expectancy of any plane fitted with this engine would be very short indeed. There was no alternative but to redesign the whole engine. By good fortune the war ended before the RFC could suffer terminal collapse.

The engine disaster also caused the collapse of the Nieuport Company and the complete abandonment of the promising Nighthawk, which in spite of apparently vibrant health had a terminal heart defect. The members of the Air Board who had ordered 11,000 of these engines merely on the designer's own recommendation were lucky not to pay a heavier price for their blunder.

It is said that even Homer 'nodded', and for a firm as efficient as Sopwith to produce a 'turkey' like the unfortunate 'Spinning Jenny', which was the nickname given the Sopwith Two-Seater Scout, was as unusual as that. Twenty-four planes only were produced, which flew with the Royal Naval Air Service in anti-Zeppelin patrols during 1915. Unfortunately, the planes had a disastrous tendency to spin resulting in numerous crashes and much loss of life. Eventually, Flight Lieutenant Brooke became the first pilot to control an intentional spin and his technique made the Sopwith an easier - if hardly popular plane - to fly.

THE ROYAL AIRCRAFT FACTORY

During the First World War the Royal Aircraft Factory at Farnborough came in for a great deal of adverse criticism, both for the planes it designed and for the effect it had on those built by private designers. Its activities were strongly resented by representatives of the infant British aircraft industry (see p.36) which saw the Factory as having a monopoly position and consequently hampering work done outside which threatened its own pre-eminent position. Noel Pemberton-Billing, the founder of the Supermarine factory in Southampton, even entered parliament to establish a voice for the private manufacturers.

It was the inflexibility of the factory that irritated the private firms, and its attempt to standardize certain of its own designs early in the war that hindered the British war effort and condemned numerous pilots to unequal battles against Germans in far better planes. One has only to consider RFC air ace Lanoe Hawker's unnecessary death at the hands of an 'outflown' Red Baron to realize that skills stood for little when the enemy had a technically better aircraft. The real problem was that the factory failed to keep pace with the extraordinary changes that were taking place in aeronautical engineering in 1915 and 1916. What had ruled the skies in 1914 was 'easy meat' only a few months later, as the Fokker Eindecker was to prove at the expense of the B.E.2c. Pemberton-Billing was to win the argument in 1916, but not until many British pilots had lost their lives in proving him right.

With war imminent in August 1914, aeroplanes were being ordered in haste and the Factory's B.E.2c seemed to be the best scout plane available. As a result hundreds were ordered for use with the Army. Its stability was one of its prime recommendations for reconnaissance, at a time when aerial combat had not even been envisaged. It required prescience to imagine that within months of war breaking out the aeroplane would be a vital weapon in the war. Unfortunately, few saw the military possibilities of the aircraft, relegating its importance far lower than that of the horse. One must resist invoking hindsight to question why the designers of the time were so naïve. Certainly individual pilots and observers took their own firearms aloft from the very start of the conflict and took potshots at each other, with varying degrees of success.

By the autumn of 1915 the 'genteel', even stolid B.E.2c had outstayed its usefulness in an increasingly ungentlemanly war that had already seen gas used on the ground, as well as U-boats sinking merchant shipping without warning. It could only be a matter of time before the aircraft was converted into an effective killer. And as usual with technological developments, it was the Germans who made the imaginative leap that converted civilian use into military employment. Bursting onto the scene during 1915 came the Fokker Monoplane (see p. 41). In comparison with the Fokker the B.E.2c was almost helpless. Apart from the obvious fact that the British had no interrupter gear (see p. 40), the B.E.2c had not been designed as an offensive weapon. The position of the observer, in the front seat and directly under the wing, reduced his visibility and therefore his capacity to operate a gun. The first guns fitted to the B.E.2c were fitted to the fuselage and fired outwards by the pilot. It was a thoroughly unsatisfactory arrangement. The B.E.2c was frankly 'Fokker-fodder' and it hardly mattered what novel arrangements were employed to fit guns, since the design was obsolete.

The German use of the interrupter gear tormented the designers at the Royal Aircraft Factory and drove them to design one of the worst planes ever to fly, the B.E.9 'Pulpit'. It was a product of desperation and everything about it spoke that language. It was in essence an 'improved' version of the B.E.2c, with the observer moved forward - and forward - beyond the end of the plane. When one came to the propeller, the observer moved further still into a little nacelle or 'pulpit' from which he operated a Lewis gun. The problems created by the pulpit are almost too obvious to need much comment. How secure does anyone feel with a propeller just behind their head, knowing that any mistake, like leaning back while standing firing the machine gun, will result either in instant decapitation or in falling out of the 'pulpit' if one leans too far forward in a high wind?

The B.E.9 was sent to France to face the 'Fokker fury' and served with

Number 16 Squadron. Lieutenant Grinnell–Milner described what it was like to fly the plane. 'There was no communication possible between front and back seat; if anything happened, if the pilot was wounded, or even if nothing more serious occurred than a bad landing in which the machine tipped over on its nose, the man in the box could say his prayers: he would inevitably be crushed by the engine behind him.' Members of Number 16 squadron won no 'dog-fights' with the 'Pulpit', for which they were heartily glad. If news had reached the Royal Aircraft Factory that the dreadful 'Pulpit' had triumphed in battle they would have built hundreds of them, assuming that they had designed a war-winning weapon. Grinnell–Milner expressed the general opinion that 'in the B.E.9 unsuitability of design had reached its acme'. But the 'Factory' was not deterred and began working on a B.E.9a. Fortunately, someone lost the design plans.

Fortunately for the British war effort, the struggle against the Fokkers was taken up by more sensible British designs. Yet the 'Factory' had not finished designing fighters that were more dangerous to their crew than to the enemy. The R.E.8 was one of them. One would be wary buying a car from a salesman who told you that you must not drive it without a heavyweight passenger alongside you, otherwise the car would turn over. How much more care might you take if this instability applied to a plane that you might be going to fly to a height of several thousand feet. However, this was the situation that confronted pilots of the R.E.8. The pilot, already having to struggle to look over the engine cowling at the front of the plane or to look down through the lower wing which seriously reduced visibility, had to be aware of the instructions written on the side of his plane: 'Do not fly with less than 150 lbs in the Gunner's Compartment.' As a demonstration of what could happen, one has only to consider an incident that occurred in May 1918 to an R.E.9 (which was

The Royal Aircraft Factory at Farnborough was much criticized during the First World War for certain of its designs. Worst of all was the B.E.9, known as the 'Pulpit', which placed the gunner in front of the propeller.

Another unsuccessful Royal Aircraft Factory design: the R.E.8, which was thoroughly unstable and unsafe unless carrying a well-built gunner.

plagued by the same design flaw as the R.E.8), flown by a Captain Palethorpe. While test flying the R.E.9, he was only saved from crashing by the quick thinking and heroism of the flight observer, Lieutenant Elliott. The R.E.9 was tail-heavy when the engine was on, and nose-heavy when it was off. In mid-air, Elliott realized that the tail was going down so he hung bags of shot around the pilot's shoulders to regain balance. When the engine was turned off the nose went down and Elliott crawled out of his seat and down the fuselage with the ballast to weight the tail. Only through Elliott's quick responses was the plane able to land safely. Fortunately, by this stage of the war Sopwith Pups and Camels were asserting British aerial mastery on the Western Front.

THE ZEPPELIN-TERRIFIER

The novelty of air warfare was immensely stimulating to private enterprise. Between 1914 and 1918 there was still room for individual initiatives because state-owned or -funded companies had no monopoly on military innovation. War in the air, though it developed fast, still contained so many surprises that nobody – even in 1918 – could be certain that they had thoroughly mastered its intricacies. Men like Sikorski and Forssman believed that the massive bomber was the way to victory; Count Zeppelin felt the future lay with the great airship (see p. 39); others, like Tommy Sopwith and Geoffrey de Havilland, felt that the fast scout/fighter with synchronized gears would command the air. Each fresh development brought forth its own antidote. It was a time for experimentation and occasionally imaginative failure – or even plain madness. In Britain one of the most progressive of the aerial 'lions' was Noel Pemberton-Billing, a 'tall, slick, monocled, iron-jawed, wealthy, young Englishman'. It is scarcely necessary to add that he was eccentric; every red-blooded young Englishman combined eccentricity with a fundamental assumption of superiority written into him by such writers as John Buchan and Rider Haggard. Pemberton-Billing, for example, had learned to fly in 24 hours. He had done so as to win a wager worth £500 from Frederick Handley-Page. P-B was a splendid chap – a bit of a gun-runner on the side but one had to earn a crust – and the founder of the Supermarine aircraft factory on Southampton Water.

For many an Englishman war had to have something of a sporting attraction, an opportunity for young fellows to let off steam in somebody else's back-yard. It was not the sort of thing that one's parents would want to see. Fortunately, it was something that the English could get out of their system in their colonies in Africa or India, before returning home and settling down. The thought of blood-crazed Huns actually crossing the Channel and inflicting their own appalling manners on England was just not on. The first appearance of German Zeppelins over England came, as one can imagine, as a tremendous shock. It was not merely a military affront, it was a social one. The Germans were simply not 'playing the game'. They were carrying death and destruction beyond the front lines to where the 'dream of England' rested inviolate, a part of every distant soldier's heart.

P-B was both a man of action and a clear thinker. He had joined the Royal Naval Volunteer Reserve in 1914 and had personally led an early bombing raid against Zeppelin hangars. But that had been war with no civilians involved. The Zeppelin raids on London, however, were indiscriminate, with women and children being killed. By January 1916 P-B was busy working on something to put an end to the German atrocities. If the new fighter planes could not stop the German airships with their bullets, he would do better with a cannon. While building his new plane – to be everlastingly described as a 'Zeppelin-terrifier' – P-B took time off to stand for Parliament. Clearly there was a need for somebody at Westminster to enforce a vigorous air policy. P-B promised that in future the Zeppelins 'will be fought in the air before they reach our shores and the sky over London will be so well-guarded that they will never dare return'.

P-B was referring to the new Supermarine (or Pemberton-Billing) Nighthawk – less a plane than a piece of flying artillery. The first version of the P.B.9 was an incredible craft, with four wings, two pusher engines and two pilots seated separately in case one got shot. Under the top wing was a stream-lined nacelle where the gunner sat, crouching over his one-and-a-half pounder Davis gun, which was strong enough to blow the Zeppelin literally out of the sky. The main problem was that the recoil of such a gun might well put paid to the Nighthawk as well as the Zeppelin. To help aim the cannon, P-B had equipped his aircraft with the first ever flying searchlight, attached to the plane's nose, which had its own independent generator. Specifications for the Nighthawk claimed that it had the capacity to carry a ton of fuel, enabling it to stay in the air for eighteen hours, sufficient time to terrify numerous Zeppelins. In case the air crew were required to stay airborne for such a long period, the gunner was equipped with a sleeping berth. The most astonishing thing about the Nighthawk was its speed. Many giant bombers had been built in Russia, Germany, Italy and Britain, and all had striven for sufficient speed to maintain

A pilot's job is to stick to his aeroplane.

FLIGHT MAGAZINE, 1913

This quote from the influential magazine mirrored contemporary views about the use of parachutes. During the First World War – and for long afterwards – British pilots were forbidden to use parachutes in case they abandoned their aircraft while they could still be saved. As a result thousands of trained personnel were condemned to a grisly death by burning.

the aircraft in forward flight. Instead, P-B had placed the emphasis on loitering in the air, almost literally 'hanging about'. It was claimed that the Nighthawk's two 100 horsepower engines could keep the aircraft aloft at just 35 mph. This provided a stable platform for the big gun which would easily destroy any presumptuous Zeppelin that might cross the Nighthawk's path. It would be pleasant to relate the success of such a bold and novel craft, but unfortunately there is none to describe. Quite simply, the Nighthawk was a crazy idea, so dangerous that only certifiable lunatics would have fired the cannon aloft. It was a desperate response to an irritating – even insulting – manifestation of German military superiority over Britain. It was appropriate that men like Pemberton-Billing should seek a solution to the Zeppelin threat, but quite inappropriate to believe that the answer lay in such a contorted monstrosity. Happily, the idea of the Nighthawk was allowed to die a natural death. Already by 1916 Zeppelins were falling victim to fast-moving British fighters, which shot them down with conventional aerial weapons.

THE ODYSSEY OF ZEPPELIN L-19

Optimism was a vital ingredient in the philosophy of Zeppelin crews during the First World War. Immensely visible as well as vulnerable, the huge airships travelled so slowly that they seemed to hang in the air waiting to be attacked by gunfire from the ground or from enemy aircraft. Yet for perhaps two years they were able to fly so high that they enjoyed relative immunity from attack, until in 1916 the new scout/fighters that the British produced made them an endangered species. However, the tiny bomb loads carried by the Zeppelins made their raids on British targets hardly worth the enormous outlay in men, money and equipment. The future of strategic bombing lay with the heavy bomber, first the smaller 'Gotha' design and then the giant 'R' series, which could carry heavy bomb loads and defend themselves effectively (see p. 53). The Zeppelin was, militarily, a 'dead end'. Nevertheless, it was the giant airship that gripped the imagination as being the first enemy ever to be seen in the skies over Britain. What would England's historical enemies, from Louis XIV to Napoleon, have given for five minutes over London? That was always presuming that the Zeppelin could find London.

On 31 January 1916, nine Zeppelins of the Naval Airship Division were sent by their commander Korvettenkapitän Peter Strasser to raid England. Unfortunately, geography was not Strasser's strong point. His instructions to the crews was to attack targets in the Midlands or the Southern area, particularly Liverpool! It may have been such contradictory orders that set L-19 off on its disastrous final trip, but we shall never know for certain. However, as the Zeppelins set out they encountered thick fog and this meant that they crossed the English coast far from where they had expected. On their return to Germany they claimed to have raided docks, factories and railway installations at Liverpool, Manchester, Goole, Nottingham and Great Yarmouth. In fact, they had dropped bombs on none of those places. L-21 claimed to have bombed Liverpool, when in fact it was 75 miles away over Birmingham. While L-13 thought it was bombing Manchester, it was shattering windows – but little more – at Scunthorpe. L-16 'battered' Great Yarmouth, but in fact bombed Swaffham, at least 40 miles away. Clearly target location was not

highly developed as yet in the Zeppelin. Still, at least eight of the nine Zeppelins sent got home safely.

The unfortunate L-19, however, got thoroughly lost and never got home again. L-19's commander, Odo Loewe, took the 'scenic route' round East Anglia and the Midlands, tracked for much of the time by ground observers who could hear the airship's engines. Poor Loewe radioed base that in the thick fog he was bombing Liverpool and then Sheffield. In fact, he was lost over Worcestershire, but did manage to drop some bombs on the outskirts of Birmingham. Nevertheless, more by luck than judgement, he managed to fly east and arrived somewhere over the Norfolk coast. German destroyers were sent out into the North Sea to search for L-19 after nine hours passed with no radio messages from Loewe. Apparently three of his four engines had failed and he was losing altitude. At last he radioed that he was over Borkum, one of the East Frisian Islands and inside German waters. He was not – he was over Dutch waters. Dutch troops recorded seeing an airship in trouble over their territory. They opened fire on her and riddled her gasbags with bullets. The grievously wounded L-19 turned away and headed out over the North Sea. German destroyers found one of L-19s fuel tanks floating on the sea, but no wreckage alongside.

We know what finally happened to the L-19. A British trawler illegally fishing in Dutch waters saw the wrecked Zeppelin floating in the distance, with part of her crew in a shelter on top of the airship's envelope. Loewe was still alive at that time. He called to the trawler captain to take his men aboard but the fisherman refused, fearing that the fifteen Germans would 'capture' his boat and make their escape to German waters. He promised instead to fetch help from a British patrol if he could find one. He failed to return and passed on his information too late to help L-19, which must have sunk later that day. A message in a bottle was all that was ever found. It was from Loewe, who blamed engine failure, adverse winds but most of all the fire of the Dutch troops for the demise of L-19. It was a dismal end to a futile operation. Admiral Scheer, commander of the German High Seas Fleet, ordered that

A German Zeppelin airship. By the time this photograph was taken in 1917, the Zeppelin threat was past its peak, but in the early years of the First World War such airships posed an aerial danger to British towns and cities that the defenders were unable to combat.

future operations over Britain must be accompanied by destroyer sweeps to prevent crippled airships being lost at sea.

The Zeppelin raids on Britain had a far greater effect on civilian morale than they did on military targets. Nevertheless, they were hardly cost-effective. For example, between 24 and 26 April, 1916 twelve Zeppelins were sent to attack London. Just one reached the outskirts and inflicted injuries on one person. And the defences were improving. It was only a matter of time before a combination of anti-aircraft fire and fighter planes made the Zeppelin a fatally vulnerable aircraft. British fighter pilots were soon being equipped with new explosive ammunition. On 2 September, the first Zeppelin to be shot down by an aircraft fell victim to Lieutenant Leefe Robinson, for which feat Robinson received the Victoria Cross. In terms of morale, the destruction of a huge airship by a tiny aircraft was in the 'David and Goliath' league. The collapse of the vast balloon in flames gave an immense significance to the event. It was if a part of Germany herself had been destroyed. Strasser refused to believe that the loss of this one Zeppelin had turned the tide but it had. Soon more and more of the airships were being shot down in flames by British fighters. As the Zeppelins dissolved in flames, huge crowds of onlookers gathered on the ground to cheer, lifting civilian morale as if they had witnessed the destruction of a Dreadnought battleship on the high seas. When a Zeppelin fell to earth in Essex, the new-born daughter of a couple who witnessed the event was named 'Zeppelina'. The Zeppelin terror was, in truth, no more than a nightly entertainment for civilians. The death by burning of the airships' crews took place too far away from the watchers to spoil the fun. But the continuation of the Zeppelin campaign after the end of 1916 was military unsound now that the advantage lay so heavily with the defenders.

THE GARROS INCIDENT

The most important development in aerial warfare during World War One was the creation of a synchronized interrupter gear which enabled a pilot to fire straight along his eyeline and through the spinning propeller. The implementation of this system on the Fokker Monoplane gave Germany such an advantage in battle that for a while they achieved total mastery of the air over the Western Front. Yet their acquisition of the gear represented a blunder on the part of its first exponent, Roland Garros. Previously the Germans had shown no interest in forward-mounted guns until Garros began shooting down their two-seater scouts in April 1915. Clearly the Frenchman had an amazing advantage in gunnery. But as yet he was alone, as no other French plane appeared to have the same gun-fitment as his Morane-Saulnier Parasol. Garros's system was admittedly crude, consisting of fitting a series a reinforced deflector blades, which deflected about 25 per cent of the bullets from hitting the propeller blades but allowed the rest to pass through. At this stage deflection was a 'hit-or-miss' business and the propeller shaft could be weakened in time. Furthermore, should the deflectors malfunction, the pilot could shoot his own propeller off – as may have been the fate of the German fighter ace Max Immelman. Nevertheless, primitive or not, Garros had a weapon which could win him at least temporary control of the skies. Believing himself immune from defeat in aerial combat, Garros succumbed instead to ground fire and he was

forced to land. He must have known that if his plane was taken intact the Germans would learn of his invention and use it themselves. Once he was free of his plane he tried to burn it before being taken away by the Germans for interrogation. The Germans wanted to know why he was burning his plane. Was there something he did not want them to see? The Germans subjected the wreck to a thorough investigation and discovered the gear.

Most of the combatants had toyed with the idea of an interrupter gear, even the Germans themselves. But Garros's gear was the first that had been seen in action and the Germans were impressed. They built replicas – adding their own refinements – and fitting them to a Fokker 'Eindecker' E.1 monoplane. This plane was to introduce a new element to aerial warfare on the Western Front – mass slaughter. The Fokker was no better a plane than contemporary French and British models, notably the Morane-Saulnier Type N, which was ten mph faster, or the B.E.2c, but with its forward-firing gun it was a natural killer. Yet the Germans were slow to build on this tremendous technological breakthrough. Instead of creating whole squadrons of the new planes they scattered them across the entire front, with just one per squadron, thus minimizing its killing potential. The two men who made best use of the Fokker were the aces Max Immelman and Hauptmann Oswald Boelcke. Against these two men and their like in Fokker E.1s the British were virtually helpless in their swarms of B.E.2c.s. Something had to be done. Fortunately, what David Lloyd George did for the question of armaments, Noel Pemberton-Billing (see p. 42) did for the 'Fokker Fury'.

A Fokker E.III monoplane. Equipped with a synchronized interrupter gear enabling it to fire through its propeller, the 'Eindecker', as it was called, temporarily won control of the skies over the Western Front, shooting down dozens of ill-equipped British aircraft.

P–B TO THE RESCUE!

'Stability Jane' does not have the ring of a war-winning weapon. It was the nickname for the Royal Aircraft Factory's B.E.2c, though 'dead sheep' would have been more suitable. As we have seen above, some of the names given to the early fighter aircraft were hardly inspiring. What, for example, does one expect to be the outcome of a fight between a Fokker and a

'Bognor Bloater'? A digression might emphasize the point. When R. J. Mitchell designed the original Spitfire he had it in mind to call the new plane the 'Shrew'. Surely generations of cartoon Germans in boys' comics could not really have said, 'Achtung, Shrew!' The name 'Spitfire' speaks for itself, so does 'Stability Jane'. With The Fokkers sweeping the skies of respectable, stable and well-behaved aircraft, Britain needed an early 'Spitfire' or 'Hurricane'. What they finally got was a 'Pup', but fortunately one with teeth. Sometimes called the 'perfect plane', the Sopwith Pup was designed as an answer to the Fokker threat, but it was far more than that. From its first appearance in the autumn of 1916 it established British predominance in the air for the first time.

By 1915 flying had ceased to be a sport, even if a 'blood sport'. Hunting rifles were out and interrupter gears were in. The 'Fokker scourge' as the British press described it had rendered all RFC planes in France obsolescent. The government would have to respond with something fast. Without a functioning synchronization gear – the RFC had not asked for one and turned down the one they were offered – attempts to botch some sort of alternative were made. These usually took the form of fixing the gun in awkward or inaccessible places, so that the gunner or the pilot had to stand up to reach above the wing, rendering him an easy target for the Fokkers. The B.E.9 (see p.35) was just one of the ghastly alternatives tried. Fortunately, De Havilland and Vickers were producing their 'pushers' – DH2 and F.B. 'Gunbus' – which featured the gunner at the front with a free line of fire, and the engine and propeller at the back. Unfortunately, though these planes offered some respite from the Fokkers, they had no answer to the more advanced German fighters being developed, as was demonstrated when, on 23 November 1916, the 'Red Baron' in the latest Aviatik Scout killed Lanoe Hawker in his DH2 pusher after a struggle lasting 30 minutes.

In March 1916, Noel Pemberton-Billing had resigned his commission in the RNAS and entered parliament as MP for East Hertfordshire. It was not long before he was weighing in to the debate about the failures of the British aerial campaign in France. He was not a man to mince his words. On 22 March, he declared that for too long the Royal Aircraft Factory had been foisting its blunders on the British public in the shape of unsuitable aircraft. To fly these planes at the front was not just risky, it was frequently suicidal. Moreover, he added, on a dramatic note, 'I would suggest that quite a number of our gallant officers in the Royal Flying Corps have been rather murdered than killed.' Sensational stuff, but P-B had no intention of retracting this accusation, referring to it again and again on later occasions. According to him it was a crime to send men into battle in machines which were little more than coffins with wings. His point was a strong one. The Factory sent 'planes' to France where it was the responsibility of the men themselves to turn them into 'warplanes'. The B.E.2c, for example, had a top speed of just 80 mph. By the time the engineers had fitted guns, that speed had been reduced quite considerably, even as low as 60 mph. The German planes, on the other hand, had guns in their design and were tested with them already in position. Their top speeds, as high as 110 mph, left the B.E.2c outclassed.

On 2 May, P-B asked in the Commons whether his detailed criticism of the Royal Aircraft Factory's machines had resulted in the halting of B.E.2c.s being sent to France. He was told it had not and more were still being sent. This was sheer 'bloody-mindedness' on somebody's part. There was uproar in the

Captain Lanoe Hawker, V.C., D.S.O., earliest of British 'aces'. Hawker was shot down and killed in the war's longest recorded dog-fight by Germany's 'Red Baron'.

Commons. Five days later the Army Council set up a Commission to enquire into what P-B had been alleging. Incredibly, orders already placed for B.E.2c.s were still honoured even though the plane was completely obsolete. One contractor even fulfilled his contract by delivering the planes in 1917. The Burbridge Report redefined the role of the Royal Aircraft Factory in terms of its experimental work on aircraft alone, and this opened the way for private manufacturers to supply the Royal Flying Corps with aircraft as good as or even superior to those of the Germans.

Ironically, the Germans played their own part in helping Pemberton-Billing to win his case. On 8 April, 1916, one of the latest batch of Fokkers was being ferried to a forward German airfield in France. By mistake it landed at a British airfield and was promptly captured intact. The Allies now had an opportunity to test the German plane against the B.E.2c and French planes like the Morane Parasol and the Nieuport Scout. The German outperformed only the B.E.2c, but not the French aircraft. Its superiority lay entirely in its interrupter gear and forward-firing gun. It is one of the ironies of the First World War that both the British and German authorities had rejected patents for interrupter gears in

1914. It had been the Garros incident that had rekindled German interest in such a remarkable way. The RFC had apparently turned down the gear designed by Captain Fisher of the War Office on the grounds of cost.

THE FALL GUYS

The low standard of pilot-training that was prevalent during the First World War (see above) leads one to the inescapable conclusion that the men who flew were regarded as 'dispensable' by those who trained them. Only this could possibly explain why RFC air crew were not equipped with parachutes. As a result a lost plane almost always meant a dead pilot, the flyer suffering a dreadful death, rarely as a result of enemy gunfire, but usually by burning to death in the crashing plane or leaping from thousands of feet to escape the flames that were an inevitable consequence of seating the pilot so near to the fuel tank. Either kind of death could have been avoided more often than not by the use of the kind of parachutes then in operation in the German Air Force. Nothing could have been more frustrating for British pilots than the knowledge that at the last moment the German pilot could escape by using a parachute designed in Britain, while the British pilot had no such opportunity. One German ace Jacobs, saved himself twice by jumping and a later Luftwaffe general, Ernst Udet, also had the British to thank for his successful parachute escape. The problem, it seemed, was that the British authorities did not trust their pilots to behave properly in action. Just as in Britain's army, the fear of the firing squad was believed to be essential to get the soldiers to move from their trenches, so in the RFC certain death by falling was what faced the man who tried to leave his crippled plane. With such a choice it is incredible that there were so many able men prepared to risk their lives by flying. This waste of trained pilots was an unforgivable blunder on the part of the RFC.

Since 1918 the world has come to appreciate that the plane is replaceable, the trained pilot irreplaceable, and this makes it difficult for modern readers to understand why the British Air Board forbade parachutes to their air crews. Yet at a time when generals could squander thousands of lives in attritional battles on the ground, it is perhaps asking too much of air commanders who came from precisely the same background as the army commanders to be any more discerning. For what it is worth, we might as well examine the arguments that were used by the Air Board to justify the prohibition of parachutes.

The overriding argument was one of morale. It was generally believed that the British fighting man – pulled out of soft, civilian life – would not fight unless he had no choice. This outrageous calumny flies in the face of all the evidence of British recruitment in 1914 and 1915, which was entirely voluntary. It was the conscripts of other nations who occasionally had to be prodded into action at the point of the bayonet. There was no mutiny in the British Army in the First World War and little sign of the collapse in morale that broke - at least temporarily - the fighting spirit of every other long-term combatant's army. Nevertheless, ignorance and prejudice on the part of military men, drawn from a social background of privilege and intellectual torpor, mistrusted a 'civilian army', just as in a later war men from the same background would suspect the civilian morale of Britain's urban lower classes. This social imbecility has been at the root of many of the military blunders that have figured in the author's examination of military incompetence. For sheer bloody-mindedness few more disgraceful arguments have been used by military authorities than that British pilots must be denied parachutes in case they were tempted to use them to escape from an enemy attack or to abandon a damaged plane. In fact, it took a very brave man to fly in the virtually defenceless planes, like the B.E.2c, with which British pilots were equipped. The authorities seem to have stood the argument on its head. Surely the pilots – invaluable as a result of training and experience – should have been encouraged to save themselves where possible rather than throw their lives away in a hopeless cause. Had the RAF Marshals in 1940 insisted that the pilot should die with his plane, Britain would have lost the Battle of Britain.

Besides the argument over pilot morale, the other points advanced against the use of parachutes are easily dismissed. It was suggested by the Air Board that whereas the crews of kite balloons might need parachutes because they were unarmed, pilots were equipped to defend themselves and their first concern should be to defeat the enemy rather than consider saving their own lives. This is palpable nonsense. During the 'Fokker Scourge' British planes were completely outgunned by German fighters with synchronized gears. To remain with a B.E.2c for very long after you had been engaged by an 'Eindecker' meant almost certain death, and once hit one faced nothing better than an agonizing and dreadful death from burning.

A third argument used by the Air Board was that parachutes were bulky and heavy, so that they would reduce the performance of the British aircraft and, moreover, they were not reliable. The simple reply is that any adverse effect they had on British planes would merely be the same as they had on German aircraft if their pilots were equipped with parachutes. And no parachute could be guaranteed, but by the time of the First World War there were reliable types in operation. The Air Board's last argument was that parachutes were irrelevant as most fatal accidents occurred during take-off or landing, when there was

The wreckage of German 'ace' Max Immelman's aeroplane, near Lens, on 18 June 1916. Some reports alleged that Immelman shot off his own propeller when his synchronized gear failed. Whatever the cause, pilots of the time suffered a dreadful death if, as in this case, they had no parachute. Most Germans, in fact, flew with parachutes, though British pilots were forbidden to wear them and had to die with their planes.

insufficient height to enable the parachute to open. This was more generally true of training accidents than of combat casualties. Most of the latter occurred at some height, but the plane was often destroyed and the pilot killed in attempting a desperate crash landing, the pilot's only option apart from leaping to his death from an operational height.

It has been suggested that the RFC had a 'pathological distaste' for parachutes as they offered the pilots an escape from combat by leaping safely from their planes, in a way which resembled an infantryman running away. Ironically, the pilots were their own worst enemies in this dispute. Many of them shared the mentality that saw parachutes as a coward's way out. As a result, it was this kind of macho behaviour that prevented a concerted effort to present the sensible arguments in favour of parachutes. On the other hand, the more thoughtful pilots – usually not called 'Puggy' or 'Squibs' and not the sort to play 'wizard pranks on Johnny Hun' – often tried to obtain their own parachutes. And, they insisted, the Air Board's arguments were wrong for the simple reason that pilots usually left themselves an escape route by not engaging the enemy *à outrance*, as they knew what faced them if they fought and lost. The knowledge that a parachute would have given them a chance of escaping would have made them fight harder and for longer.

E.R. Calthrop, a retired railway engineer, was in the forefront of parachute development and he made it clear why: 'To reduce the unnecessary wastage of our airmen.' In 1915 he presented his plans to the Admiralty and the War Office whose 'knee-jerk' reaction was later mirrored by the British Air Board's 'No, certainly not!' In the RFC both Hugh Trenchard and Major-General Sir David Henderson regarded parachutes as something vaguely effeminate. They might have reacted similarly to the idea of pink uniforms. The RFC spelled out their opposition in the words 'such an apparatus might impair the fighting spirit of pilots and cause them to abandon machines which might otherwise be capable of returning to base for repair.'

Undeterred, Calthrop continued with his work, proving without doubt that his parachute worked and naming it, 'Calthrop's Patent Safety Guardian Angel Parachute.' What was unacceptable to the British was popular abroad. In March 1917 Russia applied to buy a hundred of Calthrop's 'Guardian Angels', but was offered just twenty by the British government and on the condition that they were not used in aeroplanes. The French also tried to order some, while the Germans copied British designs to the end that no less a figure than Hermann Goering used a parachute to escape from a damaged aircraft.

THE LEGEND OF ILYA MOUREMETZ

Russia has always been a land of myth and legend rather than of history. Peopled by giants and demons – many in human shape (one has only to think of Peter the Great or Ivan the Terrible) – the Russian mentality is not geared to moderation in anything. In keeping with this, Russian scientists have often been almost magically inventive and even megalomaniac in their creative endeavours. In the early years of the 20th century Russian aeronautical engineers produced a number of planes that can only be described as monstrosities. Prominent among them was Igor Sikorski, a Russian Daedalus if there ever was one, who fled to the United States after the Revolution of 1917 and

became world famous as a designer of helicopters. Yet however American he later became, Sikorski was first and foremost a Russian, with all that entails.

Working with his colleagues at the Russo-Baltic Waggon Factory, by 1913 Igor Sikorski had produced the first of his gigantic bombers. Amazing for their time – for they were built not more than a decade after the Wright Brothers first flew – these flying pantechnicons were ludicrously ineffectual as weapons of war and more resembled conjuring tricks than the solid creations of modern, industrial man. They were triumphs of man's ingenuity – Da Vincian rather than practical. Men travelled on them as if on magic carpets, but in Sikorski's case they took the kitchen sink with them.

The prototype of the great bombers was called 'Bolshoi Baltiski' and was frankly too heavy for two 100 h.p. Argus engines to keep her airborne for very long. Undeterred, Sikorski added two more engines and created the world's first four-engined plane, which he proudly named 'The Grand', though his workman more realistically dubbed it 'the tramcar with wings'. During the 1913 military trials, the magnificent Münchhausian 'Russki Vityaz' was lost in a bizarre way. During a demonstration flight both the Sikorski bomber and a pusher biplane (with its propeller at the rear) known as the Möller II were flying together, with the smaller Möller flying above the Russki Vityaz. Crowds of officers covered the airfield, gazing up at these wonders of modern science that were soon to render them and their cavalry regalia obsolete. Suddenly, the apparently harmless Möller showed its teeth. What had resembled a skeletal moth became a deadly killer. The Möller's engine supports gave way and the Goblin engine fell from the plane like a well-aimed bomb, crashing straight through the 'Russki Vityaz' with devastating effect. Sikorski's masterpiece dived straight into the ground, killing everyone aboard, while the fragile Möller glided safely in to land.

Made of sterner stuff than his planes, Sikorski went to work to produce the greatest of all his bombers. Such a glorious work – or monstrosity as many felt it to be – had to bear the name of a mighty hero from Russian legend. It was called 'Ilya Mouremetz' after a tenth-century Russian hero who was eventually

In February 1914 Igor Sikorski's amazing Russian bomber, Ilya Mouremetz, set the pattern for all the heavy bombers of the First World War.

turned to stone – not the sort of augury most plane-makers would have chosen; it might seem to be tempting fate. However, apart from its name, it was an impressive machine for its date, with a wingspan of 113 feet and a fuselage 67 feet in length. The crew travelled in comfort – by the standards of any time – with a well-equipped cabin containing a dining room, with a pantry, toilet, full central heating provided by pipes warmed by the engine exhaust, dynamo-provided lighting and a grand view from a promenade deck on top of the fuselage with a safety rail to prevent anyone losing their balance. Its design was modern but its philosophy was redolent of an earlier age.

The great beast was a sluggard and crashed on her maiden flight on 11 December 1913, near St Petersburg, smashing her port wings. Sikorski soon discovered that his enormous machine needed a pilot as heroic as any in Russian literature or legend to handle her. Nevertheless, brushing aside every difficulty he pressed on. He took the plane up himself on 12 February 1914 carrying fifteen passengers as well as his dog 'Shkalik', in total a payload of over 3000 pounds. It was astounding that engines amounting to just 400 horsepower could keep the great bomber aloft. Recognition was not slow in coming and Sikorski's great plane received Tsar Nicholas II's approval. The Russian army immediately ordered Sikorski to build a further ten, to be ready by early 1915. The imminence of war with Germany meant that the Russians could not obtain the reliable German Argus engines, but had to fit the more powerful but less efficient French Salmson engines on the new I.M.s, as the bombers became known.

It would be happy to be able to report that the I.M.s were a success and that they paved the way for future bomber designs. In a way they were a success but their legacy was unfortunate. The megalomania that had inspired Sikorski appeared to be contagious and it resulted in an 'age of the Titans' – sad and ridiculous mutant planes – that defied gravity (just) but perverted the original human impulse to fly with the grace of birds. Sikorski had a lot to answer for with his flying tramcars.

ILYA MOUREMETZ GOES TO WAR

While Sikorski conjured up demons, other Russian designers were not so successful, bringing forth black rabbits from white toppers. Besobrasov and Ponikovin, for example, laboured long and hard to produce a triplane that had the most stagger ever seen on aircraft wings. The upper wing was ten feet in front of the pilot, the centre wing level with his eyes, thereby obscuring his vision, and the rear wing dragged along the ground about ten feet behind him. It may have been designed to clear the skies of enemy reconnaissance scouts – perhaps they died from laughing – though how it was supposed to stay in the air was anyone's guess. Incredibly, it is reputed to have flown briefly before going to meet its maker.

On the eve of war in August 1914, the Russian air force – if it can safely be called such – consisted of 224 aeroplanes, 12 airships and 46 kite balloons. In sheer size it was far bigger than that of Germany, but in terms of quality it left much to be desired, basically consisting of the cast-offs from other nations and so many different aircraft engines that it was impossible to get spare parts for them all. Many Russian planes were experimental – this usually meant that they were harebrained creations gleaned from the bottom of a vodka bottle, like Besobrasov and Ponikovin's triplane, or Porokhovshchikov's 'collapsible' and 'portable' 'Bikok' biplane. Worst of all, Russia's war effort in the skies fell victim to graft and corruption within the air ministry. Bribes and 'backhanders' were as common in the Russian aircraft industry as elsewhere, so that designers with influence in high places had their planes accepted and those who had nothing to declare but their talent went unrewarded. As a result such excellent planes as the Sikorski S.20 were abandoned in favour of fighters of French origin. Money exchanged hands to win the French manufacturers their contracts. The outcome was that Russia was frequently left with damaged goods presented as new. One French plane, the Salmson-Moineau SM1, was so bad that only three of them were ever built. These three spent most of their lives grounded with engine failure, stripped gearboxes and fractured drive-shafts. When the French government sensibly rejected the plane a company salesman sold all three to Russia. Of interest to British pilots who suffered at the hands of the Royal Aircraft Establishment B.E.9 'Pulpit' (see p.35) was the French Spad A.2., which had adopted the same deplorable 'pulpit' design, with the front gunner sitting in front of the propeller. This appalling plane was wisely rejected by the French and 57 of them sold instead to Tsar Nicholas's corrupt government, for a suitable consideration.

By now, Igor Sikorski and his redoubtable 'I.M.' bombers, as they were called, were ready to play their part in the war. Thirty-two of the bombers had been ordered and the Russo-Baltic factories had begun an expansion programme on the basis of the order, for which they received three million gold roubles. In the first weeks of the war the I.M.s underwent trials on the East Prussian border. However, teething troubles were almost terminal. So difficult to fly were the bombers that the Minister of War promptly cancelled any further building, saying 'The I.M. aeroplanes are unfit for military purposes. Do not sent them to the front. Do not order more of them. Cancel existing order.' Apparently none of the available pilots could handle the monsters and they needed to be repaired so often that no ground crew could cope. The only way to save the project was for Sikorski himself to prove the value of his own design. He therefore formed the existing three planes into a single squadron, equipped them with trained pilots and engineers, and accepted the rank of Major-General in the Russian Army. The new unit – the first bomber command in history – was to be known as the 'Flying Ship' squadron. The I.M.s at first operated from an airfield near Warsaw – which the Germans promptly captured – and carried out effective low-level bombing as well as aerial reconnaissance.

As well as their bombing duties the I.M.s also carried out photo reconnaissance, taking 7000 photographs during their operational career. However, other countries chose fast, manoeuvrable scout planes for photographic reconnaissance rather than risking such huge and expensive aircraft. Spurred on by Sikorski's great achievement, another Russian entered the field of bomber design and soon experienced the diseconomies of scale. V.A. Slearev produced his 'Svyatogor', a huge plane with 120-foot wings but just two 220-horsepower engines. His optimism was admirable but misguided. He estimated that Svyatogor would cruise at 100 mph and stay aloft for twenty hours. Instead it failed to get off the ground at all and ended its days at the edge of the airfield, with peasant children clambering in and out of its wing struts.

Meanwhile, Sikorski's I.M.s continued to contribute as much to the war as medieval knights on their chargers did to a siege. They were impressive and difficult to kill, but largely irrelevant. One of them fought an epic battle against seven German fighters, before being tumbled down like Don Quixote from Rosinante and taking three of the Germans with it. Over a period of two years the I.M.s dropped 2000 bombs over German lines, a process which would have taken the Russian artillery perhaps a week to achieve. Nevertheless, it was a stirring sight for the Russian conscript soldiers to see these monsters in action. It suggested a technological sophistication that was psychologically reassuring though in reality insubstantial. In a military sense Sikorski's great planes gave little more than an illusion of strength.

SON OF SIKORSKI - THE TARRANT TABOR

Igor Sikorski had a lot to answer for. Having opened a veritable Pandora's Box with his huge bombers, some curious contraptions now crawled out and struggled towards the skies. For some of them the effort proved too much.

German raids on London during the First World War may have been mere pinpricks when compared to the efforts of a later generation, but they were enough to damage British morale. At once the call for retaliation rang out and designers turned their attention to long-range bombers, something big enough to reach Berlin. It hardly qualified yet as strategic bombing, it was more a question of picking up the gage the Hun had cast down. In Britain the gage was picked up by a surprising personality, not, as might have been expected one of the famous aircraft designers like Sopwith or Handley-Page, but a wealthy builder from the leafy lanes of Byfleet in Surrey, by the name of W.G.Tarrant, who had never even built a plane before. Tarrant's heroic gesture went unnoticed in the general euphoria that accompanied the end of the war in November 1918. His great plane – to be known as the Tarrant Tabor – would not now bomb Berlin, at least not for the moment. Still, it would be the biggest plane in the world. To Tarrant this had a sense of rightness: that the British Empire, on which the sun never set, should lead the world in the field of aviation, or at least in the fields of Byfleet.

Official enthusiasm for the Tarrant Tabor's conception was immense. None of the doubts that had accompanied the development of Sikorski's original bombers clouded the horizon. In the 'brave new world' that would follow the Great War, Tarrant's bomber could evolve into a great civilian project, forerunner of a whole fleet of air liners spanning the empire – and all travelling at eighty m.p.h. As usual with all these 'sons of Sikorski', they were so heavy that they could hardly get off the ground and stayed in the air it seemed, only on the tolerance of the natural laws of physics.

Money appeared to be no object. Supported by the Royal Aircraft Establishment at Farnborough and by a team of expert engineers, Tarrant produced a magnificent machine which made Sikorski's I.M.s look more like a witch's broomsticks than planes. But appearance were deceptive. Sikorski's queer contraptions took off and flew. Would Tarrant's? In size the Tabor was herculean: wings 132 feet in width (far bigger than a B-29 in the Second World War), with 5000 square feet of wing area. The Tabor weighed twelve tons unloaded and stood nearly forty feet high. Tarrant was so proud of his creation he boasted that his bomber could fly from London to Bombay with just one stop, and would in time carry 100 passengers. But the first question to be answered was could it even fly to the end of the airfield? As Sikorski had found, the problem was not how to build a contraption, but how to get it off the ground, and for that powerful engines were needed. Tarrant was confident about his engines, in fact he had six of them, the top two situated between the upper wings. The problem was that some experienced observers believed that engines at that height – 30 feet up – might tend to pull up the tail of the plane. Some of Tarrant's engineers had already raised that point, but calculations proved that once the Tabor was in flight the tendency for the tail to lift would be counter-balanced by the downdraught on the tailplane from the upper wing. But would this happen as the plane took off, presumably at slow speed? The engineers scratched their heads with their pencils and decided to wait and see.

On 26 May 1919 the Tabor was ready for her test flight. The biggest plane ever built up to that time – and there were some strong competitors from Russia, Italy, Germany and the U.S.A. – was rolled sideways from her hangar at Hendon Aerodrome (she was too wide to fit in lengthways). Three full captains were to take her up, but first the lengthy process of starting the engines had to take place. Owing to the enormous height of the plane a gantry had to be wheeled out so that the engineers could climb up to start the top engines manually, a process that took nearly an hour. But before the engines could be started Tarrant began to worry in case the plane might be tail-heavy. As a result, half a ton of lead shot was fitted into the plane's nose to keep it well down during take-off. This, of course, was absolutely the last thing that the Tabor needed.

The pilot – the experienced Captain F.G. Dunn – began trying to get the 'feel' of the Tabor, trundling around and testing the controls. Then he turned the plane into the wind and began to accelerate towards take-off. The lower engines brought up the tail nicely, but when the upper engines fired the Tabor tipped over onto her nose and began ploughing a deepening furrow into the ground. Held by the nose the rest of the plane drove forward until the great

Imitating Sikorski's great bomber, Ilya Mouremetz, W.G. Tarrant of Byfleet produced his 'Tabor' in 1919, too late to carry out its prime aim of bombing Berlin. The Tabor was a failure and crashed while taking off on 26 May 1919.

bomber was vertical, with the engines ferociously revving and digging deep into the earth, propeller parts whizzing in all directions. The three captains died in their now subterranean cockpit, though the three engineers, situated further back, survived to tell the tale.

The tale was a sad one, though one better told at the inquest on three men's deaths than in the newspapers months later after some civilian version of the Tabor had crashed on the way to Bombay, loaded with passengers. Apparently, just before take-off, there had been a dispute between Tarrant's engineers and the men from Farnborough. It was a matter of balance, and the engineers had lost theirs. The Farnborough men told Tarrant that his engineers were wrong. Tarrant had wanted the issue settled by independent tests at the National Physical Laboratory. Eventually, however, he gave in to his critics and, against his better judgment, fitted the half-ton of lead shot on their instructions. In fact, it was this weight combined with the thrust from the upper engines that turned the Tabor on her nose. In reality, the Tabor was an accident waiting to happen. Had it ever got off the ground it might have gained a spurious popularity and taken a great number more lives than the three it took to prove to W.G. Tarrant that his Tabor had bombed for the first and last time.

SIKORSKI STILLBORN - THE KENNEDY GIANT

The name of Chessborough Mackenzie-Kennedy does not quite have the same Russian ring to it as does Igor Sikorski. But it is no exaggeration to describe the Scotsman as the midwife at the birth of the Russian aeronautical industry. Leaving Scotland at the age of eighteen, and with just three pounds in his pocket, Kennedy took his skills and his vision to Russia, where he was responsible for building the first ever Russian aeroplane in 1908. A year later he set up the Kennedy Aeronautic Company and attracted the interest of Igor Sikorski. Sikorski and Kennedy became friends, finding that they shared an interest not just in aeroplanes but in giant aeroplanes. While Sikorski was working on his legendary bombers, Kennedy was working alongside him. However, when war broke out in 1914, Kennedy returned to Britain to put his skills at the service of his native land.

Inspired by Sikorski's creations, Kennedy went straight to the War Office with his own idea for a huge bomber, which would become the Kennedy Giant. As was usual at the time in most countries, the idea of raining death on the heads of enemies from huge air machines was extremely popular and he soon gained official support, including the assistance of some excellent engineers. Curiously, by today's standards at least, the Kennedy Giant was to be built by the Gramophone Company, Ltd, of Hayes, Middlesex (later to become E.M.I.) as well as by Fairey Aviation. When the components were completed, the plane was ready to be assembled. Unfortunately, nobody had given any thought to housing the monster. There simply were no hangars big enough to hold the Giant and so during 1916 it had to be constructed out in the open. As it began to take shape it was soon apparent that the Giant was an offspring of the great Ilya Mouremetz, with comfortable accommodation for the crew and windows the full length of the fuselage. However, those who had not seen Sikorski's giants – and that meant everyone except Kennedy – were overwhelmed with the sheer size of the bomber. In order to move it it needed 70

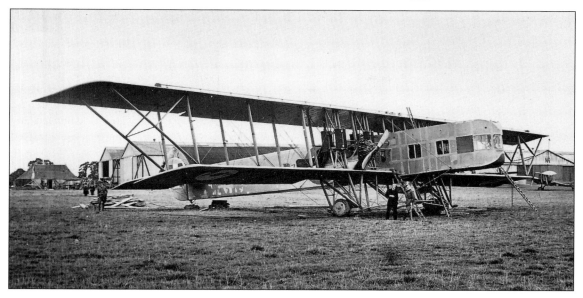

men pushing and two lorries pulling simultaneously. The Giant, unfortunately, had brittle bones. With all the pushing and pulling, it broke in half. Kennedy, undeterred, cut out a ten-foot length of fuselage and put it all back together again. But whatever Kennedy did there always seemed to be something wrong with the Giant. In an attempt to balance the great structure, Kennedy had to keep moving the wings up and down the fuselage, each time replacing the rudder which was then either too large or too small, depending on where the wings were at any one time. The undercarriage resembled a forest of stakes with four wheels cunningly concealed in it, while the engines – 200 h.p. each – laboured hard but were unable to lift such a large aircraft.

By the end of 1917 the Giant had been standing around untested for many months. Eventually, Lieutenant Frank Courtney took on the task of trying to fly the Giant. His first efforts were quite inadequate and the Giant did not even lift her skirts. Then Courtney had an idea. If he headed downhill, and into a stiff breeze, the Giant would have to fly to avoid crashing. He was wrong. At first gravity played its part and he gathered speed as he went downhill but the most that happened then was a desultory hop. The Giant had been airborne for a foot at the most. The great plane was taxied out to the edge of Northolt aerodrome and there it stayed, unloved and a prey to the ravages of the English climate. Without more powerful engines the Giant would never fly. In many ways Kennedy's dream lacked the splendour of Sikorski's. His presbyterian common-sense always held him back from making the imaginative leap that Sikorski had made. Compared to the Russian's flying monsters Kennedy's megalith was an earth-bound giant.

Igor Sikorski's colleague in the early days of Russian aviation was the Scot, Chessborough Mackenzie-Kennedy, who tried to build his own version of the Ilya Mouremetz-type of heavy bomber when he returned to Britain, which he called the 'Kennedy Giant'. Unfortunately the 'Giant', although subjected to numerous modifications, never flew.

CLASH OF THE TITANS – GERMANY'S 'R' PLANES

The nation that gave the world the epic 'Ring Cycle' of Richard Wagner was far from content to encounter Sikorski's lumbering giants in the skies over East Prussia and Masuria in 1914 and 1915 and have nothing to offer in reply. The Russian 'dragons' were slow, it is true, but they were tough fighters. Of the 75 I.M.s that flew during the war only one ever succumbed to German aerial attack.

From 1916 onwards the Germans developed their own 'giants', the 'R' bombers, which were mostly used on the Eastern Front. The concentrated firepower of the Western Front in France would have made the giant bombers unmissable targets. Moreover, they would have succumbed to the powerful British and French scout/fighters that were developing their tactics in France. However, 'R' bombers were used in bombing raids on London during 1917 and 1918. They formed the backbone of what have generally been known as 'Gotha' raids. In fact, the Gothas were much smaller and were capable of carrying relatively feeble bomb loads. On the other hand, the 'R' planes were able, by 1918, to approach the quantities carried by some Second World War bombers. Their drawback – an enormous one – was their slow speed, which made them susceptible to anti-aircraft fire.

The 'R' planes began life on the Eastern Front as a direct response to Sikorski's I.M.s. Their encounter was a veritable clash of the Titans. However, such aircraft were at the experimental edge of current technology and were subject to many drawbacks, some predictable, others less so. The prototype of the 'R' ships, the SSW (Siemens-Schukert-Werke) R.1., began operations from a muddy field near Warsaw in September 1915. During a period of heavy rain the R.1. was forced to stand for 24 hours without use. The next day it could not take off. Even with the engines working the bomber was pressed to the ground as if by a large thumb. A simple solution was found. A nearby soldier walked over, laughed and prodded the upper wing with his bayonet. Gallons of water gushed out all over the pilot and crew. The rain had run into the wings on both sides and kept the plane pinned down. As a result, a special tent was designed to cover the plane wherever it landed in future. But not all problems were so easily solved. The R.1 seemed accident-prone. Bits fell off daily, and when the undercarriage caved in completely, she was returned to Berlin without ever having dropped a bomb. First round to Ilya Mouremetz.

But prestige was now involved and manufacturers all over Germany began the struggle to match the Russians. One German army officer tried to stem this tide of madness. He clearly recognized the folly of all these great bombers: the cost in time, effort and materials that went into constructing them could be better employed producing some other weapons of war. Large numbers of men – at least 125 – were needed to keep each R-plane in the air and even when they did manage to drop their bombs these were ridiculously small in comparison with the effort that had gone into carrying it to its target. The R-planes functioned purely as aerial artillery and as such they needed to be swifter, smaller and less accident-prone. Of course this German officer was right, but this did not prevent the Germans from building dozens more huge bombers of all possible shapes. Perhaps the mistake the Germans made was not in building the R-planes but in using them in a tactical sense – merely supplementing the battlefield artillery – rather than in a strategic sense, by bombing London and other British cities. The effect of concentrated R-plane raids on the morale of British civilians, in view of the primitive air defences available in 1918, might have been more dramatic than at any stage during the Second World War.

Operationally, the R-planes were very difficult to fly. Their engines – as well as being unreliable – were prodigiously noisy and gave away their position in night operations. In addition, the glowing exhaust manifolds in the engine-room were a clear sign that the bombers were coming, as were the bright sparks emitted by the exhaust. Inside the plane the vibrations were mind-numbing. The light bulbs fell out, conversations between the crew were impossible and the radiator pipes frequently froze and burst. In addition, the window frames obscured the pilot's view, the windows had to be left open in flight and so many machine-guns were fitted that there were not enough crew to man them all.

The two-month flight of the Staaken VGO.1-RML.1 from Gotha to Alt-Auz in June 1916, a journey which was expected to take just three days, came to symbolize the problems of the R-planes. During the take-off run the landing wheel under the nose collapsed, pitching the huge plane onto its nose. Having repaired this and taken off, the pilot then discovered that his engines were overheating. With the tremendous noise inside the cockpit his mechanics had to inform him by holding up a blackboard with the temperature reading chalked in large numbers. This led to an emergency landing near Königsberg, in East Prussia. There was no alternative now but to send for new engines. Once these were installed the RML.1 taxied out to take off, only for its entire undercarriage to collapse, sending it skidding across a field on its belly. A new undercarriage was fitted. On the next attempt to take-off, the wheels collapsed again. Once a second set of wheels had been fitted, a successful take-off was achieved and the RML.1 then had an uneventful flight to its destination, arriving just under two months late. However, all had not ended well for the RML.1. On its first bombing mission, two of its engines exploded instead of its bombs. The ensuing emergency landing in a forest destroyed 69 pine trees. Only the fuselage survived, and was sent back to the factory to be refitted with wings and new engines. But that was not the last the unhappy crew heard of the ill-fated RML.1. At the factory new engines were fitted and 'phoenix-like' the RML.1 rose from the ashes of its first incarnation and returned to the front.

On 10 March 1917, the RML.1 was ready for its maiden flight. It took off

The Germans were the most enthusiastic imitators of Igor Sikorski's heavy bombers. Many German factories produced 'Giant' bombers like the Staaken-Aviatik R.VI, seen in this photograph. Such huge aircraft as the R.VI were more effective in their bombing raids on London than the smaller, but better-known 'Gothas'.

from the Staaken airfield and flew around the perimeter. Suddenly there was an explosion and one of the propellers fells off. The pilot lost control and the plane crashed into the airship hangar, killing the crew. It was the end of this ill-fated craft, yet Staaken continued to build these ungainly bombers, finally producing an R.XV before the end of the war. With a top speed of just 80 mph these planes were far too heavy for the engines available. They were examples of the mistaken belief that large aircraft were always the best.

THE INVISIBLE PLANE

The helmet of invisibility - the Tarnhelm - was celebrated in German mythology. First World War German aeroplane designers must have longed to avail themselves of its magical properties, for one of the greatest drawbacks of the giant 'R' bombers was their sheer unmissability. Unless travelling at night, they made excellent targets for machine-gunners or even ordinary ground troops with concentrated rifle fire. Designers therefore attempted to produce a less visible plane – the Linke-Hofmann R.8/15 bomber, built by a locomotive company from Breslau. The bomber was an ugly beast – more like a warthog than a bird (the usual model for most planes) – but Linke-Hofmann believed they had something that would make their unlovely bomber a winner – invisibility. The Breslau engineers covered the fuselage with Cellon, a material like celluloid. Cellon, they believed, would conceal their craft from the eyes of its enemies.

Unfortunately, this cunning plan – of almost weasel cunning – was doomed to failure. In the first place, for 'invisibility' read 'increased visibility'. Cellon was so reflective that it made the bomber incandescent, shimmering in the sunlight as if covered in luminous yellow paint. Quite apart from attracting enemy aircraft the R.8/15 also became a target for every known insect. A second drawback to the

The cult of the heavy-bomber in Germany during the First World War resulted in some extraordinary craft. One of the strangest was the Linke-Hofmann R.I which employed transparent Cellon to cover the fuselage, in an attempt to make the aircraft difficult to spot. The plan failed as sunlight made the aircraft incandescent and a particularly easy target for fighters or ground artillery.

cunning plan was that Cellon is affected by weather conditions, either tightening and cracking in dry weather or loosening and sagging in the damp.

The view from the cockpit was quite remarkable, even scenic. It was like being in a greenhouse, with the crew situated on three floors, the pilot on the top level finding it almost impossible to judge touchdowns from such a height. With the engines on the second level and the bombardier and fuel tanks at the bottom, it was impossible for the crew to communicate with each other, as they were cut off by the roar of the engines. In the event of the bomber tipping over on its nose – a common occurrence – the only protection for the crew was a cockpit almost entirely made of glass. And if the engines or fuel tanks were hit the bombardier would have suffered a fate beyond this author's pen to relate. One might surmise that this bomber had been designed by somebody's fairy godmother using pumpkins, rather than aircraft designers using their intelligence.

The first test flight of the R.8/15 was in January 1917, but it had to be delayed when the tyres fell off the undercarriage as the plane was taxiing before take-off. When the plane did fly – piloted by Hauptmann Krupp – problems soon developed. In fact, the plane was almost uncontrollable. The wings were stiffened before the second flight, on 10 May 1917, but in spite of the fact that two wings fell off, fortunately at low altitude, the pilot survived the impact as the R.8/15 went nose first into the ground. It was an ignominious end for such an unusual plane. But Linke-Hofmann did not give up so easily. A second bomber, the R.40/16, was designed on the same lines as its forerunner. It also was not a success. One pilot described the Linke-Hofmann design in these words, 'It was not an aircraft but a sickness.' On the testing flight of the R. 40/16 the pilot misjudged the landing and broke the axle of the undercarriage, so that the plane ended up on its nose. It was not rebuilt.

FORSSMAN'S FOLLY

What Germany needed was a man like Sikorski. Instead, they got a Swede called Villehad Forssman. They got the worst of the deal because Forssman was a megalomaniac with the emphasis on the 'maniac'. During the First World War money was always available for research into aerial warfare. Forssman's credentials seemed good; he had worked for the Russians in the field of airship design, but as in Russia Sikorski had cornered the market in bombing, Forssman decided he would try his hand with the Germans. Forssman brings to mind the driven scientists of the novels of H.G.Wells, beating on the door of the future while lacking the technology to open it. He eventually gained a job with the German company, Siemens-Suckert, which had already begun toying with fixed-wing aeroplanes and now hoped to do well out of the war. As has been pointed out many times, with war in the air a far more exciting and 'noble' prospect than war in the trenches, there was an enormous market for military aeroplanes, particularly for anything that enabled one to drop bombs on the enemy's heads. Bomb-carrying aircraft seemed to offer an answer to the problems of static warfare which dominated the Western Front from 1915 to 1918.

At the start, Forssman simply copied Sikorski's design for Ilya Mouremetz, coming up with a four-engined bomber powered by 110-horsepower Mercedes engines. But Sikorski was a genius, Forssman a madman. So badly constructed was Forssman's plane that the weight distribution was all wrong. Worst of all, the plane was so underpowered that it could not fly, it could only skip. Forssman redistributed weight by sticking bits on. For example, a gun turret was simply stuck on the front, where it did no good. Faced with such evidence, Siemens began to suspect that Forssman did not know what he was doing. They asked him to leave and employed a proper designer, Harold Wolff, in an attempt to save the project. Wolff simply shuffled the pieces of the bomber and dealt out a new hand. Every piece was the same but they were all in different places. This time the plane skipped and occasionally jumped. The pilot was simply too frightened to risk taking the strange contraption into the air. But Siemens were not prepared to be beaten. In their search for a willing pilot they called for the latest list of war heroes and their finger hovered over the name of Lieutenant Walter Höhndorf, a recent recipient of the 'Blue Max' (the common name for the *Pour le Mérite* award). He would do. There was nothing that a German officer could not do. In September 1915 the plucky Höhndorf took the controls of Forssman's 'folly' – sometimes called the Ladenhüter (White Elephant) – and tried to establish an aerial triple jump record. Several hops and jumps – even perhaps a skip – ended with the huge structure on its nose.

Siemens had lost heavily on the plane so far and were determined to recoup some of their losses. If only they could persuade the cantankerous beast to carry an operational load up to a height of 2000 metres, the military authorities (Idflieg) would buy the plane and Siemens would be in business. Meanwhile, the search began for a new pilot, while the remains of the great plane gathered dust in its hangar. The Siemens directors eventually bribed air ace Bruno Steffen with an offer of ten per cent of the money Siemens would get for the plane, which was being rebuilt after its earlier disaster. The problem was that he needed an aircrew, if for no other reason than to help distribute the weight evenly. But nobody would go with Steffen – none of the Siemens directors, not even his brother, and least of all the Idflieg acceptance commissioners. The risk of a fatal crash was simply too great.

Fully loaded, Bruno Steffen began to taxi down the field. Going alone because no-one else had the courage – or the foolhardiness – to accompany him, Bruno Steffen's thoughts turned to his pay packet rather than the future of German aviation. The plane was immensely heavy – it seemed impossible that such small engines could lift it into the air. But greed triumphed. Piloting the plane was like riding a bucking bronco. What looked like an acrobatics display from below was simply Bruno Steffen fighting to stay alive. After 28 minutes precisely – a lifetime to Steffen – the altimeter registered that the height required by the ministry had been reached. Now, thought Steffen, it was down to the ground as quickly as possible. The machine was reading his mind. First one engine stopped, then a second, then the third. An eerie silence followed the close-down of the fourth and last. Gliding on the back of an elephant was novel. Steffen must have felt like a leaf in autumn, circling his way to the ground where his knowledge of physics convinced him that he would be crushed to a pulp by the weight of the aircraft draped around him like an armoured coat. With the courage and strength of desperation – for Steffen wanted to live to spend his money – he coaxed the Forssman folly into producing the most elegant moment in its life, a perfect landing. The watching officials were impressed by Steffen's skills; he really had not needed to demonstrate

acrobatics and gliding skills in a bomber. Still, once the authorities were convinced by his altimeter reading, they slapped him on the back and passed the plane as fit 'for training purposes'. Siemens got their money, Bruno got his and the plane got its certificate of air worthiness.

Siemens should have quit while they were ahead. Shortly after Bruno Steffen's heroic flight they were carrying out an engine check, with engines running and the wheels chocked, when the fuselage of the great bomber simply broke in half with a startling crack. This had been the reason why Bruno's engineer brother had declined his invitation to go up with him. He had expected it to crack and now it had, fortunately when the plane was standing harmlessly on the ground. Forssman's folly was abandoned but Sikorski's shadow still lay over the field of German aviation. Better men than Forssman had taken up the challenge and soon Germany was producing giant bombers of the Ilya Mouremetz type with which to bomb London.

However, Forssman did not disappear without a single trace. He left evidence of his passage and, with Forssman, the evidence was hardly the kind that could be overlooked. At the end of the war in 1919, the allied authorities stumbled on something in a hangar at Poll, near Cologne, that showed which way Forssman had gone. Not a button off his shirt, or a thread from a coat, but a triplane wheel eight feet in diameter! The wheel is kept in the Imperial War Museum today (see photograph, above). The triplane had apparently been partly built, but though modern – in 1919 – the measurements of this plane seem redolent of an age of legends. Ilya Mouremetz would have quailed if he had seen this Fafnir or Fasolt of First World War bombers. Its fuselage was half as

The Swedish aircraft designer Villehad Forsmann was at once imaginative and yet incompetent. The planes he built for the German Air Force were beyond the technology of the time, notably in terms of being too large and too heavy for the engines available. The triplane wheel in this picture gives some idea of the problems of Forsmann's designs.

long as a football field, its wings considerably larger than that and it had ten engines. Its specifications claimed it would carry enough fuel for three days without refuelling and its warlike mission – eat your heart out Sikorski – was to sprinkle leaflets all over New York. But this plane could never have flown. It was as heavy as a houseboat, with wings far too feeble to lift it. Did Forssman design it? We will never know for certain. But who else could have indulged in such a fantasy, as the war was drawing to a close and Germany facing defeat?

Intermission: 1919–1939

LESS A PLANE THAN A MURDER WEAPON

In any competition to decide the very worst military plane ever built first place would doubtless go to the 'Bullet' designed by the charlatan doctor William Christmas of Warrenton, North Carolina. In appearance the 'Bullet' resembled a plane built from odds and ends by a blind man to a specification provided by a three-year-old. Apart from the fact that the propeller was stuck on the nose and the wings bolted to the fuselage there was little about this curious structure that resembled an aeroplane. If this seems to be too strong a criticism one need only consider the history of the plane. Two were built, both took off, both had their wings torn off by the wind, both killed their pilots – and both earned Doctor Christmas a lot of money.

Doctor Christmas dabbled in aeronautics when he was not busy dabbling in medicine and other people's finances. His theories on matters aeronautical, however, were unlikely to win him the support of any normal aircraft designer. As an exponent of the flexible wing – on the grounds that birds have flexible wings in flight – he believed that his planes would never need to have wing supports. A single bolt in the middle of the fuselage should be good enough to keep the wing in place; the rest was up to nature and the good doctor's imagination. And he had a lot of imagination. Some unkind souls thought he was simply a liar when he related the many flights he had made and planes he had built. When asked to show the evidence of his career he replied that the Christmas Aeroplane Company did not let its secrets go public. Suffice it to say that he claimed to have flown non-stop from New York to Washington in 1912 and lived to tell the tale. Living to tell the tale was Dr Christmas's raison d'être.

By 1918 Doctor Christmas decided it was time for his secrets to be revealed to the world. He was planning to build the 'Bullet', a 100 mph fighter plane that would be just what the doctor ordered for the US Army, now fighting the Germans in Europe. At first the American flyers had been dependent on French Spads and British Sopwiths, but soon, he said, they would have his 'Bullet' to carry them to glory. Christmas was only too aware that there was plenty of money to be made in building warplanes in 1918 and he intended to have his share. All he needed for starters was some money to get him off the ground. He found his financial backers – or dupes – in the shape of the McCorey brothers. Next he needed an aircraft manufacturer so down on his luck that he would even agree to build his plane. He found that too. It was called the Continental Aircraft Company and – ominously – it was based at Amityville. The

The next war could be won by bombing alone by destroying the enemy's will to resist.

AIR MARSHAL SIR HUGH TRENCHARD, 1921

An early expression of the flawed belief that 'the bomber would always get through'. Trenchard's opinions remained unaltered and influenced men like Portal and Harris in the Second World War.

Continental was putty in the Doctor's hands. He told them that his plane was being designed for a special mission – nothing less than the kidnapping of the Kaiser himself. But who was fooling whom? While Doctor Christmas was hoodwinking Continental into believing that he was really an aircraft designer, they were assuring him that they were quite capable of building whatever he wanted. In fact, they were nearly bankrupt, having built just one pusher biplane and having failed to sell a single one to the Army. In a sense the one deserved the other.

The next target was an engine. Doctor Christmas realized at this point that he was going to have to talk to the military authorities who, at that time, kept virtually all their engines for military use. He would have to bait his trap well. He persuaded a senator from New York to write a testimonial, describing him as an experienced aeronautical engineer (syringing ear wax was his most practical skill up to that time), and take it to Lieutenant-Colonel Jesse G. Vincent, who had charge of the nearby McCook Airfield. Vincent had already seen and rejected Continental's first and only product and was unimpressed by Christmas's approach. However, he got the clear impression that Christmas had friends in high places and decided to listen to the proposal. The wily doctor conveniently dropped all references to Continental in favour of a company of his own, the Cantilever Aero Company. Vincent agreed to cooperate and offered to loan Christmas a six-cylinder Liberty aero engine on the clear understanding that the plane was not to be flown until the Army had tested it. Christmas, who had no intention of taking any notice, readily agreed.

Continental now learned for the first time what kind of con-man they were dealing with. Having asked Doctor Christmas for his plans so that they could set to work straight away on this new plane, they were shocked when he admitted there were no plans and that he kept all his ideas in his head. In spite of shortages of all the proper aircraft materials, Continental got on with the job, using anything that came to hand, mainly green unseasoned wood and steel misfirings. Without plans, they made up the plane as they went along, only paying the most cursory attention to the nonsensical ideas that occasionally emerged from the Doctor's confused mind. One of their workers – a young man named Vincent Burnelli – actually tried to mitigate the worst excesses of the 'Bullet'. Secretly he tried to stiffen the flexible wings that were one of the worst features of the plane. Unfortunately, none of the other workers took the project seriously and when Al McCorey, one of the plane's backers, asked to photograph the finished article, the 'Bullet' was wheeled out of the factory complete – or rather incomplete – with the flexible wings unsecured. Burnelli's attachments had not been bolted on yet and before he could fix them, McCorey announced that the aircraft was to be flown forthwith. The smiles on the faces of Continental's workers faded as they realized that someone was going to take the monstrosity aloft. It would mean certain death.

To convince prospective pilots that the 'Bullet' was a genuine military fighter plane, Christmas had arranged for it to be painted in US Army Air Force colours. Colonel Vincent, when he heard what Christmas was doing, wrote reminding him of his promise, but to no avail. Christmas was looking for a pilot, preferably a single man. An Englishman who was the first to see the plane responded, 'You're not getting me up in that.' He wisely withdrew in favour of an American, Cuthbert Mills, who was presumably down on his luck after leaving the army. If he thought things could hardly get worse he was tragically wrong. One of the planemakers from Continental, a man with a conscience, told Mills, 'Look fella, this guy's nuts. Don't chance your life.' Mills had seen death many times in the fighting in France and believed that Death did not come out of a blue sky, not in Amityville anyway. Mills even invited his mother to watch. A large crowd assembled as Mills climbed into the Bullet and revved up the Liberty engine. At least the engine would not fail. The Bullet took off, rose a few hundred feet until a gust of wind ripped the wings off and it dropped like a lump of lead to the ground, killing Cuthbert Mills instantly. A mother wept over her lost son, a colonel raged over a wrecked engine, an aeronautical engineer agonized over his conscience, while Doctor Christmas wrote to the Army asking for another propeller and telling them that the 'Bullet' Mk 2 was already taking shape in his mind.

In March 1919 the Bullet Mk 2 was put on display at the New York Aero Show with the following sales pitch: 'CHRISTMAS BULLET – safest, easiest controlled plane in the world. Speed 200 mph–6-cylinder Hall Scott 200 hp motor. Cantilever Aero Company, 1265 Broadway, New York City.' When the Army got wind of this they refused absolutely to allow the doctor to use one of their airfields to test the new plane. They should have known better. Doctor Christmas had no intention of testing anything. There was no need. He had found himself a genuine RAF pilot – with the appallingly inappropriate name of Captain Allington Jolly – who was going to demonstrate to the world the qualities of the new Bullet. The maiden flight was from a farmer's field and ended in the farmer's barn. Captain Jolly got the plane into the air, the wings became very flexible indeed, and the Bullet crashed straight into the barn, killing the pilot instantly.

Undeterred, Doctor Christmas now took his idea before a House of Representatives Committee at Washington. Insisting that his plane was the most impressive ever built, 60 mph faster than any other plane flying, he also claimed that he was being inundated with orders from European buyers. There were, in fact, no orders: the Europeans had seen enough premature death for the time being. He told the Congressmen that in 1914 only his loyalty to his country had prevented him taking up an offer from the Kaiser for a million dollars in gold if he would divulge his secret design to the Germans. In the end, as far as we know, Doctor Christmas built no more planes. However, he entered the business to make money and he did just that, the US Government paying him $100,000 for a patent he had filed for the Bullet's aileron.

One is left to reflect less on Doctor Christmas' morality than on the technology involved in building the Bullet. Was it really a plane? It flew, certainly, and it crashed. But was it controllable? Certainly not by the pilot. The only control exercise was by Doctor Christmas himself and that made him responsible for the deaths of the two pilots. It has been observed that the Bullet was less a plane than a murder weapon – a fitting epitaph for what was certainly the world's worst aircraft.

CAPRONI'S FAT LADY

During the First World War, the craze for huge bombers did not pass Italy by. If these flying monstrosities seemed like something from an operatic set - Wagnerian in Germany, folkish and fantastic in Russia - in Italy they were a cross between Verdian bombast and opera buffa. Even

Sikorski and Forssman had not managed eight engines and nine wings. In fact, as far as this writer is aware nobody ever matched Count Caproni's Ca60. Even the Italians maintained a proper sense of balance when viewing the count's creation. As one said drolly, 'It would not have looked out of place sailing up the English Channel with the Spanish Armada in 1588.'

Following in the footsteps of Igor Sikorski and his huge bombers, Count Caproni decided that Italy must have aeroplanes of the same size and potential for her war against Austria in 1915. As a result he produced the huge Ca31 and Ca32 bombers, each with a capacity to carry several 1000-pound bombs. His final bomber – the Ca42 – was a vast triplane with a wingspan of over a hundred feet. Hundreds of such bombers saw service with the Italian Air Force during the First World War. Until this point there was little so far in his career to suggest that Caproni was anything other than a capable designer of bombers. It is true that his planes did suffer from the same problems as the huge bombers did in every other country: they were too heavy for their engines, and were generally not cost-effective in labour or capital. Nevertheless, he was not a madman like Forssman – or at least one might have supposed not.

When the war ended in 1918, Caproni attempted to transfer the skills he had acquired in wartime design and production to civilian transport. In 1920 he hoped to build the first great transatlantic airliner to carry 100 passengers across to New York. But what had been good enough to lumber through the skies, carrying six or seven men in abject discomfort, to drop half a ton of explosives on the heads of his enemies, was not going to prove good enough – or indeed big enough – for fare-paying passengers travelling 3000 miles without stopping. Comfort became the prime consideration.

The count began his 'Capronissimo' Ca-60 as a seaplane, by choosing a 77-foot long houseboat, which was moored on Lake Maggiore, as the fuselage. The houseboat had a de luxe interior, with ample window space, and looked exactly what it was – a boat. The problem came when Caproni began to try to convert it into a flying machine. As a bomber-designer he had been responsible

Count Caproni's massive nine-winged aircraft was far too heavy for its engines. It began and ended its life on Lake Maggiore.

for lifting a plane weighting up to 15,000 pounds. With the 'Capronisimo' he was facing a weight of 55,000 pounds. It was quite a challenge. But the second decade of the century was an age of aeronautical dreamers whose imaginations outran their technical capacities. Three great wings had been enough to lift the bombers. If the Capronisimo was three times as heavy, the Count reasoned, let it have three sets of triplane wings – nine wings in total. To power the plane Caproni used eight American-built 400-h.p. Liberty V-12 engines.

On 4 March 1921, before a vast crowd of dignitaries and well-wishers, the Capronissimo made her maiden flight – maiden being an inappropriate word for so matronly an aircraft – on the smooth waters of Lake Maggiore. The engines revved madly and pulled as only three thousand horses could, the nine wings bent with the effort, the crew filled the air with every known assault on the Italian language, and the Capronissimo raised its nose some sixty feet out of the water. The crowds held their breath as if to keep the great craft aloft with willpower alone but, alas, it was not enough. The end, when it came, was as dramatic as the death of the heroine in an opera by Puccini. With a resounding crack the Capronisimo broke her back, the wings collapsed and giant cocktail sticks filled the air like the English arrow storm at Crécy. Soon, all that was left of the aircraft was floating débris on the lake.

The search for scapegoats began. Suspicion fell on the pilot whom, it was said, preferred to crash on the water and from just sixty feet rather than in the North Atlantic and from many thousand feet. Many suspected that he had merely precipitated the inevitable end of a machine that could never have flown. Caproni dismissed such talk and made it known that he intended to rebuild the plane. He salvaged part of it and dragged it ashore. Mysteriously the remnant was burned to a cinder before he had managed to reconstruct it. It seemed that fate was against him. Caproni never completed his airliner and for a while returned to bombers. But he was no longer in step with the spirit of the age and suffered neglect and virtual oblivion.

THE WORKS OF MAXIM GORKY

Following the defection of Igor Sikorski to the United States after the Revolution of 1917, the mantle of master-magician of the Russian aircraft industry fell upon the shoulders of A.N. Tupolev, who carried the flame of 'monster bombers' right through to the Cold War. As early as 1932 he devised an aerial battleship – the six-engine AM-34 RN – which had a wing span of 175 feet and carried ten guns. But it was an expensive failure and for just a moment it seemed that the Russian love of the large and ungainly might be coming to a halt. Then help came from an unexpected source. In 1932 the Union of Soviet Writers and Editors – known as YURGAZ for short – wanted to celebrate the fortieth anniversary of the start of the literary career of the great Soviet author Maxim Gorky. They therefore approached Tupolev with a commission, financed by a public subscription, to build a huge aircraft to become the flagship of a 'Maxim Gorky Propaganda Squadron'. The huge A-20 would be a bomber of sorts – it would drop leaflets and extracts from Gorky's works in all parts of the Soviet Union, as well as spread the word abroad.

A man as important as Gorky needed a big plane and that is what he got. It was staggeringly big. Its wingspan was 260 feet and the length of its fuselage was

106 feet. It could carry more than a hundred passengers and had a crew of twenty. As its field was propaganda, it was equipped with a cinema in the rear fuselage, a printing press in one wing (left wing), a photographic studio in the other wing, a telephone exchange, printing press, radio transmitter, a laundry, a pharmacy as well as cabins, toilets and a galley. It also boasted the biggest loud-speakers in the world, which reached the parts of the Soviet Union that other planes could not reach. And for the totally deaf peasant, there were lights on the underside of the fuselage which flashed simple messages.

Unfortunately, this triumph of Soviet aviation had a rather short life. On 18 May, 1935, as a propaganda stunt, the employees of the Central Aerodynamic Institute in Moscow were invited to bring their families for 'joy-rides' in the great aircraft. Huge queues formed at the airport and the first lucky people flooded aboard. In order to demonstrate the size of the *Maxim Gorky* two Polikarpov I-5 fighters flew alongside, one to make a documentary film of the event. One of the pilots got more than he bargained for. The other fighter pilot, one Comrade Blagin, feeling somewhat upstaged by the giant aircraft, decided to show off in front of the crowds by trying some acrobatics. He began by bar-rel-rolling his tiny aircraft, lost control and crashed on top of one of the *Gorky*'s wings, becoming stuck between two of the engines. At first it seemed that all would be well, and the crowds on the ground were torn between screaming and cheering. Then, from a height of several thousand feet, the *Gorky*'s wing fell off and part of the fuselage ripped open, throwing the passengers out and killing people on the ground. Finally, the great plane itself crashed to the ground, killing everyone on board. It was a catastrophe and a scapegoat was necessary. As the *Maxim Gorky* had been a propaganda aircraft its destruction was to have a significance for the Soviet peoples that went beyond the mere loss of a plane. Comrade Blagin had to carry his guilt beyond the grave. From 1935 onwards the word 'Blaginism' entered Russian dictionaries as meaning 'selfish exhibitionism and the lack of a proper socialist discipline.'

Critics of the Soviet Union's obsession with large planes, like the *New York Times*, tried to draw a moral from the disaster, equating the pursuit of national pride with a lack of appropriate humility and care in their designers. But the Soviets were not listening. A huge national subscription raised the money for three more of these absurd planes. Two were eventually built, one serving as an airliner and the other seeing service as a transport during the Second World War.

As if to prove that anything Tupolev built he could build better – or perhaps bigger – K.A.Kalinin built an experimental bomber to match the A-20. 'Experimental' is certainly the right word for a plane that carried its bomb load – an incredible 20,000 pounds – in an undercarriage which appeared to be a curious cross between seaplane floats and ordinary wheels. The K-7, as it was called, was well-protected, with enough machine guns to keep nine crewmen busy, but it was underpowered for such a vast plane – 4500 h.p. engines as against the A-20's 7200 hp – and had a wing area even bigger than *Maxim Gorky*, thick enough and wide enough to accommodate 120 people. On its test flight violent vibrations shook the tail boom, which were promptly reinforced with slabs of steel making the entire plane too heavy for its engines. On the next test flight the reinforced tail boom fell off and the great bomber did a nose dive into the ground, killing its crew. Kalinin soon fell out of favour with Stalin and was executed as an enemy of the people.

REPERCUSSIONS

During the inter-war years Soviet designers toyed with the idea of building heavy fighters equipped with very powerful 102mm recoilless cannon. The problem with this idea, of course, was the need to integrate the large cannon into the structure of the plane and of carrying the additional weight. A number of different planes were designed but none was successful. A.N. Tupolev, more renowned for his huge bombers than his fighters, supervised two separate research teams and from their work developed the Ant-23 and the Ant-29. The Ant-23 was the product of V. N. Chernyshev's team, and adopted the highly original idea of turning the gun barrels into lengthened tail booms, so that the escape of exhaust gases when the gun was fired could be dispersed beyond the tail plane.

In appearance the Ant-23 was one of the strangest of all Russian experimental planes, being little less than a flying cannon, with a propeller at both ends. In some ways it resembled a First World War 'pusher', though it had, in fact, two engines, with a propeller at the nose as well. Unfortunately, the rear engine – the 'pusher' – did not push to much effect, and the plane's maximum speed was only 186 mph, poor when one considered by this date – 1933 – Italian aircraft were achieving over 300 mph. Moreover, and this can hardly have come as much surprise, the Ant-23 was sluggish and unmanoeuvrable. To make matters worse, it was an aircraft more dangerous to its pilot than to the enemy. The risks of the design were truly horrifying. For example, as pilots pointed out to the designer, should they be forced to abandon the plane they would be blown backwards by the wind as they left their seats and minced up by the rear propeller. Test pilot I.F.Kozlov very nearly suffered this fate. Flying on cannon-firing trials he fired one shot and the gun exploded, shattering its barrel which was, it should be remembered, the tail boom of the plane. Normally Kozlov would have leaped out and escaped by parachute. But, fearing a grisly end in the rear propeller, he stayed in his seat and miraculously managed to land the front part of the plane that was still in one piece. It was enough to condemn the design and no more work was done on this plane.

Attention turned to Tupolev's other protégé, A. A. Arkhangelski, who had adopted a more conventional approach in his heavy fighter, which carried the designation Ant-29. The plane was a two-seater, twin-engine monoplane, with two 102mm cannon built into the fuselage, one above the other, and dispersing the hot gases by the tailplane. Arkhangelski's plane had a top speed of 218 mph, but it was very unstable and so slow was its cannon in firing that if it missed with its first shot it would be helpless against a machine-gun firing enemy. The development of an efficient 20mm cannon put an end to Russia's search for a flying cannon and Tupolev, for once, was left with egg on his face and two failed designs.

No bomb heavier than 500 pounds will ever be needed.

AIR VICE-MARSHAL BURNETT, DEPUTY CHIEF OF THE AIR STAFF, TO AIR VICE-MARSHAL DOWDING, 1932

The whim of the supremacy of the bomber in air warfare reflected a thoroughly conservative mode of thinking, as witnessed by this suggestion that bombers will never be more capacious than existing models.

THE BOMBER THAT DID NOT GET THROUGH

The contribution made by R.J. Mitchell to the British war effort between 1939 and 1945 cannot be over-estimated. Although he never lived to see his masterpiece, the Supermarine Spitfire, in action – he died in 1937 – he must have known that there was no plane in the world that would prove its master. Yet if the Spitfire was to save his country during the darkest days of 1940, another of Mitchell's designs might have won the war a year early had it ever been built. For the Type 317 Mitchell bomber was as much a masterpiece as the Spitfire and even further ahead of all other of its world rivals than its more famous stable-companion. The fact that Britain never built this potentially great plane is one of tragedies of the British war effort, which – it has been suggested – cost Bomber Command many thousands of lives lost in four-engined bombers like the Stirling whose specifications were so far inferior to the Mitchell design. More darkly, perhaps, the use of the Mitchell bomber would probably have cost the Germans heavier casualties during the area bombing campaigns. The projected speed of the Type 317 - as high as 370 m.p.h., which was at least a hundred m.p.h. faster than the Lancaster, Britain's best bomber of the war – might have overwhelmed Germany's night–fighters and even proved too much for the Me–109 day–fighters. This would have allowed Bomber Command to bomb during daylight, with a consequent increase in bombing accuracy. The advantages of the high-speed bomber were demonstrated by the later Mosquito, though this was merely a light-bomber. To have that much speed, as well as a capacity to carry an average of 14–17,000 pounds of bombs, would have provided Britain with the finest bomber of the whole war.

The story of the Mitchell bomber is, like so many such stories in British aviation history, one of lost opportunities. It began with the Air Ministry specifications of December 1936, for a four-engined heavy bomber. Vickers, Short Brothers and Supermarine all entered designs and the latter two were awarded contracts to build prototypes. The design submitted by R. J. Mitchell was such an improvement on the specifications that had they even approached them, rather than met them, the bomber would still have been a super-plane. With a

This painting of R.J. Mitchell's Type 317 bomber gives some idea of one of the Second World War's greatest missed opportunities. Britain might have had a 'super-bomber' in 1941, far superior to the Avro Lancaster and so fast that it could carry a vast bomb load to Germany at a speed that would have made it difficult for German nightfighters to intercept.

In October 1937 the chairman of Vickers, A.A. Jamieson, accompanied by J.D. Scott, Vickers' test pilot, visited Germany and was shown the latest Luftwaffe planes and equipment by Luftwaffe general Ernst Udet. Scott reported his important findings to the Air Ministry only to get the above response, typical of British complacency.

maximum speed of 370 m.p.h. it would have been faster than a Spitfire – as well as the fastest of German fighters – and it would have been able to go into production during 1941, a year before the Lancaster. Its maximum bomb carrying capacity might have reached 21,000 pounds and its maximum range would have been 3000 miles carrying 8000 pounds. It would have carried three turrets, the central one retractable but, above all, at such high speed its need for protection would have been far less than other four-engined bombers. The great Lancaster – beloved of almost everyone at Bomber Command – would have been left for dead by a plane that flew 100 m.p.h. faster.

While Supermarine worked on the prototype of the Mitchell design, Short Brothers produced the very disappointing Stirling bomber. It is perhaps unfair to compare the Type 317 with the Lancaster. The true comparison should be between Mitchell's design and the Stirling, which was the design that the Air Ministry chose to adopt. The Stirling began badly. As a result of RAF hangars being a mere hundred feet wide, the Stirling had its wings reduced to just 99 feet 10 inches. This had a disastrous effect on the bomber's ceiling, which was kept at 17,000 feet, well within the range of German anti-aircraft guns. Because the Air Ministry had not moved with the times, the new bomber would be unnecessarily exposed to danger with consequent effect on flight operations and increased loss of life. The compartmentalization of the bomb bay in the Stirling also meant that it was unable to carry bombs larger than 1000 pounds, once these became widely available. Again, its designers had not looked ahead. The Stirling was very much the poor relation when compared with Mitchell's design.

However, during the latter stages of the Battle of Britain, fortune smiled on the Luftwaffe in a way that it was never to understand. In September 1940 a raid on the Supermarine factory at Woolston, near Southampton, gutted the building and destroyed the two fuselages of the Mitchell prototypes. It was a loss, but it hardly had to be permanent. The German aircraft industry was later to withstand three years of saturation bombing compared to which the raid on Woolston was a mere pinprick. Yet it continued to produce prototypes for new aircraft, including high performance rocket and jet craft. However, the Air Ministry took the soft option and went ahead with the Short Stirling, consigning Mitchell's potentially war-winning design to the dustbin of history's 'might-have-beens'. It was a crass decision. Conceivably today we might remember Mitchell's Type 317 bomber as the greater of his two masterpieces, the one that not only saved Britain from defeat but the one that hastened victory in Europe with a saving of countless lives.

PART THREE:
WORLD WAR TWO

IS IT A BIRD ? IS IT A PLANE ? IS IT...ONE OF OURS ?

The misidentification of aircraft in wartime has been one of the main causes of aerial 'friendly fire' incidents. It is almost always a human failing, resulting from poor training or panic on the part of the anti-aircraft gunners or pilots involved. Losses caused by such misidentification have generally been classified under the title of 'friendly fire' ('blue-on-blue' in US parlance), but as General Norman Schwarzkopf explained during the Gulf War, no fire is ever 'friendly'.

It will come as no surprise to students of the Battle of Britain (see p.96), of all aerial struggles the 'most pregnant' with consequences, that not all British casualties of the three-month battle were inflicted by the Germans. No fewer than twenty British aircraft were lost to British anti-aircraft fire, while a further nine planes were shot down by British pilots; in fact, in total more than two whole squadrons were lost to 'friendly fire'. Just how 'trigger-happy' the British gunners were could be seen from the treatment meted out to one young hero, Flight Lieutenant Roderick Learoyd, on 2 November 1940. Learoyd had been awarded the Victoria Cross and was to be given the freedom of his home town in a ceremony at New Romney. He set out in a Handley Page Hampden from Scampton for the airfield at Hawkinge, but just after he had taken off he came under fire from machine-guns on the airfield perimeter. Surviving these he approached Hawkinge only to be subjected to heavy anti-aircraft fire and was driven off, finally having to make a forced landing at Manston. Surprisingly – at least in view of the reception they gave him – the authorities at Hawkinge had been told to expect Learoyd and he had flown in low, obviously intending to land. How the gunners could have mistaken this slow approach for a low level attack by a Dornier Do17 – the explanation they later gave – is difficult to understand. Nevertheless, when the young hero arrived at Manston, his Hampden was found to have suffered more than twenty bullet and shrapnel holes, while his co-pilot had suffered a shrapnel wound in the leg and missed the ceremony because of his injuries.

THE BATTLE OF BARKING CREEK

On the morning of 6 September 1939 – with the war just three days old – a searchlight battery on the Essex coast reported a flight of unidentified aircraft passing over them towards London. It was the spark that ignited the short fuses that many officers in the RAF were carrying at this early stage of the war. Equipped with enthusiasm, 'gung-ho' courage, itchy trigger-fingers and roaring torrents of adrenalin, hundreds of young men were soon involved in a tragi-comedy of errors that has earned itself the mocking title 'The Battle of Barking Creek' – Barking Creek being a notable outlet for London sewerage.

Whatever be the lengths to which others may go, His Majesty's Government will never resort to the deliberate attack on women and children, and other civilians for purposes of mere terrorism.

PRIME MINISTER NEVILLE CHAMBERLAIN IN THE HOUSE OF COMMONS, 14 SEPTEMBER 1939

The prime minister was not misleading the House (see p. 119). Neither Britain nor Germany began the war with any intention of bombing civilians. However, once defeat seemed imminent Britain was prepared to use any means to avoid it.

The report of 'raiders' went to RAF Sector Operations at North Weald and thence on to XI Group Fighter Command HQ at Uxbridge. The course of the incoming planes was tracked at both places. However, as the enemy flight was near the borders of XI Group's responsibility, XII Group Fighter Command at Nottingham was also informed. It now fell to Group Captain D. F. Lucking, Sector Controller at North Weald, to order up a precautionary flight of fighters. Lucking began by scrambling a flight (six planes) of Hurricanes from 56 Squadron at North Weald. This should have been enough to cope with the initial 'sighting', after which reinforcements could be summoned as appropriate. However, Squadron Leader E. V. Knowles, acting on his own initiative, decided to scramble the whole of 56 Squadron (twelve planes) as well as two reserve pilots, who took off five minutes after the other twelve Hurricanes and followed them at a half-mile distance and a thousand feet below. Unfortunately, Lucking was still under the impression that his orders had been carried out and that just six British fighters were in the air, instead of the fourteen that actually were. At this moment Lucking received further reports from Observer Corps posts of the original 'sighting' and decided that he needed more planes in the air. He therefore ordered six more Hurricanes – this time from 151 Squadron – to join the search. Meanwhile, right and left hands were not acting together. At XI Group HQ reports from a radio-location station that multiple plots of aircraft approaching from the east had been recorded prompted XI Group to scramble four flights of Spitfires (24 planes) from three squadrons (74, 65 and 54) at Hornchurch to 'intercept' the Germans. Interception altitude was to be above the level at which the Hurricanes already scrambled were operating. A 'friendly-fire' incident was now virtually guaranteed.

Air raid sirens were by now sounding throughout London and in South Essex and North Kent. But the truth was that the British were chasing their shadows. As yet there had been no visual confirmation of the incoming German planes. One side was ready for battle, but who was going to provide the opposition? As hysteria grew anti-aircraft batteries began opening fire on the planes overhead, all of which it soon transpired were 'friendly'. In the air the two flights of Spitfires from 74 Squadron, operating out of Hornchurch, soon sighted the Hurricanes from 56 Squadron, but failed to identify them correctly. The leader of 'A' flight radioed, 'Bandits ahead!', and two pilots – Flying Officer 'Paddy' Byrne and Flying Officer John Freeborn – dived in to attack two stragglers (in fact, the reserve pilots from 56 Squadron). Crying 'Tally-ho!' the pilots of the two Spitfires dived onto the Hurricanes with guns blazing, while the rest of 56 squadron scattered. Byrne and Freeborn latched onto their prey and pursued them towards Ipswich. But now the farce took on a darker hue. The Spitfires began scoring hits and soon one of the Hurricanes, flown by Pilot Officer Montagu Hulton-Harrop, crashed in flames, killing the pilot. The other Hurricane, flown by Pilot Officer Tommy Rose, though damaged, managed to make a forced landing. Meanwhile, the skies over Essex were filled with the whirling shapes of a further 24 Spitfires and 18 Hurricanes, all diving and weaving away from the gunfire of the anti-aircraft guns. Luckily at least one man kept his head: Squadron Leader Teddy Donaldson, commanding 151 Squadron, who managed to recognize an engagement with friendly forces for what it was. Radioing the warning 'Do not retaliate. Bandits are friendly!' Donaldson managed to restore some order to the proceedings.

Unfortunately so much of this activity had occurred on the borders of XII

Group's responsibility that the Duty Controller in Nottingham decided to be safe rather than sorry by scrambling two full squadrons of Spitfires from Duxford. What followed was an embarrassing shambles. Frankly, 19 and 66 Squadrons were simply not ready for scrambling and as they tried to take off they found they were heading straight into planes approaching from the other end of the airfield. Meanwhile, the survivors from 74, 65 and 54 squadrons, trying to return to their bases, were subjected to a heavy bombardment from the coastal batteries at Sheerness and Chelmsford. Only one plane was badly damaged, but most of the others had narrow escapes. The whole episode boded ill for the future when the real enemy was engaged.

Such an incident warranted immediate investigation. A full court of inquiry ordered the arrest of the two Spitfire pilots Byrne and Freeborn, while Group Captain Lucking was also taken into custody, pending court martial. The two young pilots had in reality done nothing more than follow their instincts. In another situation their actions might have won approval rather than disgrace. They were as much victims as the pilots who were on the receiving end of their fire and both were acquitted of any blame. Lucking was a different case. A senior officer, he had lost control of a situation which might have cost the lives of hundreds and the loss of valuable aircraft. It will be some time before we know what happened at his court martial, the findings of which became part of a general cover-up. The fiasco was downgraded to a mere 'incident' and the fatality was not acknowledged by the authorities.

The truth of what happened at the 'Battle of Barking Creek' will never be known for certain. Official allegations that a flight of German planes was sighted, but that it then turned back are almost certainly just part of the cover-up. The initial sighting was probably just a distant formation of ducks or geese removing to their daytime feeding grounds. After the Hurricanes of 56 Squadron had been scrambled they became the 'bandits' through a misreading of their plots. Once these planes found that there were no 'bandits' they would have turned inland and thereafter been seen as the 'bandits' themselves, approaching from the east. And once the anti-aircraft guns opened fire on them, the Spitfires approaching from the opposite direction would have assumed that they were the enemy. In the heat of the moment, and with the adrenalin pumping, the Spitfire pilots would have lost their inhibitions and dived into the attack. The reaction of the authorities was predictable: what could not be accepted must be brushed under the carpet. Understandable in wartime, the continued suppression of this tragic military blunder is less easily justified some fifty years afterwards. The details of Group Captain Lucking's court martial rest in a closed file at the Public Record Office, apparently stamped 'To remain closed.'

FALSE LANDINGS

In wartime it is a wise pilot who knows his own side of the lines. In both world wars there have been numerous occasions where, by mistakenly landing behind enemy lines, a pilot has revealed something that had best been kept secret. The most famous example, perhaps, was named the 'Mechelen Incident' and was believed to have forced Hitler to cancel the invasion of France he had planned for January 1940.

The 'Mechelen Incident' contained elements of both farce and intense seriousness. For the sake of some dirty washing the future of Western Europe was put into the balance. On 9 January 1940 a German major from a parachute division, Hellmuth Reinberger, was called to attend a secret conference at Cologne the following day. Complete with top-secret air plans he set off by train and had gone about half way when he stopped for dinner. By chance he was invited to dine at the local air base. He dined well and after a few drinks he got into close conversation with the station commander, a reserve major named Hoenmanns who offered to fly Reinberger to Cologne to save him a boring train journey. He said that he needed the practice and, in any case, wanted to drop in on his wife and take home some dirty laundry. Reinberger was only too pleased to accept and the next day, in perfect flying conditions, the two men set off in a tiny Me-108 trainer.

Reinberger had on his knees a briefcase, which contained top-secret plans for Germany's proposed invasion of Holland and Belgium, which had only recently been drawn up and was apparently a re-run of the 1914 Schlieffen Plan. Although visibility had been perfect when they took off, there was a sudden change in the weather. Hoenmanns began to panic, realizing that he was losing his way and drifting towards the west. Before he could make adjustments to his flight path his engine suddenly cut out and he was obliged to make a forced landing, losing both wings in a line of trees. Nevertheless, both men survived the crash and scrambled clear into a snowy thicket of bushes. They studied their map only to discover that they were no longer in Germany, having crossed the Belgian border a few miles from Maastricht. Realizing the danger Reinberger hid behind some bushes and tried to burn his secret plans, but his lighter would not work. An amused peasant came up and offered Reinberger a match. The major built a small fire and began to burn the papers one by one, but could not burn them all. As fate would have it, the plane crash had been witnessed by a troop of Belgian troops led by an officer, who now reached the scene and proceeded to arrest the two Germans. They were marched off to a command post, Reinberger carrying the plans under his arm. Left for a moment in an empty room heated by a stove, Reinberger made another desperate effort to burn the plans. Though badly charred, they were rescued by the Belgian officer and handed over to his superiors. They in turn passed the papers onto the French and British, who immediately recognized their significance. Reinberger had been carrying nothing less than the German invasion plans. Surely this was too good to be true. When the news reached Berlin Hitler was furious with the Luftwaffe, dismissing senior officers left, right and centre, and abusing Goering publicly. Goering's wife suggested using a clairvoyant to gauge Allied reaction to the plans. This lady, incorrectly as it turned out, convinced the Nazi leaders that Reinberger had been successful in burning the plans. Belgian intelligence conformed this. Nevertheless, Hitler decided that he would wait. French and Belgian troop adjustments told him what he needed to know. The plans had not been burned. His enemies would be waiting for him if he persevered with the existing plan of attack. On 16 January the plan was postponed and was in due course rewritten according to the inspiration of General von Manstein: Plan Yellow was born and with it victory over France. The two German majors spent the war as prisoners in Canada. The fate of the laundry is uncertain.

Sounding like an episode from *Dad's Army*, the story of the German bomber that landed on the beach at Bridport, Dorset, in November 1940, has one of the most bitter of outcomes. As related by the brilliant young British scientist, Dr R.V. Jones, it was an episode in the 'battle of the beams', during which Jones and his colleagues struggled to break the German system of navigation beams that allowed German bombers to mount accurate attacks on British cities. German bombers were returning after one bombing raid over the Midlands, when one of the planes suffered a compass failure. It was then misled by a British beam into landing on the beach at Bridport, assuming that it was over France. This was a coup of unimaginable importance for Jones, as the plane was carrying a complete X-Gerät system, which would have enabled British scientists to misdirect the German raiders by using a false beam. It was absolutely vital that the plane with its prize should be taken intact.

As fate would have it an army unit of no great distinction – and even less initiative – took complete control of the situation. Told of the importance of the plane, which had landed on the sand at low tide, the officer in charge of the coastal defence unit allocated two soldiers to guard the plane 'with their lives'. One can imagine Private Pike and Lance-Corporal Jones both elated and terrified by the responsibility. As a parting shot the officer told the two not to let anyone touch it, adding 'I don't care if even an Admiral comes along. You are not to allow him near it.' Our two worthies fixed bayonets and defended their prize against the world.

Unfortunately, the tide began to come in, a circumstance for which their officer had not prepared them. Some sailors nearby offered to help pull the plane out of the water but the soldiers kept them at bay and stood resolutely by as the water rose and rose until much of the plane disappeared from view. Technical Intelligence officers arrived just too late. By the time the tide had retreated the inside of the bomber was filled with sand and light alloy components of the beam system had been corroded. Dr Jones bluntly suggests that if the plane had been saved intact the devastating raid on Coventry, just eight days later, could almost certainly have been prevented.

RADAR TRAP

Luck plays a major part in warfare. Just as, in 1940, Dr R.V. Jones lost the chance to gain a complete X-Gerät machine which might have saved Coventry from devastation (see above), so, four years later, he was delivered a Lichtenstein SN-2 wide-angle-radar unit by the Germans themselves.

Just after dawn on 13 July 1944, at Woodbridge air base in Suffolk, a young pilot officer, W.D.Raymond, reported seeing what he believed to be a British Mosquito aircraft circling the base. He thought it was returning from a mission over Europe and was, perhaps, low on fuel. So he fired green flares telling it that it was safe to come in to land. The plane promptly did so. Raymond collected a truck and drove out to pick up the crew. What first raised his suspicions was that there were three airmen, when Mosquitoes only carry two! As he drew near the men he suddenly realized that the men were German and the plane was the newest kind of Ju88 G-1 nightfighter, which was bristling with all the latest gadgetry, including radar systems unknown to the British. Raymond pulled out a pistol and the Germans surrendered. Apparently, they later admitted, they had only just completed their flight training and had been on their first operation. They had been flying by compass heading and had flown in exactly the opposite

This Junkers Ju-88, complete with its secret Lichtenstein radar system, landed by mistake at a British air-base in Suffolk in July 1944 and helped the British counteract the German night defences, which had been costing Bomber Command an exorbitant number of lost planes.

direction. Instead of landing at their base in Holland as they had expected, they had landed in Suffolk. As it happens, they were out of fuel and had they flown over the North Sea they would never have reached land.

The find was a precious one. Within hours Dr Jones and his specialists had arrived to investigate the plane. What they found was of vital importance to Bomber Command's campaign over Germany. British Intelligence had heard rumours of new German equipment which fed off British signals but they had seen no evidence of it. Now here it was, delivered and gift-wrapped. The success of German nightfighters recently had caused heavy casualties to British bombers, notably in the Nuremberg raid (see p.121). The reason why the nightfighters were achieving greater success was now apparent. They were homing in on the signals from the bombers' Monica radar, which was supposed to beep when nightfighters were approaching. Moreover, the British H2S blind-bombing device was enabling the Germans to locate the bomber-streams from 90 miles away through their Naxos airborne radar. When this news was passed on to Bomber Command, Air Chief Marshal Harris swiftly ordered all the Monica warning devices to be removed from the tails of his bombers. During investigations carried out at Farnborough it was also discovered that Lichtenstein SN-2 radar operated on a frequency of 85 megahertz, thus enabling the British to devise counter-measures. It was an astonishing stroke of luck and one that virtually ended the Luftwaffe's ability to defend Germany from Bomber Command's strategic offensive.

A COOL RECEPTION

The British military operation at Narvik in Norway, in April 1940, has been generally viewed as one of the most incompetent ever staged by this country. The fate reserved for Britain's aerial effort on that occasion was a particularly cruel one.

Although a decision to evacuate British troops from Norway was imminent, eighteen Gloster Gladiators of 263 Squadron were flown in from the aircraft carrier *Glorious*, at the request of Major-General Paget, to challenge German air superiority over Aandalsnes, south of Trondheim. The Gladiators left their carrier in a snowstorm and were guided to a makeshift airfield on the frozen Lake Lesjaskog. Here ground crews had cleared the snow and piled it up alongside the runways, thus marking them out. Unfortunately, the Germans had flown over the lake and seen what the British were doing. An unkind idea occurred to them. They would wait until the British planes had arrived and made themselves at home, then they would pay a little unexpected visit. As night fell, so did the temperature. Standing out in the open in thirty degrees of frost the Gladiators froze, with controls and engines like solid blocks of ice. The ill-prepared ground crews had battery starters but no acid to put in the batteries. Moreover, there was just one armourer to check and service eighteen planes, carrying 72 Browning machine guns, if the latter could be defrosted, which was doubtful.

At daylight frantic efforts were made to get the planes operational again. Only two were working when the German bombers flew over and started bombing the lake. In many places the ice cracked and the planes sank into the water. Elsewhere, they were blown up or severely damaged. During this one-sided combat, their ground crews hid in the trees at the edge of the lake while the pilots and air crew rushed about trying to refuel and re-arm the surviving planes to make a fight of it. Of the eighteen Gladiators that had landed at dusk, thirteen of them were destroyed by midday. The five surviving Gladiators managed to get away from the ice-trap and land at a Norwegian army camp. After a brave struggle against Germany's overwhelming aerial superiority the Gladiators were withdrawn to their carrier and were all lost when the *Glorious* was sunk by the *Scharnhorst* and *Gneisenau* (see pp.8-20). It cannot have been pleasant for the pilots of these old biplanes to realize that they were only in Norway because they were deemed expendable. Hawker Hurricanes had been available to accompany the British troops, but the RAF considered that they were too valuable to be risked in such a hare-brained operation. Ironically, some Hurricanes were eventually released to help the troop evacuation. They too tried to hitch a lift home aboard the *Glorious*.

A WARM WELCOME

To the people of the warring nations in both world wars, airmen comprised a race apart. Their exploits were so far outside the normal experience of ordinary people that their intrusion in the everyday life of country folk sometimes took an unusual form. Pilots baling out from stricken aircraft who descended by parachute were sometimes not accorded the sort of welcome they might have expected.

During the Italian invasion of Greece in 1940, one of the Bristol Blenheims of the Greek Air Force was damaged in action and its pilot looked for a suitable place to make a crash landing. He glimpsed some fires on the ground and assumed that they had been lit to guide him in to his base at Larissa. He landed in a field only to discover, to his consternation, that the field was alight because the local peasants had been burning old grass. He and his crew clambered out to be confronted by a hostile mob. The peasants would not believe that the flyers were Greek and insisted that they looked and spoke like Italians. The pilot pointed out that his plane carried Greek markings, whereupon the peasants stated that the Italians were well-known for carrying false markings. Then the pilot pointed out that he and his crew spoke perfect Greek. But again the peasants were unimpressed: the Italians were now employing Greek-speaking air crew. The pilot was becoming desperate at this stage as the peasants were growing increasingly threatening. Suddenly the navigator, Lieutenant Maravelias, began singing a Greek song with the accompanying dance. The peasants were convinced at last and joined in the celebration, only remembering at the last moment to wheel the Blenheim away from the burning grass before the fuel tank exploded.

A more bitter reception was accorded to a Polish pilot of the RAF who baled out from his damaged Spitfire over Wapping in 1940. Injured and partly blinded in his cockpit, the Pole fell into a street crowded with people furious at the damage they had suffered at the hands of the German bombers. The Pole appeared to be jabbering in a foreign language assumed, by the mob, to be German. Ignoring the RAF 'wings' on his uniform, the crowd beat him to death without attempting to identify which side he was on.

BETWEEN 'FRIENDS'

Neutrality is very difficult in 'Total War' as both Sweden and Switzerland found to their cost, since both countries were overflown and occasionally bombed by planes of the belligerent states (see p.151). Switzerland finished the war with a powerful strategic bomber force of her own made up of 186 interned American four-engine Liberators and Flying Fortresses. Some Swiss and Swedish fighter pilots might even have qualified as 'aces' for the number of foreign fighters they had shot down in 'dog-fights' over their own territory. But if it was difficult to be neutral, how much worse it must have been to be, like France, a defeated ally of Britain, whose delivery from Nazi oppression became one of Britain's main war aims. To liberate France the Germans would have to be driven out of French territory and this could not be achieved without the sacrifice of French lives during the fighting. Just how many French lives were lost to British and American actions between 1943 and 1945 is not known but it was considerable. And what made things worse, many of these lives could have been saved.

The destruction of the French city of Royan is a striking example of military incompetence linked to bad luck. In the early hours of 5 January 1945, a strong force of 354 British Lancasters attacked the town, which was being stubbornly defended by the Germans against a siege by the French Resistance. The garrison at Royan was preventing the allies from using the great port of Bordeaux. At SHAEF (Supreme Headquarters Allied Expeditionary Force) headquarters it was understood that French citizens had been evacuated from the town and that there were only Germans inside. This was wrong – there were still 3500 civilians living in the centre of Royan, with the Germans holding the perimeter. By a ghastly misunderstanding the Lancasters were ordered to bomb the centre of the town – where there were no Germans at all – and proceeded to obliterate it with 1651 tons of high explosives, more than was dropped on Cologne during the 'Thousand Bomber Raid'.

This tragic error could have been averted. The previous day a telegram had been sent from SHAEF to the headquarters of the US Sixth Army Group, commanded by General Devers. It ordered the following message to be circulated: 'From the air force staff at SHAEF headquarters. Inform all Allied units engaged in that sector, that on 5 January 1945, RAF Bomber Command will bomb the city of Royan with 250 aircraft at 4:00 and with 100 at 5:30 a.m..' Through sheer inefficiency the Americans took four hours to decode the message and then circulate it. Last of all they decided that they had better let the French know. The American sergeant who delivered the message spoke no French and was unable to warn the French commander what his message involved. By the time the confused message was relayed it was too late for the French to call for the operation to be cancelled. They knew there were 3500 French civilians still in the city, but had no prior knowledge of what the Allies were planning.

Of the French inhabitants of Royan, nearly 2000 were killed or severely wounded in the bombing, which destroyed the residential centre of the city. The German defences on the periphery were unscathed. So severe was the destruction and the fire that followed that French fire engines were allowed in from La Rochelle. The French were astonished by the raid, which they could only imagine was delivered by the Germans.

Royan was only one of many instances of French civilians paying a high price for liberation.

ITCHY FINGERS

During the German invasion of Poland in September 1939, Polish anti-aircraft gunners suffered from a severe case of 'itchy fingers'. For some reason the gunners were not instructed in the art of aircraft identification. The outlines of Polish and German aircraft was oddly regarded as classified information and was kept safely locked up, out of the sight of the flak gunners who might have benefited from knowing the difference between friend and foe. The outcome was entirely predictable. Polish anti-aircraft guns shot down twice as many Polish aircraft as the German guns did. In fact, ten per cent of the entire Polish air force was lost to 'friendly fire', one out every three crews dying in this way. The Polish authorities were entirely responsible for this unnecessary slaughter, ordering that Polish planes should fly no higher than 1600 feet while flying over Poland. With their relatively slow speeds, they made easy targets for the gunners. Even those crews that managed to parachute from their planes were frequently beaten up by their own compatriots because they had been warned that men found parachuting over Poland should be regarded as German agents.

After the Japanese attack on Pearl Harbor (see p.141) one can understand why the American anti-aircraft gunners developed a bout of 'itchy-fingers', but one cannot excuse it. It was yet further evidence of the kind of panic among American gunners that was apparent around Gela in Sicily in 1943 (see p.131).

On the evening of 7 December 1941, six fighters from the aircraft carrier Enterprise, which had fortunately not been in the harbour during the Japanese attack, flew past Diamond Head and asked permission to land. In view of the nervous condition of the anti-aircraft gunners throughout the island of Oahu, clear instructions were circulated to every unit that six friendly aircraft were coming in to land. There could have been nobody in charge of a gun in Oahu who was not made absolutely aware that the incoming planes were American. Yet it was not enough. As a naval officer said later, 'Kids were sitting on these guns who had been shot at all morning, and they were jittery and trigger-happy.' As the planes flew over the battleships in 'Battleship Row' the flagship *Pennsylvania* opened fire with every gun it had got. Where the flagship led, everyone else followed. The problem was that the panic was infectious. Even those gunners who knew the six planes were Americans joined in firing because everybody else was firing. One fighter tried to crash land at Wheeler Field, but it was so full of bullets that it cartwheeled in and burst into flames. Another of the aircraft was brought down over a residential area and exploded, causing heavy civilian casualties. One plane crashed on Ford Island and was machine-gunned even after it had landed. Fortunately, the firing was as inaccurate as it was wild and the pilot sprinted away from the wreck, dodging bullets as he ran. Two other pilots parachuted down from their stricken planes, but when Ensign Eric Allen tried to follow suit he was machine-gunned as he hung in the air and later died in hospital. As if this was not bad enough, the gunners kept firing and inflicted casualties on nearby ships. The loss of the six planes ended the 'Day of Infamy' for the American people.

At the end of 1944 Hitler was unprepared to accept that the war was lost and launched a tremendous counter-attack against the Americans in the Ardennes which has become known as the Battle of the Bulge. Alongside the ground assault he also drew together all the remaining strength of the Luftwaffe and launched them in surprise attacks on British and American airfields around Brussels. As many as 439 Allied aircraft were apparently destroyed on the ground, including B-17s, Lancasters, Spitfires and Typhoons. It was a stunning achievement which cost the Germans just 93 aircraft shot down by Allied fighters or flak. Unfortunately, the butcher's bill became much larger as the triumphant German squadrons returned to their bases. The German anti-aircraft defences had been kept in ignorance of the operation and when the low-flying German aircraft flew over them they massacred them with a violent explosion of flak, which shot down an incredible 184 'friendly' planes, including 59 unit commanders and senior staff. It was a death-blow to the old Luftwaffe, which was never able to launch so powerful an operation again. It was also probably the most expensive 'blue-on-blue' mishap ever recorded, certainly in terms of material if not in lives lost.

AN UNWELCOME NIP IN THE AIR

Probably the most unsuccessful weapon of the Second World War was the Japanese balloon bomb, over 30,000 of which were launched from Japan with the wind towards the west coast of the United States. Although some of these did reach the forests of Oregon – one killed a mother and child having a picnic by the side of a lake – the rest were lost without trace in the vastness of the Pacific Ocean. Almost certainly the bomb was the least successful weapon – in terms of numbers sent and materials used, as well as results achieved – to be employed in man's long history of warfare.

The Phoney War

THE SHADOW OF THE BOMBER

So great was the fear of the bomber on the part of the British people and their leaders, during the inter-war period, that their reaction to the possibility of aerial bombing was, for a while, more damaging to the country than the bombing itself would have been, given the available forces in the German arsenal. The British people, like a patient fearing a visit to the dentist, suffered far worse agonies of anticipation than the realities of the treatment could possibly have produced, so that the extraction of a tooth came as a welcome relief.

The blunders described below were the product of an over-reaction to a perceived threat. In previous books I have referred to commanders 'painting pictures' rather than reacting to actuality. The fear of the bomber had its roots in something similar to this. Significantly, neither Germany nor France reacted with the kind of panic shown by the usually phlegmatic British, on whom the influence of the Italian military theorist Douhet had a surprising effect. He predicted that bombing of cities would lead to destruction on a scale found only in the Book of Revelations. A German commentator observed, wryly, that the panic that Douhet predicted was what might have been expected of an Italian population. The British drew the wrong lessons from the bombing in 1937 of the undefended town of Guernica during the Spanish Civil War by the German Condor legion. No British city – least of all London – would have been as helpless as Guernica had been. Stuka dive-bombers, which did much of the damage in Spain, would have been ineffective against the sort of fighters that Britain already had in 1938 - Hurricanes and Spitfires. But British politicians and other 'experts', as I describe below, predicted that bombers would bring Armageddon to Britain's cities. Any responsible government, instead of preparing its people for devastation, should have devoted its attention to how it was going to enforce its political will on the enemy by military means. Otherwise, the government had no right whatsoever to begin a war that could only lead to the extermination of its urban dwellers. Precautions were one thing, panic quite another.

The 'Phoney War' (the name traditionally used in Britain to describe the period between the outbreak of the Second World War and Hitler's invasion of Western Europe) was a war the British fought against themselves. It was a struggle in which characteristic British virtues and vices contended, while the national love of the absurd reached some of the highest levels in our history. The French understood the experience perhaps better than us. Their description of 'La Drôle de Guerre' got closer to the atmosphere of the time. It was a 'funny' kind of war.

In 1939 the British shrugged their shoulders and got on with preparing for annihilation. To understand why they did this we need to ask the Conservative politician Stanley Baldwin.

THANK YOU, STANLEY!

Stanley Baldwin was one of the most anonymous of British statesmen. When he was prime minister in the 1930s a casual acquaintance from his schooldays, who met him on the train, asked him what he had been

I think it is well . . . for the man in the street to realize that there is no power on earth that can prevent him from being bombed. Whatever people may tell him, the bomber will always get through.

STANLEY BALDWIN IN THE HOUSE OF COMMONS, 10 NOVEMBER 1931

One of the most damaging – and inaccurate – statements ever made by a British prime minister. Significantly, at this point Hitler had not even come to power in Germany. It was this sort of weakness on the part of democratic leaders that paved the way for Hitler's aggression and British appeasement.

doing since leaving school. He was that kind of politician. He was not a man to stir the emotions of a nation. Yet with one phrase he was elevated to the pantheon of memorable orators. With only the counsel of despair behind him he had announced in 1931 that in the event of war, 'the bomber will always get through'. Baldwin predicted that there would be 'tens of thousands of mangled people – men, women and children – before a single soldier or sailor' suffered so much as a scratch. There was no defence, he said; one might as well prepare for the end by making enough papier mâché coffins for the dead of London and closing all swimming baths in the capital to house the corpses. Hospitals were to prepare three million beds for casualties of the first few air raids. Later in the decade, when Winston Churchill thundered out his call for rearmament, the Treasury insisted that it was a waste of time as there was no defence against the bomber.

In the last months of peace in 1939 British leaders, both political and military, prepared to fight an enemy of their own creation – fatalism. Without intelligence reports – or indeed without using their own common sense – about the actual capacity of the German Luftwaffe to bomb British cities, Britons were told to prepare for little less than mass extermination. As late as 1937 the Committee of Imperial Defence, apparently drawing on expert opinion, expressed the view that no sooner had the prime minister issued the dreaded words 'war with Germany' than the sky over London would be filled with German bombers which for 60 days would hover like a cloud of locusts, killing more than 600,000 of the capital's citizens and maiming twice as many more. It would be Armageddon; and the Four Horsemen of the Apocalypse, suitably decked out with swastika armbands, would vie with the Angel of Death to ride unfettered through England's 'green and pleasant land' raining death and destruction. In 1938, Bertrand Russell did what he could for the nation's peace of mind by publicizing what would happen in time of war. According to Russell, London would become, 'One vast raving bedlam, the hospitals will be stormed, traffic will cease, the homeless will shriek for peace, the city will be a pandemonium.' The problem was that the politicians believed this sort of mistaken prediction and framed their policies accordingly. In fact, pessimism in the face of the perceived destructive threat of the bomber caused the 'establishment' to look to its own defence rather than the nation's. The maintenance of public order took top priority, with plans devised for troops to suppress 'panic and riot' rather than to minimize the effect of the bombing or to actually fight the Germans.

As a defence policy panic is always inappropriate. Nobody seemed to have asked where the Germans were to acquire the planes to equip these legions from Hell. Surely every piece of evidence suggested that the Germans had a tactical air force prepared for ground support rather than a strategic one, designed for area and civilian bombing? And if, as everyone appeared to believe, the bomber always got through, what was the point of all the warring nations building fighter aircraft, faster by far and more heavily armed than any extant bomber? Surely the much vaunted Hurricanes and Spitfires might be able to shift the locust swarm of German bombers from time to time during the first 60 days of war? And were the numbers of German bombers – not to mention the quantities of air fuel for them – limitless? A moment's thought by a mind not thoroughly immersed in the fiction of H. G. Wells would have shown that the apocalyptic scenario presented by the British government was no safe basis for entering a war and was certain to do more harm than good to any war effort.

With our present available resources, only a harassing effect can be counted upon. Whether this can lead to the attrition of the British will to fight depends in part upon imponderable and, in any case, unforeseeable factors … A war of annihilation against England appears to be out of the question with the resources thus far available.

GENERAL DER FLIEGER HELLMUTH FELMY, 22 SEPTEMBER 1938

This influential opinion was a clear indication that there was no question of a massed German bomber attack on London in 1939. British Intelligence must have been aware of this. Why then were the public fed scare stories about a 'holocaust' in 1939?

TAKE COVER!

It was believed that the Germans would prove to be prompt with their aerial destruction of London. And when the first bomb alert was heard at 11.27 a.m. on the 3 September, it was considered that the Germans had politely given the Prime Minister time to finish his announcement on the radio that Britain was at war with Germany. The expected panic did not immediately set in, partly because the 'enemy plane' that set the sirens wailing turned out to be a French one and also because the British do not panic on a Sunday morning. Too many Sunday roasts were at stake.

Air raid sirens soon became part of everyday life, and it was not long before the British had taken them to their hearts and were making fun of them. Sir William Davison led the demand for a more interesting sound, more musical or perhaps more stirring; something like a bugle-call or a 'tally-ho'. Naturally there were letters sent to *The Times*. One correspondent suggested the opening bars of 'Colonel Bogey', while the all-clear could be 'Who's afraid of the big bad wolf?'. The Bishop of Chelmsford hoped to keep people's spirits up with 'Cock-a-doodle-do' repeated several times. Others suggested the national anthem, though the thought of everyone leaping to their feet in a crowded Anderson shelter was enough to put paid to that idea.

An act of Parliament of 1937 had called for the provision of bomb shelters and the recruitment of air-raid wardens. A year later, when war over Czechoslovakia became a very real threat, the pace of preparation accelerated. But the question of bomb shelters proved to be one of the most contentious issues of the entire war. The example of German bombing during the Spanish Civil War had indicated the need for deep underground shelters, but the problem, at least in peacetime, was who was going to foot the bill for building them? The councillors of West Ham were sure of one thing: it was not going to be them. It was a 'capitalist's war' and they wanted no part of it. West Ham was a Labour Party stronghold and its councillors were generally elderly party hacks

The London Underground system provided the British capital with the best deep shelter protection imaginable against air-raids. Incredible to relate, the government at first refused to allow the shelter-less Eastenders to use the tube stations as a refuge.

who were still committed to pacifism even when the threat of German bombers metaphorically hung over them. They disapproved of the Nazi regime as strongly as anyone but they would not help Britain fight and nor would they pay for the building of public shelters. So it was that the residents of the borough would be unprotected when the bombers came.

The most obvious – and the most effective – form of shelter available to Londoners was the Underground system. It had been widely used in the First World War during the so-called 'Gotha' bombing raids, but some experts believed it encouraged a 'deep shelter' mentality, persuading the general population to stay under cover when their lives were at risk. Although there was no real evidence for this, it reflected the 'establishment' contempt for the British masses who, once they had gone to ground – or under it – would not come up again, at least not until the Hun had been put in his place. Those whose families could escape into the bourgeois safety of the coastal towns of North Wales were incensed at the idea that the workers could find safety in a rabbit warren of tunnels at Bethnal Green Tube Station. As a result the use of the tube as air raid shelters was forbidden. East Enders responded by buying tickets and occupying the platforms. It was democracy in action.

For most people air raid shelters meant the Anderson shelter. This consisted of two curved sections of corrugated steel, bolted together and dug into the ground. Covered with at least eighteen inches of soil, it proved to be remarkably successful. Naturally, it had its drawbacks, flooding being one of them. In

The Anderson shelters were the simplest imaginable. Even so, these women would have needed help to dig them into position in their gardens - if they had gardens. Many Eastenders could not use the shelters for lack of garden space.

big cities there was a bigger drawback – Anderson shelters were intended for gardens. In the back-to-back houses of Britain's Victorian cities there were no gardens. Once again poverty could be synonymous with danger. The East Enders of London would be dependent on public shelters and yet the government at first tried to resist making the tube stations available. But for the British the weather came before German bombs as a matter for concern. Both the Anderson shelters and the coal-holes that many poorer people used as shelters flooded in the autumn rains of 1939. If it came to a choice between shivering with cold in a muddy trench in the garden or quivering with fear in their warm beds, most people chose the latter. Women carried placards to town halls proclaiming, 'Is pneumonia better than bombs?' Significantly, when the bombing began in earnest, most people found they already knew the answer. For the middle classes, the Anderson shelter in their garden became a 'feature', a kind of gazebo, offering numerous opportunities for the horticulturally-minded. Flowers and vegetables of all kinds flourished in wartime gardens, including prize marrows. Poorer folk remembered the toads who moved in alongside them in the shelters and kept them awake at night practising diving into the water which seeped in to a depth of several inches.

The urgency of the government response to the incipient 'panic and riot' – as yet just simmering – can clearly be seen from civil defense preparations. Three weeks into the war one group of air-raid wardens assembled for the first time only to find their hall locked and bolted. Without a key they were obliged to force an entrance. The hall was empty, had no chairs nor any lighting. If the Germans came Britain would be ready – but not quite yet. On the other hand, the Church had no intention of being caught napping. In order to comfort the legions of dead and dying who would succumb to the German bombers, Canon Barry of Westminster undertook a first-aid course. He was surprised to find that his first lecture was on the treatment of snake-bite.

ARP (Air raid protection) drills were rarely taken seriously by the general public. The members of one golf club told a group of wardens who arrived at their establishment on an exercise to 'go away and play somewhere else'. One London borough took the view that women wardens would be unable to face the challenges that might lie ahead. During practice sessions gramophone records of exploding bombs were played to add a touch a reality, but when women wardens were involved the volume was turned down so the explosions sounded like 'gentle plops'. It was easy to laugh at the enthusiastic young girl fire-fighter, in her dungarees and rubber boots, who kept falling over as she ran. She had forgotten to cut the string with which the shop had tied the boots together. But six months later – in the inferno that London was to become – nobody was laughing at the wardens – male and female – who were all that stood between Londoners and a conflagration that would not only have taken their lives but even scorched the trophy room and the nineteenth hole.

DON'T PANIC

To compound the folly of its own propaganda, the government of Neville Chamberlain now began to evacuate major cities, ordering millions of women and children to leave their homes and move into safer areas. What followed was little less than a social revolution, as the previously

There has been a tendency in the past to over-state the case that 'the bomber will always get through', and perhaps also to lay too much stress on the claim that the counter offensive is the only means of defence in the air.

AIR STAFF
MEMORANDUM, 1938

Now they tell us! But advice of this kind was slow to trickle through to the political leaders who continued to spread gloom and despondency for another two years.

A primary school teacher instructs her class on how to wear gas masks. The fear of gas far exceeded that of high explosive bombs. In 1939, everyone was provided with gas masks, but gas was never a viable weapon and was never used by either side during the war.

unthinkable came to pass: the working classes and the middle classes were forced to mix. Much of what happened, amusing though it appears to late generations, served to lower morale in a way that shared suffering during the later Blitz could never do.

In the first place most of the evacuees did not want to go; in the second the country folk did not want to receive them. The typical attitude of the latter was summed up by one rural MP, 'Compulsory billeting would be far worse than war.' The Government, as usual, judged the British people by the lowest common denominator. There must be orderly evacuation or else there would be panic and pandemonium. What might appear as an emergency measure, inspired by thoughts of public safety, smacked all too often of social regulation designed to minimize discomfort for the ruling classes. Winston Churchill showed himself no friend of the people by predicting in 1934 that bombing of London would lead to three or four million fleeing the city. In his mind, the proletariat was bound to crack, lacking as they did the courage and self-discipline of their masters. As we now know this proved to be quite untrue. Evacuation may have begun as a product of panic, may have lowered morale by separating families and exposing urban children to profound culture shocks, may have exposed the country to disruption and dislocation on an unimaginable scale, may have created virtual refugees by the million in a country as yet untouched by war, but in the end it paved the way for profound social reform when the war was over, by exposing the appalling living standards of many urban families. Significant anecdotes of the period have a disturbing as well as an amusing side. Lack of toilet training among evacuated city children never failed to shock. One case of a Glaswegian child illustrates the point. The six-year old, evacuated from a tenement with her mother, was unused to using the communal toilet at home. Billeted in a middle class household, she defecated in the middle of the carpet. Her mother responded angrily, 'You dirty thing, messing up the lady's carpet. Go and do it in the corner like you've been shown.'

The evacuation policy has been condemned as being drawn up 'by minds that were military, male and middle-class'. Only middle-class thinking can have believed that a fracturing of the family unit – by sending children away and by separating husbands and wives – was likely to cement public resistance to Hitler. For this response to the outbreak of war was the result of an unfounded fear of German bombers – which simply did not exist in the numbers conjured up by fainthearts. Significantly, the French did not black out Paris or flee in their multitudes until the Nazis were knocking at their doors.

The bombing scare had already seen an earlier evacuation – by the middle classes themselves. When war became imminent advertisements began to appear in newspapers offering salvation for those who could afford it. For Londoners wishing to avoid the inconveniences of war the city of Bath offered itself as an ideal alternative, as it claimed to be 'immune from all air-raid dangers'. Aldwick Bay, on the south coast near Bognor Regis, ambitiously claimed that it was 'immune from the international situation'. Clearly, Bognor and its environs had a prior arrangement – missing from the textbooks and ranking somewhat below the Moltov–Ribbentrop Non–Aggression Pact in the German archives – with the Third Reich. Readers of *The Tatler* were pleased to learn that – to ensure that the British way of life suffered no serious disruption – a hotel at St Leonard's-on-Sea assured its guests that 'the ballroom and adjacent toilets have been made gas- and splinter-proof'. Other advertisements promised, 'A Garden of sunshine absolutely free of war's activities' and invited readers to 'Live safely and comfortably during the war period in one of the many delightful out-of-the-way beauty spots of North Wales.' These tantalizing glimpses of a 'happier land' were not available to everyone. Most advertisements specified who the fortunate few would be: 'British gentlefolk' or 'good-class people' with 'refined children only'. This was not the British at their best. Rarely can the sanctimonious and ungenerous have had such an opportunity to display themselves as in the early months of the war, when self-preservation masqueraded in so many guises. One advertisement read, 'Doctor in safe area would receive MILD MENTAL case (lady) in perfectly appointed country house.' And this was at a time when London was preparing to become a necropolis . . .

THE MASSACRE OF THE INNOCENTS

One extraordinary effect of the threat from the air in September 1939 was a veritable holocaust of British pets. Germany's first victory in the war was one they did not even recognize: Britain's first defeat was a bitter and self-imposed one. With grim determination and the best will in the world the British people put the interests of their pets before their own and had the majority of them killed. While the communal graves dug all over London yawned empty of human cadavers, the veterinary surgeries of Britain worked overtime until the victims spilled over and were laid outside under tarpaulin. It was a microcosm of what was happening in the human world, with working- and middle-classes unwillingly intermingling. In the 'Killing Fields' of Britain, pedigree and mongrel lay together in the brotherhood of death.

The disposal of these 'casualties' replaced in the public interest the problem of the vast number of humans who apparently should have been dead but were not. At least 600,000 Londoners were living and breathing who were supposed to have succumbed to the German air threat. Clearly they were not taking their shots. Could the special graves dug for them at such cost in time and energy – as well as lowered morale – be used for the animal casualties? Apparently not. Eventually a 'secret burial ground' was found somewhere in the East End, where more than 80,000 animals were buried in one night. But as the weeks passed and the Germans did not come to bomb London, many people reflected on their precipitate action in consigning their beloved pets to an early grave. Precise figures will never be known for the number of dogs destroyed, but it may have approached one million. It had been just another aspect of the panic that the government had failed to control as war approached. Ironically, if the British leaders could have heard what the Germans were saying at that moment about their plans to bring 'fire and sword' to the struggle with Britain there would have been many red faces. Herman Goering, head of the Luftwaffe, had made it clear to his whole command: 'Under no circumstances would London be bombed without written permission from myself and from the Führer.' Furthermore, it was feared that the massacre of cats might result in a plague of rats as during the Spanish Civil War – and even a reappearance of the Black Death. After all, a people that had turned its backs on its loyal but dumb friends might expect to suffer any kind of visitation of God's displeasure.

However, British animal lovers – having temporarily lost their senses – regained a sense of proportion when the fate of the German ambassador's chow was in the balance. Baerchen – for that was the creature's name – rather than suffering the anti-German abuse that had been directed at dachshunds in 1914,

It was a dog's life in Britain in 1940. Here Airedales practise wearing gas masks at the kennels of Lt. Col. E.H. Richardson, in Surrey.

was instead offered a 'good home' by some two hundred families. Unfortunately, Fascism did not leave British shores with the German ambassador and his staff. It surfaced among British dog-breeders who demanded, 'Kill all the mongrels! Keep all the good strains alive!' One expert remarked, 'I should say that the present time offers an opportunity to wipe out all mongrels and cross-bred dogs . . . and if the authorities could or would carry that out it would clear the streets of a lot of danger and filth.'

One grand lady pronounced: 'I do not want mongrels to multiply because they are ugly, ill-mannered curs, usually dirty and cross and have no value, whatsoever, either to the senses or the pocket.' It was not long before the true dog-lovers responded. Lady Kitty Ritson took up the fight on behalf of the mongrel, emphasizing the right of every Englishman to own a mongrel if he wished. Prolonged chorus of barks. Had the Germans followed this 'dog fight' in the newspapers it would, even more than usual, have convinced them that war against such people was really a waste of time. They would have read advertisements recommending owners to evacuate their dogs to neutral territory for the duration of the fighting and press reports of columns of cars and vans carrying dogs to safety in the countryside. Apparently budgerigars could be evacuated for just a penny a day. But for those dogs and cats who braved the war in the cities there were special fleets of animal ambulances which were prepared to tour the streets after an air raid. Some insurance companies actually covered dogs from risks of enemy action. Although dogs were not formally issued with gas masks as a matter of policy, it was only on the grounds that they would do more harm than good. Instead, the People's Dispensary for Sick Animals sold gas-proof kennels. The British were getting their priorities right again.

PUT OUT THAT LIGHT!

On the flawed assumption that what could not be seen from the air could not be hit, the British government enacted rigorous blackout legislation throughout the land. And so began the first real struggle of the Phoney War, between official 'blackness' and the various levels of darkness thought appropriate by Britons at large. Even after four months of 'war' an RAF observer described London as resembling a 'starlit night', with intermittent flashes of light and long strings of winking clusters like 'diamond necklaces'. Yet if Londoners were proving recalcitrant it was not from a lack of effort on the part of the self-appointed guardians of the blackout, the ARP wardens, and soon their peculiar cry, 'Put out that light!', was ringing through the land.

The first casualty of the aerial war was a martyr to the struggle for perfect blackness. In London's Harley Street a young policeman fell 80 feet to his death after climbing up a drainpipe to try to reach a window from which a light was shining. In other parts of the country the police took more direct action, shooting the bulbs from any lights that had been left on in error. Offenders were brought before magistrates for a mandatory fine, but excuses were inventive if not always convincing. One man claimed that a starling had flown into his house and had turned on the light switch with its wing; another said that the culprit was an ornament displaced from a shelf by the vibrations caused by anti-aircraft fire.

Sometimes blackout offences seemed to have an altogether darker side, at

The blanket black-out of Britain in 1939 was an enormous undertaking. In Worthing children formed a 'Black-out Corps', volunteering to paint the windows of large premises. Here two girls paint the windows of the local hospital.

least in the spy-clouded minds of the general population. Was the man 'puffing hard to make a big light' on his cigar really signalling to German planes as was suggested by one zealot? Anything was possible. After all, Londoners had been advised by one First World War pilot not to gather together in crowds and gaze up at the heavens. He warned that, 'The white blobs of numerous upturned faces can be seen from an aeroplane at a considerable height and form a good and tempting target.' With that kind of advice it is hardly surprising that magistrates fined a man who struck matches in the street to try to find his false teeth that had fallen out, and the keeper of an aquarium who failed to screen the tiny heating lamp in his fish tank. Fear of the German bomber was producing bureaucratic 'over-kill'.

The psychological damage inflicted by the British on themselves assumed more dangerous proportions with the blackout regulations for road transport. In fact, throughout the Phoney War, road casualties far outweighed anything German bombers inflicted on the British mainland. Cars were forced to drive without lights, and deaths from road accidents exceeded those from any action of the armed services until April 1940. The first British soldiers to die in the war were killed by a bus, as they sat in the middle of the road singing a hymn, after a night's drinking. By Christmas 1939 4133 people had been killed on Britain's roads. To these figures must be added the many others who died as a result of the 'blackout', walking into rivers, canals or lakes in the darkness, falling down steps and through glass roofs. Attempts to reduce the speed limit for cars to 20 miles an hour were met with a rebuff from the Royal Automobile Club, which regarded attempts to stop the murder and mayhem on the roads as 'a sop to those who kicked up a row'. Government regulations to impose the new speed limit were little less than an example of 'Nazi-methods against the motorist'. One pressure group smartly countered the new speed limit with the argument that drivers would need to light their dashboards to judge their speed, thus breaking 'blackout' regulations. Dogs could be a menace on the roads during the blackout, until a firm brought out a new white dog-coat, fitted with bells. How long this stayed white when a cocker spaniel found an interesting patch of ground to roll in is best left to the imagination. However, one use was found for white Pekinese. Ladies of the smarter set carried them at night for increased yet genteel visibility.

While ladies carried their Pekinese and drivers eyed the open roads proprietorially, at least one politician thought things had already been taken too far. Winston Churchill soon made it known that Britain was scoring an own goal by killing more of its own people than the enemy, cutting down on its war production without a single German bomb having fallen on mainland Britain and depressing the morale of her people in a way that the enemy had striven for four years from 1914 to 1918 to achieve. The 'blackout' had not been a response to a real threat but to a fear. Churchill suggested that the right time to react to German bombers was when they presented a real threat. In the meantime, there must be a relaxation of the blackout, before it drove the whole country mad. One farmer in the West Country, for example, had been prosecuted for showing a light in the middle of one of his fields. He complained that he could not identify the cows for milking but eventually resorted to painting large white numbers on each cow. To preserve the New Forest ponies from rampant motorists, the authorities first tried painting them to increase visibility but later found that their foals would not go near them in such camouflage and the idea was dropped. The criminal community – both greater and lesser – soon adjusted to the blackout. While burglars could no longer be certain which houses were occupied and which empty, pick-pockets and bag-snatchers had no difficulty making their escape with their loot. On a lesser, but in some ways more significant level, bus conductors reported that they were being given more dud coins and buttons as fares than ever before.

In the country the blackout presented even greater difficulties than had been imagined by the planners in Whitehall. But ingenuity often triumphed. One magical example was the West country land girl, bereft of batteries for her torch, who found her way home by the glimmer given off by a handful of glow-worms. Perhaps Shakespeare's Puck might have set his bombsights by just such a light but surely no Luftwaffe pilot. Anecdotes abound of the problems and possibilities of the blackout, like the one about the young lady in the blacked-out train who was heard to announce in the pitch darkness, 'Here, take your hand off my knee! No, not you, you!'

For some people it seemed Hitler had already arrived in England and was wearing a policeman's or an ARP's helmet. Officialdom in all its forms often failed to interpret the spirit of the blackout legislation. Everyone who survived

It is very disputable whether bombing by itself will be a decisive factor in the present war. On the contrary, all that we have learnt since the war began shows that its effects, both physical and moral, are greatly exaggerated.

SIR CHARLES PORTAL, 1940

Bomber Command had had its fingers burned after its early attempts to prove that 'bombers will always get through'. Most of their bombers did not get through, being easily shot down by fighters and ground fire. Some bombers would get through, but not the feeble types Britain was using at the start of the war.

the war has his or her own story of 'little Hitlers'. One particularly unreasonable reaction was by a policeman who stopped a car on the outskirts of London and ordered the driver to extinguish his lights. Inside the car was a Lincolnshire couple who had been on holiday in the capital and, having just heard that reservists were being recalled, were hurrying back to Lincoln and had to drive 200 miles in total blackness. And all for fear of the bombers that Germany did not have and would not have used had they possessed them. Significantly, when in the House of Commons it was suggested to the Minister for Air, Sir Kingsley Wood, that the RAF should bomb the Krupps armaments factory, he refused on the grounds that Krupps was private property. It was indeed a 'Phoney War'.

THE WAR OF THE WORDS

One of the strangest manifestations of the 'Phoney War' was the commitment of British Bomber Command to the propaganda war against Hitler. On the assumption that morale inside Germany must be vulnerable to a 'war of words', aged British bombers struggled deep into hostile territory for the sole purpose of scattering 'confetti' – as the leaflets were called – all over the German countryside, adding no doubt to the problems of litter collection but otherwise not harming the German war effort one jot. One critic of the leaflet campaign, Air Vice-Marshal Arthur Harris, commented that it was doing little more than providing Europe with toilet paper for the duration. But why Henley-on-Thames should be singled out to receive anti-Nazi propaganda was a deeper mystery that will be explained in due course.

The leaflet campaign 'Operation Nickel' or the 'Confetti War' as it was generally known, was the final stirring of appeasement in the declining Chamberlain government. As the leaflets had already been printed before war was declared it is a clear indication that the British Prime Minister still hoped for 'jaw-jaw' instead of 'war-war'. On the night of 3–4 September ten Whitley bombers left Leconfield airfield carrying thirteen tons of leaflets packed into brick-shaped bundles, which were scattered over Hamburg, Bremen and the Ruhr. The same process was continued nightly, until some actually reached Berlin by the beginning of October. The leaflet campaign was one of the worst blunders perpetrated by the Chamberlain government. At a time when Hitler needed to be convinced of Britain's steely commitment to war, the leaflets seemed a feeble response from a weak old man and a moribund administration. Hitler's attitude to Chamberlain had been clear from a joke he made after the Munich Agreement. With reference to the 'piece of paper' Chamberlain had held triumphantly aloft when he returned to England, promising peace in our time, Hitler quipped, 'I only signed it because I thought the old gentleman wanted my signature.'

The Minister for Air, Sir Kingsley Wood, was proud of the leaflet campaign. He declared, 'The distribution of messages to the German people over large areas of enemy territory has, I believe, been of considerable value in giving information to the people of Germany.' This announcement was greeted with hoots of derision by the general public. The Minister was in so much confusion that he decided that the text of the leaflets could not be seen by the British people, even though the continent was knee-high in them. When an American journalist asked to see a copy of one of the leaflets he was refused permission on the grounds that, 'We are not allowed to disclose information which might be of value to the enemy.' The leaflets themselves, produced by the Political Warfare Executive, were in fact so amateurish that Arthur Harris offered the suggestion that they were kept from public knowledge because they were too embarrassing to be seen by anyone but Nazis. One leaflet told the reader, 'You, the German people, can, if you will, insist on peace at any time.' In view of the stranglehold the Nazi regime exerted on Germany by 1939 this was wishful thinking. Moreover, it displayed a total ignorance of how most Germans felt about Hitler. In many ways, the ordinary German citizen had a far better lifestyle than ever before and believed they had Hitler to thank for it. A later leaflet – on the day before Poland collapsed under Germany's blitzkrieg – claimed, 'The French army crossed the frontier into Germany on 6 September . . . The British and French fleets have swept German merchant shipping from the oceans . . . Night after night the British Air Force has demonstrated its power by flights far into German territory. Germans note.' Most Germans must have suspected that these British leaflet raids were all part of the British love of irony, something that was alien to the Germans since they generally said what they meant. By the beginning of October 1939 the British were getting desperate. The next round of leaflets informed them they (the German masses) were starving, while their leaders had enormous bank accounts. One imagines the baffled Germans waiting expectantly for the British bombers to drop food parcels with the next leaflets.

The 'Confetti War' was lampooned by cartoonists and humorists everywhere. In Punch A.P. Herbert coined the word 'bomphlet' to describe Britain's new weapon. Nevertheless, the government insisted that – through astute forward planning – the leaflets had been printed at a very cheap price. Do you know, the public was told, that one could drop a million leaflets for the price of a single medium bomb? Airmen, trained for war, sometimes confused the purpose of their aircraft's payload. One airman was warned against dropping a whole package of leaflets without unfastening them: 'Good God, you might kill somebody,' he was told.

Meanwhile, as it became apparent that the German people had not abandoned the Nazi party and overthrown Hitler, the British bombers flew even further into the German Reich. Vienna, Berlin, Hamburg and Leipzig all received the 'white bombs' from these modern-day British missionaries, who carried the 'word' like St Boniface to the heathen Germans. One Whitley crew actually landed inside Germany imagining they were in France. They were able to take off again safely because the German peasants who had surrounded them were so busy laughing at their leaflets.

In the 'Confetti War' the only casualties were the bomb crews of the Whitleys and Hampdens who drew the short straw for these operations. Six per cent of the planes involved in the leaflet campaign were lost, either to enemy fire or to aircraft malfunction. In view of the fact that they faced hardly any opposition from the Luftwaffe, this was a high figure. The flights were by no means the 'piece of cake' that some people have suggested. The British bombers had relatively few comforts for the crew and were not designed for such long journeys, some of which reached as far as Prague and Warsaw. It was deeply depressing for the aircrews to risk their lives – or at least their health – in delivering letters. They were servicemen not postmen. Moreover, the navigation of these bombers was often poor, with the result that often the streets of Dutch, Belgian and Danish cities were swathed in British propaganda, exhorting the bewildered citizens to abjure the Nazi party.

As the fiasco became more widely known, the Air Ministry sought a way to find a new significance for their early raids on Germany. The phrase 'special reconnaissance' was the euphemism chosen for dumping paper on the continent and watching it blow in every direction but the right one. The Germans used the 'Nickel' raids to practise their anti-aircraft fire, with the Whitleys as live targets. The crews of the Whitleys learned from the raids how cold it can be on winter nights over Germany, with the bomb bays open while they threw out handfuls of circulars. So cold was the experience that the crews, with no oxygen or heated suits, almost froze to death. Visibility in the cockpit was often hindered by the ice, inches thick, that gathered on the windscreen, while every moving part of the aircraft's controls usually froze solid on each journey. As the enemy below was smothered in paper, the skies above the bomber were peppered with gunfire at regular intervals, in order to stop the guns freezing.

In February 1940, the aged Whitleys were replaced on the 'Nickel' run by Hampdens, which enjoyed rather better weather. Unfortunately, the Hampden was even less user-friendly than the Whitley had been. Each trip to Germany and back – a flight of eight to ten hours – was accompanied by much inconvenience. For example, the air crew had no toilets provided and had to improvise. Furthermore, the task of releasing the leaflets required two men to leave their duties to throw them out. As a result, for ten minutes the bombers flew on with no protection from their turret gunners. Even the leaflets themselves caused technical problems. Sometimes they blew back into the fuselage and wrapped themselves around radio aerials, as well as seriously inconveniencing the pilot who was desperately attempting to fly a steady course.

The Americans eventually joined the British in the propaganda war. By 1945 it has been estimated that Anglo-American planes had dropped over thirty leaflets for every single man, woman and child in Western Europe. Sadly, there is no evidence that the campaign served any real purpose. The Nazi regime, though repellent to many Germans, was not seriously threatened by internal opposition. At the same time as the leaflets were dropped, saturation bombing of German cities stiffened resistance to the Allies and worked counter to their own propaganda. German morale proved to be no more brittle than that of the British people under strategic bombing. Most Germans had no real alternative but to grin and bear it, even had they believed the propaganda of an enemy who held out the hand of friendship and yet slaughtered women and children without mercy.

The leaflet run was the most unpopular task for any bomber crew. In the first place it was as uncomfortable and dangerous as normal bombing operations and, furthermore, it was a complete waste of time and paper in the eyes of the aircrew. In their search for an alternative, the Political Warfare Executive fell back on a system used in 1918, the propaganda balloon. The Germans, following their own curious logic, had already threatened serious action against British aircrew spreading leaflets. While they took no exception to British bombers massacring civilians in Hamburg and Cologne, they were so incensed when they captured bomb crews with leaflets aboard that they sentenced them to ten years' imprisonment. To circumvent this problem a balloon was used instead of a bomber. The system was primitive in the extreme. Below the balloon hung packets of leaflets attached to strings. A slow burning wick burned through the strings at given intervals and the leaflets cascaded to the ground. As with all balloons, of course, the whole system depended on the vagaries of the wind. There were many other teething troubles. For example, the burning wick was extinguished by wet weather and it was found that a favourable wind was available only seven times a month. Of the balloons released from Britain, only just over half reached Germany, the rest travelled as far off course as Spain or Scandinavia. Some seemed to have a will of their own.

During April 1941, a curious event took place in Henley-on-Thames, Oxfordshire. Overnight, it seemed, the town had been littered with leaflets, which started to clog the drains. The police began to receive complaints from the general public that they were being accused of being Nazis and were being threatened with dire consequences if they failed to abandon their support for Hitler. Furthermore, the leaflets were written in German and presumably represented some cunning trick by Goebbels and his crew. When the nearby RAF base at Benson heard what had happened they contacted the Air Ministry to insist that they were still the Royal Air Force and not the German Air Force. Moreover, they felt it was unnecessary to urge the good folk of Henley to leave the Nazi Party as few of them belonged. However, if anyone doubted Henley's loyalty the commanding officer at Benson would be happy to give the Balloon Unit satisfaction. The Balloonatics could have the choice of weapons. The Air Ministry conceded their error in doubting Henley's loyalty and matters were resolved amicably. The reputation of the Balloon Unit was hardly increased by incidents such as this or the occasion when, in June 1944, the Royal Navy was put to flight – they raised anchor and left harbour – to escape a fleet of balloon mines that they supposed the Germans were floating in against them. The balloons were eventually all shot down by the naval anti-aircraft crews. The Air Ministry answered the Royal Navy's complaints with the observation that perhaps Their Lordships had slightly over-reacted. What had began as a farce in 1939 ended just as ridiculously in 1945. In between millions of pounds as well as thousands of man-hours had been wasted in a propaganda exercise that was more embarrassing than effective. Leaflets teaching German soldiers to say, 'Ei sörrender!' when they encountered British or American troops were presumptuous to say the least. As any serving soldier realized far better than the deskbound civil service types who prepared the leaflets, it took more than a piece of paper to persuade a German soldier to give up.

BRITISH KAMIKAZE

The Fairey Battle should have been designed in Japan. As an aircraft it was so helpless that it required an aircrew of men of suicidal courage. As examples of British kamikaze go, the Battle was without peer. Unfortunately, it had not been designed as a 'one-way' flyer, but was a serious attempt at building a light bomber. Designed to 1933 specifications, it was an example of mass-produced obsolescence. Most Battles were built by Austin Motors and in many ways the aircraft resembled an 'Austin 7' of the skies. It was a homely, comfortable, stable aircraft, that was a distinct improvement on the biplane Hawker Harts and Hinds that it replaced. But by the time it saw action in 1939–40 the world had changed. It was slow – its top specified speed of 241 mph was never met in practice – feebly armed and was easily ignited, having no self-sealing fuel tanks. Attacked from behind or below it was dead meat. It began service in the RAF in 1936 in a peaceful period when such raptors as Me-109s were not even slivers of steel in their maker's eyes.

The public remains amazingly cheerful … The success of the Defiant fighting planes … has raised everyone's spirits considerably.

MOLLIE PANTER-DOWNES, OF THE NEW YORKER, SUMMER 1940

The success of British propaganda can be seen by this incredible statement by an American reporter, sent back to the USA for domestic consumption. In fact, the Boulton-Paul Defiant had been a disastrous failure, most being shot down by German Me-109s. The few that were able to return fire often shot their own tails off.

The Avro Manchester was one of the least successful bombers of the Second World War. Its 'Vulture' engines made it thoroughly unreliable, but when it was transformed into the four-engined Lancaster and fitted with Merlin engines it became a great success.

In keeping with the undistinguished military demonstration put on by British forces in the early part of the Second World War, the Battle was in the forefront of Britain's air effort. Ten squadrons carried out reconnaissance during the 'Phoney War' and one Battle gunner actually shot down an Me-109. The Luftwaffe had been caught napping. Ever afterwards when Me-109s met Battles the result was different, usually entailing the complete destruction of the Battle units. The Battle's greatest moments came in three days after the German invasion of France began on 10 May, 1940.

Unable to spare fighters to escort the Battles on their missions, and in the full knowledge that the aircraft had no chance whatsoever against Me-109s, the RAF commanders opted for low-level attacks for the Battle. What technology could not supply must come instead from the courage of the aircrews. And what courage! Even the Germans were astounded. If the Battles were vulnerable to Me-109s, they were simply 'sitting ducks' at 250 feet to anti-aircraft fire. They earned the reputation of being 'flying coffins'. Yet in their attack on the Maastricht bridges the Battles fought one of the most heroic actions of the entire air war. It was what the British liked best – courage in the face of long odds. By 10 May things had got so bad that only volunteers were available to fly the Battles. The Germans were annoyed at the behaviour of the British air crews and soundly lectured them after some were taken alive. All this futile courage was not professional, they told the Battle's crews. Why had the British waited to attack the bridges until they, the Germans, had fortified them with anti-aircraft guns? Why had they not attacked before the guns were in place? There was no answer to that. Such questions played no part in British military conduct. Two officers aboard one Battle received posthumous V.C.s, while oddly the third man – not an officer – received no award, even though he gave his life as willingly as the others. The inscrutable face of the British military machine imperceptibly stiffened its upper lip and gazed on.

In three days the Battles were almost exterminated as a species. They were suffering 60 per cent losses on each mission and for the little they achieved were a disgraceful waste of trained personnel. The planes that survived this holocaust in France found quieter pastures, patrolling the coasts of Ireland or Iceland. Yet these 'coffins' continued to be popular with aircraft manufacturers, who continued to make them well after they had proved to be far more dangerous to their own crews than to the enemy. In all, over 3000 were built, and most spent the war as trainers or as target-tugs. The waste of valuable spare parts was never questioned. But at least the Battle was no longer part of the 'British kamikaze'.

Defiance was about all the Boulton-Paul Defiant could offer to the German aircraft it encountered. It had seemed like a good idea at the time, and had been built in 1935 to specifications which looked backward to the problems of First World War pilots, since the plane was vulnerable to attack from the rear. In order to defend its tail, the Defiant had a large turret armed with four Browning machine guns, but with no forward firing gun. A more perceptive name for the aircraft would have been the 'Parthian', as it always fired over its shoulder. The difficulty of negotiating the aircraft into a position where it could fire at oncoming enemy fighters must have been immense. Moreover, the observer/gunner was always in danger of shooting off his own tail as he followed a fast-moving German fighter. The few Defiants that saw action at Dunkirk in 1940 and during the Battle of Britain fared badly and the aircraft was withdrawn from day action and tried as a night fighter, though without radar. It had no more success here, because the same problem existed, whereby the pilot was constantly swinging the plane round to allow the turret gunner to fire at the enemy, only this time in the dark.

It may have the best football team in the land and it has bid unsuccessfully for the Olympics but Manchester must take second place to its small northern neighbour Lancaster on two counts. In the first place Lancaster is the county town of Lancashire and in the second the plane of that name was a darned sight better bomber than the Manchester, which contributed little to the British war effort whilst its bigger brother contributed so much. They both came from the same 'stable' – or hangar if you are feeling pedantic – from the designers at A.V. Roe, but there the similarity ends. Where old pilots purr with pleasure at the memories of the Lancaster, they awake sweating at night from their dreams of flying the Manchester.

The problem was that the Manchester was born with a 'dicky' heart – the Vulture engine, designed especially for the plane by Rolls-Royce. The ominously named 'Vulture' was as bad an engine as the same company's Merlin was a marvel. It was just a question of luck really, and the Manchester was definitely an unlucky aircraft. Its first test flight on 24 July 1939 was a bit of a shock for its pilot, Captain H.A. Brown. It took him just seventeen minutes to decide that the Manchester was quite unstable and the Vultures were not producing the expected power. In spite of reservations the Manchester went into production and began its short and disastrous operational career in February 1941. As famous a flyer as Guy Gibson took over a Manchester squadron in March 1942. Off the record he was called a 'clot' for accepting the command as the plane was no good and kept crashing for no good reason. It was the 'despair' of ground crews who could never get everything right at the same time. There was always something wrong. While the original Manchester limped from disaster to disaster, its designers had decided to produce a Mark III with four Merlin engines instead of the two Vultures. It was the old story of the 'ugly duckling' and the 'swan'. Changing the name of the new four-engined design from the much-hated 'Manchester' to the new 'Lancaster' transformed the situation. Suddenly the Lancaster was born, widely regarded as the finest bomber of the war from any country. Why the authorities had persevered so long with the 'Vulture' engine when the Merlin was available is anybody's guess.

But many, perhaps most, of the Whitleys produced during the war scarcely left the Aircraft Storage Units.

THE STRATEGIC AIR OFFENSIVE AGAINST GERMANY – DESIGN AND DEVELOPMENT OF WEAPONS

During the Second World War some major aircraft firms were paid to continue producing obsolescent aircraft to maintain the workforce. For example, the Fairey Battle was an unwanted aircraft. Yet even after its decimation in France in May 1940, a further 3100 were produced to complete orders. The same was true of the Blenheim, which also was shown to be quite inadequate. 5421 were built, most after the plane was shown to be operationally useless. Even after the Lancaster was being built, scarce resources were still devoted to building 1812 two-engined Whitleys, whereas only 300 had originally been planned. This production of largely irrelevant aircraft was designed to maintain the impression of high production figures regardless of the uselessness of the aircraft built.

The Battle of Britain

MYTHS

The Battle of Britain became the subject of myth almost before it had entered into history. Everybody who lived through that summer of 1940 believe they know what happened. A handful of British pilots, known as the 'few', triumphed over Hitler's aerial legions and saved Britain – nay Western civilization – from Nazi oppression. Their Spitfires and Hurricanes – outnumbered many times over – won an incredible victory when all had seemed lost. Losing control of the air, Hitler had abandoned his plans to invade England. He had missed his chance to drag a caged Churchill through Whitehall to Buckingham Palace where King George VI would offer him the hand of his youngest daughter in marriage.

Myths are like pearls, they grow around a piece of grit into something far more splendid. The grit remains, but the pearl has enwrapped it in so many layers that it is impossible to recognize it any more. And such is the relationship between truth and myth. They start from the same place but end as far away from each other as human imagination takes them. It is the British way with history. They write it afterwards as if everything happened as they had predicted it would. Unacceptable facts are hastily disposed of under the carpet and everyone joins in a celebration of the myth. As a result lessons are never learned, problems never solved, corners never turned. The blunder of believing a myth is seen everywhere in the economic decline and the social stagnation of post-war Britain.

THE MYTH OF THE 'FEW'

The Luftwaffe could never have won the Battle of Britain and never even came near to winning it. Its attempt to destroy the R.A.F.'s Fighter Command was a blunder in view of Hitler's intention to invade the Soviet Union as soon as he had persuaded Britain to make peace. Hitler never had a realistic plan to invade Britain and the German admirals had no confidence in their ability to control the Channel and transport enough troops to ensure a landing on the south coast. If an invasion of England had ever been even a long-term aim, Hitler would not have squandered his navy in Norway. He hoped for a negotiated peace with England and Goering's futile attempt to break the R.A.F. merely ended by breaking the Luftwaffe instead.

Did Hitler or Goering give any serious consideration to what they would face in an all-out air war with Britain? The answer is 'No', because they saw the Battle of Britain not as a separate battle but as a continuation of the great offensive in the West that had overthrown France. As such, they did not act in a way which suggested that they needed different aircraft – or tactics – from those that had won them control of the skies over France. The Nazi leaders – as against the experienced Luftwaffe officers – underestimated the qualities of Britain's aircraft and her pilots, always a formula for defeat in wartime. Worse even than that, they overestimated the strength of the Luftwaffe which, since the beginning of the Polish campaign in September 1939 had suffered heavy losses and needed a period of rebuilding. German losses since the start of the war had seen fighter strength reduced by a third, dive bombers by over 40 per cent and

In spite of its fame and the favour it found with pilots the Spitfire never acquired any sanctity in the eyes of the Air Staff; it certainly possessed none at the time of Dunkirk, when there was talk of stopping its production in favour of the Beaufighter.

J.D. SCOTT IN VICKERS HISTORY

In view of the specifications of the Spitfire and its known capacity to match the best the Germans had, the above statement seems incredible. Clearly those in authority had not yet grasped the fact that the defence of Britain rested on the ability of this plane to stop the German bombers from having free rein over British cities.

bombers by nearly sixty per cent. Over Dunkirk the Luftwaffe had lost 240 planes against British fighters and the thought of engaging these same fighters over their home territory should have urged caution on the Luftwaffe command. It did not, even though such a man as Adolf Galland warned that, 'The Luftwaffe would not have a walk-over against the RAF . . . The British had a fighter arm which was numerically stronger and better controlled than us.'

Galland's comment strikes at one of the main tenets of the 1940 myth – that British fighters were outnumbered. In fact, as Galland asserts, the British fighter force was to be numerically superior at various points in the battle for a number of reasons. In the first place, the German aircraft industry was a shambles, and absurdly complacent. Incredibly, between September 1940 and February 1941 there was a 40 per cent reduction in aircraft produced. In the very month – September 1940 – that the Battle of Britain was won and lost, German factories produced fewer planes than were lost to the RAF in battle. This does not conform with the myth of the 'few' but is nevertheless statistically correct.

The inadequacies of the German aircraft industry in 1940 were a result of Germany's decision to fight 'short, sharp' wars, concentrating on the production of dive-bombers rather than strategic bombers. Moreover, the intensity of the fighting would cost the Luftwaffe relatively high loss rates which would not have to be made up quickly because the war would only last a matter of months. This high rate of attrition could only be justified if the war did in fact only last months. But when it became apparent that an attritional struggle in the air would be necessary against Britain the Luftwaffe had no hope of victory in view of the state of the German economy. While British factories concentrated on building fighter aircraft in the early stages of the war, the Germans had to build bombers, as well as tanks and artillery to equip a vast army and U-boats and surface ships for the Navy. The decisive decision made by Sir Hugh Dowding in May 1940 during the Battle of France to keep the majority of Spitfires in Britain for national defence condemned the Luftwaffe not only to defeat in the Battle of Britain but to a position of inferiority that she never overcame.

It is increasingly obvious that the myth of the 'few' is simplistic, as are all such myths. The heroism of Britain's fighter pilots – not to mention the fact that there were pilots in the RAF from all parts of the old empire, as well as from conquered Europe – was an example to a nation suffering in wartime, but was it any greater than that of the Me-109 pilots, fighting with just five minute's fuel and the English Channel to recross? Heroism alone did not win or lose the Battle of Britain. The battle was really won in Britain's aircraft factories and lost in Germany's. Statistics show how little chance there ever was of Germany winning the Battle of Britain. These are the production figures for single-engine fighters (Hurricanes, Spitfires and Me-109s), which were the main fighters that contested the Battle, during the relevant part of 1940.

1940	Britain	Germany
June	446	164
July	496	220
August	476	173
September	467	218
October	469	144

Moreover, during the period of the Battle, the 'few' averaged over 700

Hurricanes and Spitfires available at any one time, as well as over 1,300 Fighter Command pilots to fly them. With the Germans unable to replace their losses it was the Luftwaffe Fighter Force that was facing elimination by October 1940, not RAF Fighter Command.

MAKING A MESS OF THE MESSERSCHMITT

It is sometimes pointed out that the Messerschmitt Me-109 might actually have been a better plane than the Spitfire. Opinions vary. But nobody would deny that this was one of the world's outstanding aircraft of its period. It was a design that ran to over twenty marks. Yet, excellent as it was, was it the right plane to fight the Battle of Britain? Or, to put it another way, was the Battle of Britain the right battle for the Me-109 to fight? In fact, did the Luftwaffe have a plane suitable for fighting so far from their bases? Some might suggest that the twin-engine Me-110 was the answer. In fact, they would be wrong. The Me-110 was part of the problem, not part of the answer. It had been designed to overcome the main weakness of the Me-109, namely its short range. But what was eventually built, the Me-110, was technically inferior to many fighters of the time and its top speed – 288 mph – was 65 mph slower that the Spitfire so that Hurricanes and Spitfires were able to shoot it down with an ease similar to that with which the Mitsubishi Zero had slaughtered the Brewster Buffalo (see p.144). In truth, the Me-110 was slow, cumbersome and needed a second crewman to observe what was happening on its tail. Frequently it had to abandon its role of protecting the bombers in order to protect itself. Groups of Me-110s were often forced into a caracolle, a manoeuvre in which they flew round in circles protecting each other's tail. This ridiculous manoeuvre might have saved their tails, but it was no way to win a war. The Germans had, in fact, overlooked the real answer to the Me-109's short-range problem: the installing of drop-tanks to enable the Me-109 to enjoy a longer range. Oddly enough, drop tanks had been used by the German Condor Legion in the Spanish Civil War. Why not use them now? There is no obvious answer, except possibly the fact that it would have lowered the fighter's performance. Yet this drawback would have been minute compared with the advantage of enabling the Me-109s to fight on equal terms with the British fighters.

JUNKING JUNKERS

If the Messerschmitts were a problem, then the Junkers were little better. The war had started with the old Heinkel-111 as the mainstay of German bombing, but it had soon been superseded by the Junkers 88. If the British had their Blenheims and Battles to mourn over, the Germans had their Ju 88s. This plane had a nasty habit of catching fire without warning, especially in mid-air, and found difficulty in taking off with full fuel tanks. Among bombers crews operating this plane morale was very low, unsurprising since they had presented Goering with a list of 32 complaints about their plane. Goering later reflected, 'It's not the enemy the squadron's frightened of – it's the Junkers 88.'

The most famous Junkers aircraft – the Ju 87 'Stuka' was a 'bully' of an aircraft. It functioned best when there was no opposition. Against British fighters

A German Me-109 fighter plunges to the earth after receiving a direct hit during the Battle of Britain. Messerschmitt 109s were a match for the British Spitfires but always fought at a disadvantage so far from their bases owing to fuel limitations.

over Southern England in 1940 it was out of its depth. Its maximum speed of less than 200 mph made it redolent of an earlier war and its complete helplessness at the end of its dive made it easy meat for Spitfires and Hurricanes, as well as anti-aircraft artillery. It soon became obvious that against this kind of opposition the Stuka was a 'death trap'. Moreover, the Stuka's real function was 'dispersing crowds' of helpless ground troops. Its tiny bomb load – one 1000 pound bomb or a cluster of 110 pounders – was ridiculous against well-prepared enemies and its fate was similar to that of the British Fairey Battle light bomber. So heavy were losses of the Ju-87 that they eventually had to be withdrawn from the battle to escape extermination.

One blunder by the Luftwaffe planners was unforgivable given the usually high standards of German Intelligence. Underestimation of the enemy may be typical of military parvenus like Goering and Hitler, but German professional servicemen were not noted for such inaccurate judgments as was made by one senior Luftwaffe officer, Joseph Schmid, who declared that his reports showed that 'the Luftwaffe is clearly superior to the RAF as regards strength, equipment, training, command and location of bases.' Furthermore, he reported that British aircraft factories could build just 250 fighters a month (the true figure was double that). He concluded, 'In view of the inferiority of British fighters to German fighters the Luftwaffe is in a position to go over to decisive daylight operations owing to the inadequate air defenses of the island.' This must rank as the worst piece of intelligence since the Trojans believed the Greeks had given them a wooden horse as a present. There was not even any mention of radar, which meant that every German raid was anticipated and met by fighters already in the air. This sort of nonsense represented a severe decline from the standards of the Luftwaffe established by General Seeckt in the 1920s. It clearly indicates that the courage and efficiency of the German air crews was being squandered by their leaders. It is impossible not to agree with the modern view that the Luftwaffe was incapable of overcoming the RAF in 1940. Significantly, by the end of that year British aerial strength was growing far faster than

German Stuka bombers flying over Russia in May 1943. The Stuka was the tactical aircraft par excellence. In ground support its capacity to dive-bomb precisely and to scatter and terrify enemy troops with its siren made it a great success. However, when Goering used the Stuka over England in 1940 it was massacred by the fast-flying Spitfires and Hurricanes. So slow was the Stuka that it was driven from service in the West and could only find a use on the Eastern Front after 1941.

German. It was for this reason that RAF Fighter Command – unwisely as it happened – went on the offensive during 1941 and 1942, culminating in the failure of the 'Rhubarb' attacks and defeat in the skies over Dieppe (see p.101).

'WHAT A TIME FOR BULLSHIT'

'Cleanliness is next to Godliness,' as the RAF ground staff at Lympne airfield found when the Inspector-General came to call. Moreover, on 11 August, 1940, the Luftwaffe found itself upstaged by Air Chief Marshal Sir Edgar Ludlow-Hewitt. While Luftwaffe generals Sperrle and Kesselring had it on their agenda to destroy the RAF fighter airfields at Lympne, Hawkinge and Manston, they were unfortunate enough to find that their appointments clashed with the RAF's Inspector-General, Sir Edgar Ludlow-Hewitt's inspection of these sites. Even a Luftwaffe attack on the airfields was not enough to prevent a man of Sir Edgar's disposition from carrying out his duty. The war would just have to wait.

On the morning of 11 August German bombers, escorted by Me-109s, were attacking airfields along the south coast. However, at the same time the station commander at Lympne was 'in a tizzy', ordering everyone to tidy up the base as the Inspector-General was due to arrive. Cooks, office staff, orderlies and batmen rushed in every direction, beautifying, straightening the curtains and the cushions, clearing desks and swopping round the 'In' and 'Out' trays. Outside, men were cutting the grass, pulling up the weeds, shovelling this into that and putting it into sheds. It was going to be a hard day.

As the Air Chief Marshal drew up at Lympne in his staff car, the Luftwaffe arrived at the same moment, and the two vied for the attention of the harassed airfield personnel. The Inspector was first dragged into a shelter while Ju-88 bombers plastered the airfield with bombs, reopening the craters that the station ground crews had just filled in for the inspection, as well as uprooting the newly planted flowers and wrecking the new paintwork. It was a heartbreaking sight after such a hard morning's work. The Inspector-General humphed, how did the Luftwaffe know that he was coming? Still intent on doing his job, he tried to inspect some of the offices but was driven underground again when a wave of Dorniers flew over and deluged the field in showers of anti-personnel bombs.

When Ludlow-Hewitt emerged from the shelter it was getting late for his next inspection. 'I'll return in a few day's time,' he told the station commander. He drove away as the German bombers headed back across the Channel. With an air of resignation, the station commander ordered his men out again to fill in the craters and get the station working again for fighting a war. Oh, and by the way, he said to an aircraftsman as he passed, that window frame is smudged...

RHUBARB OVER DIEPPE

No sooner had the defensive victory in the Battle of Britain been achieved by Fighter Command, than their new commander, Sholto Douglas, went over to the offensive by a campaign of 'dragging a coat' across the coast of France in an attempt to force the Luftwaffe fighters to come up and fight. At first glance it seems an absurd idea. The main reason for the Spitfire's supremacy over the Me-109 was the fact that when fighting over England the German fighter suffered from an insufficiency of fuel to stay long enough to fight on equal terms. Surely by conducting the duels in France, closer to the German bases, the Me-109 might prove the master of the Spitfire? Sholto Douglas had been a First World War fighter 'ace' and these tactics seemed redolent of an earlier, nobler war. Appropriately, these massed fighter sweeps over France were called 'Rhubarbs', which is a fair way of describing the sense behind them. The Germans hardly bothered to get out of bed when the fighters arrived and only showed interest if bombers came with the fighters (these combined operations were known as 'circuses').

Shocks were in store for the RAF. In the first place, the Spitfire Mark V was soon shown to be inferior to the Me-109F. Worse was to come. Suddenly, onto the scene came the new Focke-Wulf FW 190, which was greatly superior to any current British fighter. And so the numbers game began again. Air Marshal Sir Trafford Leigh-Mallory, once described by Montgomery as 'that gutless bugger', began to claim remarkable successes for his fighters. During the summer of 1941 his Spitfires shot down every German fighter twice. In the second half of the year, the Germans lost 731 aircraft according to Leigh-Mallory - 154 according to everybody else. The truth was very different from that imagined by Fighter Command. 'Rhubarb' was thoroughly rhubarb and the British were losing four aircraft for every one they shot down. Wiser heads than this author's have wondered at the strategy of maintaining 75 fighter squadrons in the United Kingdom during 1941, so that they could conduct chivalrous mêlées with about a quarter as many German planes, all the time suffering a 75 per cent erosion figure. Meanwhile, in the Far East – notably Singapore and Malaya – the wretched Brewster Buffalos faced imminent destruction by Mitsubishi Zeros, while in North Africa German Me-109s ruled the skies for the lack of British fighters and in Malta three Gloster Gladiator biplanes alone cocked a snook at the Germans.

The 'rhubarb' policy came to a head at an appropriate moment, on the day of the Dieppe Raid on 19 August 1942. Yet, as if some sort of luck accompanies divine fools, the British were baled out again when on 23 June, a brand new Focke Wulf FW 190 landed by mistake at RAF Pembrey, in South Wales.

Everything that made the German fighter superior to British fighters was available in one easy test-flight. And Supermarine were just releasing their new Spitfire – Mark IX. It was possible to test the new Spitfire against the Focke Wulf. The Spitfire was inferior in many ways, but was far better than any other British fighter and would give the FW 190 a close 'run for its money'.

It would be inappropriate to spend much time explaining why the Dieppe Raid was a ghastly mistake and how hundreds of Canadian troops were wasted in an ill-judged demonstration of combined operations. From the aerial perspective, the battle over Dieppe was the biggest air battle of the Second World War and one of the biggest in history. The British employed 67 RAF squadrons as an air umbrella over Dieppe – 48 of which were Spitfires – but by doing so Fighter Command was sacrificing the advantage it had enjoyed in the summer of 1940 of fighting at home. Now the situations were exactly reversed with an inevitable outcome. German fighters, operating from bases in France, had the opportunity to refuel and return to the fight, while the Spitfires could stay for just five minutes over Dieppe before heading home to refuel. Shot-down British pilots were captured or drowned in the Channel, while downed German pilots were able to return to duty. It was the Battle of Britain in reverse. The RAF also flew four Mustang squadrons out of Gatwick and lost ten planes, some shot down by friendly guns as their shape was not recognised by AA gunners. Mustangs found themselves chased by FW 190s even while being shot at by British gunners – an unenviable situation.

The aerial fiasco was at first acclaimed a great victory for Fighter Command. Newspapers claimed 280 Luftwaffe aircraft were destroyed. The Germans would have been surprised to know they had so many aircraft available that day. Winston Churchill, unwisely believing Leigh-Mallory's figures, crowed about the victory in the Commons, saying, 'Dieppe was an extremely satisfactory air battle which Fighter Command wish they could repeat every week.' In fact, the RAF had lost 112 aircraft against 48 Luftwaffe losses, including just 23 fighters. It was the RAF's biggest defeat of the entire war as well as her heaviest losses, with 59 Spitfires falling to Me-109s and FW 190s. The writing was on the wall: 'trailing a coat' over France must stop. There had been far too much 'rhubarb'.

The Blitz

LATE FOR SCHOOL

One of the most tragic incidents of the entire Blitz on London occurred in the Silvertown district of West Ham on the night of 9 September 1940. It was perhaps inevitable that such a tragedy would occur in West Ham. Some people at the time believed that West Ham was asking for it and that her councillors had not realized the risks they were taking in not providing underground shelters for their people.

A school right in the middle of the bombed-out area – known as 'No.1 Bombing Area' – was being used as a shelter. After the previous two nights' bombing it was filled with hundreds of people who had lost their homes and were now crowded into the classrooms. There were whole families, sitting with their baggage around them, waiting for help though from what quarter they did not know. The Germans had been probing the dockland area for several nights before dropping their bombs, and Silvertown was right on the bombing line.

On Sunday they had been told that coaches would be coming to collect them at three o'clock but hours passed and no coaches came. Helpless local officials kept repeating to the restless people that they must be patient, the coaches were coming. The children wanted to play outside in the playground but the playground was one huge crater where the bombs had fallen. Part of the walls of this school – designated a 'rest centre' by harassed officials – were bulging where the foundations were giving way beneath. The school had suffered almost as much damage as their homes, yet it was considered safe enough to house a thousand homeless people.

And still no coaches came. Instead hundreds of other refugees squeezed into the school until it was filled to overcrowding. Some of the families were marched to another school only just across the road, but for the original residents of the rest centre there was to be no relief. Their ears strained to hear every vehicle as it passed, but no coaches came. And so the thousand in the 'rest centre' stayed a third night in danger.

On visiting the area, the journalist Ritchie Calder, who knew the East End well, was struck by a premonition of doom. Somehow he knew that unless these people were moved the school would be bombed with them in it. He hurried back to Central London and three times warned the authorities in Whitehall that they must do something. They assured Calder that the people would be removed when the coaches arrived.

But that night – Monday 9 September – the Germans got there first and as expected planted a bomb into the school building, killing 450 of the Eastenders inside. Those who had left the school the previous afternoon had been saved by little more than the width of a street. They crowded in horror round the huge crater where the school had been, wondering why the coaches that were supposed to have ferried these people to safety had not arrived.

An inquiry was begun, but it was all too late now. As usual in wartime it was a mixture of human error and bad luck. The coaches had been ordered on the Sunday and had set off to collect the homeless of Silvertown. The drivers had been told to rendezvous at a pub called 'The George' in a neighbouring borough. The driver at the head of the convoy claimed he knew the pub. He certainly knew a pub called 'The George', but it was the wrong one. It was a mile away from where he was supposed to be. Unable to contact the local officials, who were waiting at 'The George', the coach drivers gave up and went home. The next day a few coaches did arrive at the school, but as some of the homeless were transferring to the vehicles an air raid siren was heard and they were rushed back inside the school. Local officials deemed they were safer in the school than in the coaches and they decided to try to make the transfer the following day. There was to be no next day for many of the people. Time had run out.

The Silvertown disaster was a disgraceful example of official ineptitude. Some people had spent four nights in the school, all the time in the midst of the most acute danger. One can blame the coach drivers for not trying harder. Perhaps they were never made aware of the desperate nature of their work. One can blame the local officials, who were probably in over their heads, facing impossible conditions and suffering as much as the people they were trying to help. But most of all one must blame the councillors of West Ham who cared so little for their people that they provided no safe shelters for the victims of the bombing.

The rest of the story is a savage indictment of the treatment suffered by many Eastenders during the Blitz. When coaches eventually arrived to remove the survivors of the school bombing, they were taken to the middle-class area of Epping Forest, where no arrangements had been made to receive them. Some of these wretched people – bombed twice – actually had to sleep in the forest. For a week many slept in cinemas or in the theatre, but most were put back in another school, one made of glass, hardly a reassuring shelter from the bombers above. Ironically, this was the Prime Minister's own constituency and when the scandal was revealed to him improvements quickly followed. Nevertheless, five coachloads of the Silvertown homeless were taken to the old workhouse building of a borough in North London. Here they were received as if they were – by some timeshift – in Dickensian England. The local officials welcomed them with the announcement, 'The first thing we do here with you Eastenders is to scrub yer!' At this the Eastenders got back in their coaches and were taken to yet another school, which felt the blast of another bomb that night. They were still not safe after nearly a week of travelling. Ritchie Calder, a month later, found some of these homeless people living under arches back in Silvertown.

A LITTLE NIGHT MUSIC

During the Blitz, there were two main problems with London's anti-aircraft guns. They hit German bombers about as often as they brought down flying ducks from lounge walls and their shells killed more Londoners than Germans. Apart from that they served the important function of boosting morale by keeping everybody awake all night. Anyone suspecting irony in the last sentence would be wrong. The Londoners wanted to hear the soothing sound of big guns blasting the night sky – it reassured them. It showed that not only could London 'take it', but it could give it back as well.

On the assumption that 'the bomber will always get through', little attention was given to anti-aircraft guns and searchlights at the end of the First World War. Nor was AA defence any more urgent a priority during the inter-war period. After all, why should time and money be spent producing guns that could not stop bombers? It was surely far better to put every effort into building more and more bombers so that whatever the enemy did to you you could do back to him. So poor was marksmanship in this 'Cinderella' service that in 1926, during exercises, only two hits were scored out of 3000 rounds fired at a stationary target of fixed and known height. An embarrassed officer reported that the effect of AA guns was mainly on morale. Even as late as 1938, the total anti-aircraft defences of the whole of Britain amounted to just one hundred guns and 800 searchlights. A contemporary report had said London alone needed 216 guns and a thousand searchlights. This moribund service had, until the outbreak of war, been under the command of General Alan Brooke, a part of this famous commander's curriculum vitae about which he preferred to remain silent. His successor, General Pile, found his new command full of 'terrible inefficiency'. It was peopled at first by what has been called 'the dregs of the call-up'. It is doubtful if Falstaff could have equipped the service with so handy a bunch of misfits and 'square pegs'. In October 1939, one battery received 75 recruits, of whom one had a withered arm, one was mentally deficient, one had no thumbs, one had a glass eye that was for ever falling out if he moved suddenly and two were ill with advanced syphilis. In the 31st AA Brigade, of one thousand recruits, fifty had to be discharged immediately as being unsafe to be allowed out on their own, twenty were mentally deficient and eighteen more were suffering from a variety of medical conditions that should have seen them turned down as medically unfit. Many of the others were simply too young to serve elsewhere and were transferred as soon as they grew up. With this 'band of heroes' Britain felt ready to take on the best the Luftwaffe could throw at her.

In addition to its deficiencies in both manpower and guns, the AA service had a philosophy geared to a different war. General Pile again pointed out that the AA would be best suited to facing the bombers of twenty years before – the German Gotha or Giant bombers travelling at about 100 mph – or better still, Zeppelins. Fire control was by a system of sound locators and a very complicated Fixed Azimuth system that depended on bombers flying in straight lines and at fixed heights and speeds, otherwise it could not cope. More problematic still was the question of identifying friend from foe. So many errors of identification occurred that many batteries preferred not to fire at all unless they could be sure, which they rarely could. As a result, in the early part of the Blitz – 7–9 September 1940, when there were heavy raids – Londoners were frustrated at hearing plenty of bomb blasts but virtually no return fire from the AA guns. Their feeling, not unnaturally, was that the Germans had a free hand to bomb them without the consequent fear of being shot down. This was apparently more disturbing than the bombs themselves. General Pile felt the same as millions of Londoners: 'It was obvious to me, sleeping in my bed, that our system was no good. I became both angry and frightened at the same time, and lay awake the rest of the night thinking how to deal with this business.' Churchill was already thinking the same thing. Bristling with his usual bellicosity, he announced that he would only feel safe if every gun in London was firing at the German raiders – preferably at the same time. Noise might prove to be an antidote to fear. In any case, let the German pilots have a share of the fear.

Pile assembled his commanders and spelled out the lesson. It was noise that was needed. It mattered less how many planes were shot down than that it sounded like they were being shot down. And it might make the German bombers raise their ceiling, thereby reducing the accuracy of their bombing. There is evidence that approaching German planes, witnessing the sight of so many guns firing and of searchlights criss-crossing the sky jettisoned their bombs on the London suburbs rather than fly into the inferno. This was a victory of sorts, though a doubtful one for the people of the southern and eastern suburbs. Moreover, it is clear that the thousands of shells that were pumped into the air 'fell to the ground I know not where'. The shells and shrapnel that emanated from London's AA guns undoubtedly killed and wounded more Londoners than they did German airmen. Even so, most Londoners would still have opted for firing the guns at whatever cost rather than feeling impotent under the bombs of an enemy.

One Londoner who followed the barrage carefully was the Prime Minister. His ear was so well attuned to the sound that once, when some of the guns were 'rested' to prevent their gun barrels from wearing out, he phoned Pile to ask why all the guns were not firing. Pile replied that if he did not rest them he soon would have none, to which Churchill pointed out that he could rest the guns when there were no more enemy bombers over the capital. Not everyone was

Flattering to deceive, these searchlights and AA rocket-guns give the impression of irresistible power. In fact, at no time during the 1940 London Blitz did Britain's anti-aircraft services achieve more than a token effect on enemy planes.

impressed by Pile's efforts. One man wrote to him, 'Dear Sir, As a citizen of London, I think the Anti-Aircraft defence of London is the biggest scandal since Nero . . . Why you don't understand the meaning of the word barrage.' Others, less bellicose, complained that it was all too much. One local council complained that the vibrations of the guns were cracking the lavatory pans of the council houses. Could General Pile kindly take his barrage somewhere else? Some Londoners thought they had better solutions to the aerial threat. Construct the guns on balloons, Pile was told, and fly them up to the level of the German bombers and shoot them at close range. Another 'bright idea' was for fleets of British bombers to fly over the Germans and drop sand in their engines.

Without radar control the anti-aircraft fire was ineffective. During September, 1940, it has been estimated that 30,000 shots were fired for every German plane shot down, though by October the ratio was reduced to 11,000 to one and by January 1941 to just 4000. At least the ack-ack was forcing the German bombers to fly higher with the result that the accuracy of the bombing fell off. But this merely meant that the bombs fell somewhere else instead of on their military targets, on civilian houses for example. Yet nobody was truly satisfied if the guns were not firing back. Even churchmen warned the Prime Minister that there would be anti-war riots if the guns could not be heard. They boosted morale and as more of them were brought in to defend the capital the common man could be heard boasting, 'Now we'll give them hell.'

FIREWORKS

The second 'Great Fire of London' took place on 29 December 1940, and was the result of blunders by government ministers, of whom Herbert Morrison must take the greatest share of responsibility. It came close to destroying St Paul's Cathedral – hit by 28 incendiaries – and succeeded in destroying eight of Sir Christopher Wren's churches, as well as much of the Guildhall and many of London's oldest and finest medieval buildings. At one stage there were over 1400 separate fires in the City, yet incredibly the Old Lady of Threadneedle Street survived. As one observer wrote, 'The whole of London seemed alight!', while one East Ender concluded, 'Blimey, we've lost the war.'

From the government's point of view the fire marked the failure of the voluntary system that had seemed to be working well in the prevention of the threat from fire bombs. If, as we have seen above, the anti-aircraft defences were helpless to prevent the Germans dropping bombs and could offer only psychological relief to suffering Londoners, there had to be a way to minimize the damage that the bombs would do after they fell. Fire was recognized by both the British and the Germans to be the most potent weapon against heavily urbanized areas, and so during the Blitz the Germans dropped thousands of incendiary bombs. It was possible to prevent these incendiaries from doing too much damage if fire-watchers were quick to reach the scene and take appropriate action. But speed was essential and it should have been government policy from the outbreak of war in 1939 that all adults should by law have been made responsible for fire-watch in the immediate vicinity of their homes and places of work. Instead, a voluntary fire-watch scheme was operated until 29 December, 1940, when the conflagration demonstrated the consequences of popular neglect of their responsibilities.

It would be wrong to suppose that no effort had been made to instruct London's population in the rudiments of self-protection, notably from incendiary bombs. A Public Information Leaflet had been issued by the then Home Secretary, Sir John Anderson, to every household at the outbreak of war in 1939 emphasizing, 'IF YOU THROW A BUCKET OF WATER ON A BURNING INCENDIARY BOMB. IT WILL EXPLODE AND THROW BURNING FRAGMENTS IN ALL DIRECTIONS.' The leaflet explained in the simplest manner possible that such bombs should be smothered in sand or earth. Incredibly, by the time of the Blitz it was found that only one in every three people remembered how to deal with incendiaries or claimed ever to have known. When questioned most responded that they would throw water on an incendiary bomb, while others brightly suggested that they would, 'Lay on it', 'Throw it in a sewer or anywhere where there was water', 'Leave it where it was and run' or 'Put on my gas-mask'. Basically, most people refused to read the leaflets sent, either because they were: 'too complicated', 'too boring' or 'an insult to the intelligence.' When the incendiaries fell and caused fires, the general public blamed 'the authorities' for not 'putting them out'.

In the first four months of the Blitz, however, the more determined of British adults had taken their responsibilities for dealing with incendiary bombs quite seriously. And so effective had the diligent fire-watchers been that the public had begun to lose its fear of these bombs. At the merest suggestion of one falling in the street it was common practice for several active people within earshot to rush towards it equipped with a bucket and sand or earth to smother the incendiary. To the complacent, it seemed that the threat was more apparent than real. However, on 29 December 1940, a Sunday night between Christmas and the New Year, the city was empty, buildings were shut and locked up and people were at home celebrating the Christmas festivities. As a result there was nobody available to snuff out the threat of the incendiary. Those that landed on the roofs of churches, offices and warehouses burst into flame and kept burning because there was nobody there to put them out. Of London's historic buildings only St Paul's Cathedral had created its own team of fire-watchers and it was this alone that saved the great building that night.

Once the fire-watchers had failed and the fires had started it was the job of the firemen to try to save as much of the city as possible. For any fire emergency in the centre of London there existed a natural source of water, the River Thames. But on this occasion the Thames was lower than anyone could remember it. Within minutes of the fires starting hundreds of firemen and appliances were on the scene only to find that there was not enough river water to power the pumps. It was an incredible and an agonizing discovery for the firemen. After a last muddy trickle the pumps ran dry. A conjunction of extraordinary events conspired to keep London's firemen short of water. The emergency main which ran through a 24-inch underground pipe through the City from the Thames to the Grand Junction Canal had been cracked by the bombs. With that gone, the vast number of pipes soon lowered the pressure from other sources and the static water tanks were soon empty. With the Thames at low tide and the firemen unable even to reach the water that was available from the bridges or the embankment, it was a 'worst-case' scenario beyond the greatest pessimist's construction. Even two fireboats were unavailable; one had collided with a submerged wreck and another was downstream of London Bridge, held back by an unexploded parachute mine. For several hours the firemen could do little but watch the City burn.

Even four months of bombing had not taught the authorities of the dangers that could occur. Admittedly what happened that night would hardly happen again in the entire war, yet it should have been considered. No large building – office, church, cathedral or whatever – should have been left unguarded from the threat of incendiary bombs. This blunder – a general rather than a particular one – was going to cost the capital many of its most historic buildings. With a westerly 50 mph wind whipping up the flames, acres of fine Victorian and Edwardian buildings were consumed while the modern ferro-concrete blocks of buildings survived.

The firemen fought on with what few weapons they had. They were the true heroes of the Blitz, enduring more danger in a single night of fighting London's fires than most soldiers did in the entire war. They had to fight not only the

London's docklands ablaze after a German air-raid in 1940. Residential areas near the docks bore the brunt of civilian casualties because of the shortage of deep shelters.

devastation caused by the German bombing, but the maladministration that flung them back upon their seemingly limitless reserves of initiative and good humour. What they had to put up with was often unforgivable rather than unavoidable, and the product of petty bureaucratic incompetence as well as public apathy. One has only to read of the chaos that followed the raid on Coventry on the night of 14/15 November 1940, when fire teams from throughout the Midlands and even London joined in the battle to beat the flames, only to find that there were as many types of pump fittings and hose screws as there were different brigades. The result of the lack of standardization of equipment meant that many appliances stood unused while Coventry burned. Only the nationalization of the Fire Service after the 'great fire' of London, by grouping together an incredible 1666 fire authorities, meant that the lesson of Coventry had been learned, but at what price?

The fire of 29 December has been described as the 'Great Fire of London that need not have been'. The following day in a cabinet meeting Winston Churchill was furious at what had been an avoidable tragedy. Measures were immediately taken to ensure that it could never happen again. But it was too late. Through carelessness Londoners had squandered their heritage. Fire-watching now became the legal responsibility of every adult citizen and this time nobody objected. Londoners began to realize the truth of that most frustrating of epigrams: you never really appreciate what you have got until you have lost it. One woman commented: 'It is so terrible that because of sheer wanton neglect of the obvious precautions, millions of pounds' worth of damage should have been done, and hundreds of brave men's lives risked and lost: the loss of beautiful old buildings, tragic as it is, is of minor importance to a people who can look after them no better than this . . .Ours is the guilt for the irresponsible apathy and heedlessness which made possible this lunatic negligence on the part of our elected rulers.' It was a bitter start to 1941.

On New Year's Eve Home Secretary Herbert Morrison broadcast on the radio to 'the slackers' who had let London burn. But their fault was less than his. He failed to provide the leadership, and the compulsion the people needed. It was all very well for Churchill to rage, but why had the protection of London not been in the forefront of everyone's mind? London had been allowed to suffer from the kind of firestorm that was to engulf Hamburg and Dresden later in the war. And all this had been caused by just 136 German medium bombers.

THE 'MYTH OF THE BLITZ'

Where was the safest restaurant in London during the Blitz? There were many contenders for the title, but it always seemed to be presuming too far on one's luck to stake a claim. It was also dangerously misleading if the general public took too much notice. This was the case with the Café de Paris, in Coventry Street, Piccadilly. Advertising itself widely as 'London's safest restaurant', since it was underground, it allayed the public's fears and persuaded them to congregate there to forget their troubles and enjoy a splendid evening with the best food and entertainment in London. But if it was the 'safest' restaurant, how safe was 'safe'? It was the sort of claim one hoped would never be put to the test. On 8 March, 1941, it was tested.

There had been no raids on London for six weeks. It seemed as if the Blitz was over and the memories of the terrible days in Autumn and Winter 1940 were just bad dreams. People began to relax their vigilance. They emerged from their shelters as if from hibernation and began to sniff that Spring was in the air. Nobody had been sure what to do in 1939 and mistakes had been made. But now the fire service had got the bombing under control and everyone had a story to tell of what they had done with incendiaries. Life was returning to normal again, at least as normal as you can make it in wartime. The Germans were no longer threatening to invade England, and the Luftwaffe had acknowledged their masters in the RAF. Already, Hitler and his Nazis seemed further away than before Christmas. With a new spirit in the air it was time to have some fun – time, in fact, for an evening at the Café de Paris.

The Café de Paris was reached by a long flight of stairs leading down between the Rialto Cinema and the Lyon's Corner House in Coventry Street, Piccadilly. Sunk below ground level, it counted itself 'safe' because it had two roofs, its own and that of the cinema directly above. Its regulars pointed to the fact that it was so subterranean that it was far away from the noise outside and gave the impression it was safe because one could not hear danger from guns or bombs. Ironically, the café's dining-room and ballroom were modelled on those of the ill-fated liner *Titanic*, another public receptacle noted for its 'safety'. It was an ominous coincidence.

The restaurant had re-opened at the height of the Blitz, and was a place to be 'seen', defying the worst that Hitler could do. It seemed almost patriotic to be there, dancing to the music of 'Snakehips' Johnson's Caribbean Band and eating well. It was light years from Silvertown or the railway arches of Bermondsey, where the 'real' victims of the Blitz were. This was a place for the rich, the young and the beautiful. On the evening of 8 March, 1941, Lady Betty Baldwin, daughter of the former Prime Minister, was off duty from her ambulance shift and thought an evening at the Café would cheer her up. When she arrived she found that her favourite table was taken and had to be 'squeezed in' to a corner of the crowded restaurant, which was full of uniformed Dutch and Canadian officers, and well-dressed ladies. It was her lucky night. Within an hour everyone at her 'favourite table' would be dead.

Everyone seemed to feel especially safe in the restaurant that night. One young lady later said that she and her friends had regarded it as a kind of underground shelter. After all, it advertised itself as 'so deep and so safe' it was a natural place to assemble in the event of a raid. She had walked through the darkened streets with a 'tin hat on her head' and had not felt safe until she had arrived at the café.

Someone should have stopped the Café de Paris advertising itself as 'safe'. There was no sound evidence that the premises were particularly free of risk, and the two roofs that protected the customers were far too flimsy to offer real protection. The café's customers were living on borrowed time. A direct hit on the cinema above would condemn the *bon viveurs* below to a dreadful death. And at 21.45 on 8 March, two small 50-kilo bombs hit the Rialto, and fell through the two roofs to explode in the café, killing 'Snakehips' and decimating his band. In fact, one of the bombs did not so much explode as burst open, scattering yellow explosive powder everywhere. The lights were all out and the dining room was strangely silent for a moment, before the injured began groaning. Apart from the explosive effects of the bombs, many of the dead and wounded had been hit by the flying glass from the mirrors. Up at street level, passers-by peered into the smoke billowing up the stairs from below.

Within five minutes of the bomb exploding, word reached Westminster Control Centre that the Café de Paris had been hit and before ten o'clock ambulances and stretcher parties were despatched. Strangely, they did not all arrive for thirty minutes, during which time many of the injured died of shock or loss of blood. The wardens who had been nearby rushed to the Café, but were simply overwhelmed by the numbers of dead and injured and got involved in first aid work, rather than taking command of the situation. Unfortunately, nobody had the experience necessary to correctly identify the help that was needed. As a result, the message that reached the Control Centre spoke of above a hundred 'trapped' casualties. This was quite wrong, as the bomb had done little structural damage to the buildings but within such a confined space had caused terrible injuries. The result of the mistaken message was that the Control Centre sent out two Heavy Rescue Parties to extricate the buried victims. What was needed, in fact, was a Mobile Aid Unit and lots of ambulances and stretchers. More and more of the wounded were having to be carried up to the surface and laid out on the road. As a result of the powder that had scattered from one of the bombs, the skin of the casualties had turned yellow. The bodies on the pavements of women in their evening dresses lying stiffly in death gave the impression to some passers-by that they were dolls.

A remarkable sense of order existed below ground, where the survivors were trying to help the injured. Lady Baldwin's Dutch officer was cleaning wounds in champagne, while a nurse was trying to staunch a heavy wound in a man's back with a table-cloth. The wounded man, with commendable good humour, muttered, 'Well, it's not everybody who's been cut in on by the Luftwaffe.' But if this was a symbol of the 'London can take it' image of the Blitz, a darker and disreputable feature of the period was also present in the

The London underground did not always provide safe shelter. Bank Station, much closer to the surface than most tube stations, took a direct hit in January 1941.

Café de Paris that night. One wounded lady felt somebody take hold of her hand. She relaxed, thinking that help was here. Then the hand let go of hers and she realized that it had removed the rings from her fingers. Another survivor noticed two figures with caps on their heads whom everyone assumed had come with the rescue services. But they had not – they were looters, picking over the bodies and taking handbags. One man was apprehended with a handbag full of jewellery. Apparently, the rescue services never reached the scene of a disaster before the criminal fraternity. The looters kept men on watch during a raid to report on bombed areas so that looters could get there before the fire brigade. It was dangerous but it was profitable. Nor were London's cabbies always as lovable as most people recall. On this dreadful night Lady Betty Baldwin, who had escaped with cuts to her head, had used her ambulance training to good purpose in tending the injured and was covered in blood. Feeling faint, she was carried upstairs by her Dutch officer, who called a taxi. The cabby looked at Lady Baldwin's bloody dress and said, 'I don't want no blood in my cab,' and drove off. The 'myth of the Blitz' requires a better ending than that. Below ground in the smoke-filled dining room the dead still lay where they had fallen and the gravely injured waited for medical attention. A voice was heard: 'Well, at least we haven't got to pay for our dinner.' Laughter rippled through the room, up the steps and into the crowd waiting anxiously for their missing relatives.

Absolute priority must be given to the long-range bombers for this work ... The training of these bomber crews must be given priority over the training of crews for Coastal Command aircraft, Army Co-operation squadrons, the Fleet Air arm, Photography and Fighters, and this priority must be maintained despite the pressure on the Air Force by various departments...

MEMORANDUM BY MARSHAL OF THE ROYAL AIR FORCE LORD TRENCHARD TO THE PRIME MINISTER, 19 MAY 1941

The narrowness of Bomber Command's strategic thinking is seen here. Seemingly unaware of activities in other areas of the war, the bomber chiefs lacked the vision to conduct a successful war against as powerful an enemy as Germany.

British Strategic Bombing

Britain's strategic bombing campaign over Germany has become, in the eyes of most modern historians, the most controversial military campaign in British history. Even the murderous attritional campaigns of the First World War had the justification that, misguided though they may have been, they were aimed at the military personnel of the enemy. Unless one interpreted 'Total War' as an invitation to regard all Germans as 'military personnel', in that civilians worked in war industry and were therefore legitimate targets and that civilian morale was liable to crack more quickly if family life was disrupted by homelessness or death, then one has to regard the strategy as indiscriminate, militarily wasteful and morally questionable. These accusations have frequently been made against Bomber Command's four-year campaign over Germany and also against the philosophy adopted by its leaders, not just Sir Arthur Harris, but Sir Charles Portal as well, sustained by the intellectual and scientific arguments of Lord Cherwell (see also p.116). Sir Winston Churchill bore a burden greater than any one military commander. As has been observed before, in 1940 Churchill had to fight the war he was able to fight rather than the war he would have chosen to fight. Through strategic bombing alone could Britain harm Germany before 1944 and as Prime Minister it was Churchill's responsibility to use whatever methods were available to him. It must be pointed out - uncomfortable as it may be for some readers - that at the height of the V-weapons campaign in 1944, Churchill discussed with his colleagues the use of anthrax weapons against Germany. By this stage of the struggle morality and 'total war' were uneasy bedfellows, as the Americans were going to discover in 1945 with the use of the atomic bomb on Japan.

Professor Lindemann, Lord Cherwell, was Prime Minister Winston Churchill's chief scientific adviser during the Second World War. He lent his intellectual weight to the argument in favour of strategic or area bombing. As a result, Bomber Command continued its bombing of German cities long after it was proved to be wasteful and ineffective.

THE BOMBER WILL NEVER GET THROUGH

After the outbreak of war in 1939 it did not take Britain long to realize that the bomber, in daylight, was never going to get through without a lot of help from fighter escorts. Douhet had been wrong. And, as if to prove it, the RAF made a series of bomber raids on the German Fleet that were both heroic and yet futile, a dangerous and typically British combination of qualities.

On 4 September 1939, Britain began her shooting war with Germany. Blenheim and Wellington bombers took off to attack the German pocket battleship *Admiral Scheer* at Wilhelmshaven. The crews were under strict instructions to avoid civilian casualties and to hit nothing but the ship. The *Scheer* was

All the evidence of the last war and of this shows that the German nation is peculiarly susceptible to air bombing ... if you are bombing a target at sea then 99 per cent of your bombs are wasted ... If however our bombs are dropped in Germany, then 99 per cent which miss the military target all help to kill, damage, frighten or interfere with Germans in Germany.

MEMORANDUM BY MARSHAL OF THE ROYAL AIR FORCE LORD TRENCHARD TO THE PRIME MINISTER, 19 MAY 1941

Generalizing about national characteristics has always been a rich source of military blunders. One wonders if Trenchard realizes how close he was to declaring war on the German 'people' (genocide) rather than on the German military machine or Nazism.

attacked from a height of 500 feet by three of the bombers whose crews later reported that they could see washing hanging from a line on deck. The bombs from one Blenheim hit the *Scheer* but simply bounced off into the sea without exploding. The Germans, taken by surprise, soon began firing their flak guns and of the 29 British bombers taking part seven were shot down. The only damage suffered by the Germans was when one of the stricken Blenheims crashed into the cruiser *Emden*. It had been an expensive practice run and had proved nothing except that low-level attacks were far too costly in the face of modern anti-aircraft defences.

The British decision to confine their attacks to the German fleet alone was referred to as 'expediency reinforcing the dictates of humanitarianism'. Killing civilians was unacceptable at this stage of the war and even destroying military installations was questionable as some of these might be 'private property'. It was a funny kind of war, with German Blitzkrieg in the east devastating the Polish state, slaughtering soldier and civilian alike and bombing their cities to destruction.

On 29 September, eleven Hampden bombers set out in clear weather to attack German shipping. Off Heligoland they sighted two German destroyers, but before they could attack them they were in turn attacked by a squadron of Messerschmitt Me-109s, which proceeded to shoot down five of the Hampdens and would have almost certainly shot down the rest had not the need for the fighters to refuel saved the British bombers by the skin of their wing-tips. The Hampdens' guns had failed to hit a single 109.

Unflustered by the dismal performance of their medium bombers, Bomber Command decided to force the issue by unleashing their powerful Wellingtons, whose twin turrets – front and rear – would soon re-establish the superiority of the bomber over the interceptor. On 3 December, 24 Wellingtons took off to attack two cruisers off Heligoland. It was expected that if they encountered the 109s, as had the Hampdens, this time the result would be very different. In fact the 109s did appear, but seemed puzzled at first by the tactics of the British bombers, whose rear-turret gunners prevented the German fighters from following their normal attack pattern. In fact, the Wellingtons succeeded in sinking a minesweeper with a bomb that passed through the ship without exploding and then returning home without suffering any losses. The pilots were jubilant. They had demonstrated their quality in battle. The Germans had been quite impressed by the way the Wellingtons had held them off, but they had also identified the bombers' weakness – an attack from the beam. From side on the Wellington would be completely helpless. On 14 December, a dozen Wellingtons flew over Heligoland, challenging the Germans to come up and fight. Travelling at just 1000 feet, the Wellingtons were quickly engaged by the anti-aircraft guns and six or them were shot down. As the damage had been done by the guns rather than the fighters, this raid seemed to prove nothing, except that at 1000 feet bombers were 'sitting ducks' for the flak. Nevertheless, although they had lost no bomber to a fighter Bomber Command could hardly be satisfied with a 50 per cent loss rate.

On the same day, still in clear conditions, 24 more Wellingtons set off for Wilhelmshaven and though two aborted and returned through mechanical failure, the rest reached their target, being picked up by German radar and intercepted by four *Gruppen* including both Me-109s and Me-110 'heavy fighters'. There began a running battle, with the Wellingtons keeping a tight formation and initially holding the fighters off. Forbidden to risk civilian casualties, the bombers felt unable to drop their bombs as German ships were in dock. It was therefore when the bombers turned for home that things began to go wrong. Having learned from their previous encounter how not to attack the Wellingtons, the German pilots attacked from the beam. Over the North Sea, they began to shoot down the Wellingtons, one after another. Ten were shot down in flames, two others ditched in the sea and three more crashed on passing over the English coast. Fifteen losses out of twenty-two that had made the trip comprised the heaviest losses ever suffered by Bomber Command during the entire war. The Germans had lost four fighters and were generally impressed by the British turret gunners. Nevertheless, as one German pilot said, 'It was criminal folly on the part of the enemy to fly at 5000 metres in a cloudless sky with perfect visibility.' One of the German commanders concluded, 'After such losses it is assumed that the enemy will not give us any more opportunities of target practice with Wellingtons.' It was a cruel but accurate judgement. The British were testing - and to their surprise - disproving a theory: the bomber will not always get through.

From 18 December 1939 until the last weeks of the European War, the British bombers were driven to abandoning the daylight hours and only flying on missions at night. The effectiveness of German aerial defences – fighter-interceptors and anti-aircraft guns – showed that Bomber Command could not sustain the losses they would suffer over Germany in daylight.

THE BUTT REPORT

Following Britain's heroic retreat from Dunkirk, when all the little ships had gone back to their river moorings and their pleasure trips, the stark fact remained that the British Army had suffered one of its most humiliating defeats. Shorn of all its equipment and facing a German army superior in men, machines, morale and, most of all, leadership, Britain could not for the foreseeable future envisage a way in which she could return to the continent to overthrow the Nazis. Even the Royal Navy was stretched so far that it would take a miracle if she could keep the homeland safe and the people fed. So if victory was to come it must come through the offensive force of Bomber Command. Britain's bombers would have to carry the war to the German homeland so that, just as in the First World War the Navy's blockade had strangled the German people, this time British bombers would destroy German homes and reduce morale to such a degree that the tortured German masses would rise up to overthrow Hitler.

It was a far-fetched scenario, yet it was one to which Churchill clung, notably during the dark days of Britain's isolation in 1940 and 1941. And so Bomber Command conducted its 'strategic' air war against Germany in these two years during which Britain fought alone. Nightly raids by British bombers rained death and destruction on Germany's cities. But the Germans seemed to notice it more as an insect sting than a lion's bite. Was the bombing campaign effective? There were numerous stories of destruction from neutrals but there was absolutely no sign of German morale cracking. Photographic evidence seemed to be inconclusive. Or was it? At Lord Cherwell's suggestion, Mr D.M. Butt, a civil servant in the Secretariat of the War Cabinet, was asked to present a report on the success of British bombing of Germany up to the summer of

The number of British planes operating in the district of Cologne itself did not exceed seventy.

HERMANN GOERING, 1942

Goering had told Hitler and the German people so many lies about the condition of the British RAF that he left no grounds for believing that the British could have possibly sent a thousand bombers against Cologne. According to Goering, they did not have a tenth of that number. Being a liar himself, he expected the enemy to be lying, hence his figure of seventy. Those who had been in Cologne during the raid knew that Goering's figure was risible.

1941. Butt reported on 18 August and what he had to say caused a profound shock. Essentially, British bombers could hardly guarantee to hit Germany at all let alone a particular part of it.

Butt's findings were alarming to say the least. Of British aircraft attacking French ports only two out of three reached the target (according to Butt 'reaching' the target meant being within a five miles radius of it). This became one in four for targets in Germany as a whole and for the Ruhr it was an incredible one in ten. On moonless nights or when the moon was new just one in fifteen reached the target and even with the full moon only two out of five succeeded. Having reached the target those plucky air crews then had only the slightest chance of hitting what they were aiming at. Precision bombing was a thing of the future.

Two weeks before Butt issued his findings, Bomber Command's leaders told Churchill, 'We give the heavy bomber first priority in production, for only the heavy bomber can produce the conditions under which other offensive forces can be employed . . . Then only shall we be able to return to the continent . . . and impose our will upon the enemy.' Churchill refrained from adding 'Amen' and, armed with Butt's report, he asked the Chief of Air Staff, Sir Charles Portal, to explain how he reconciled Butt's findings with his view of the bomber as the war-winning weapon. It was a fair question. For example, in revenge for the Luftwaffe's raid on Coventry in November 1940, Bomber Command had attacked Mannheim. Accompanying the bombers had been a photographic unit which showed that hardly any British bombers had even reached Mannheim, a city twice the size of Coventry. Claiming to have dropped 300 tons of bombs on Mannheim, it was admitted, meant no more than that 300 tons of bombs were exported in the general direction of the city. The outcome of research into Bomber Command's efforts up to 1942 was that they had amounted to an almost complete 'dead loss'. Given this evidence it is extraordinary that Britain continued to allocate the vast majority of its resources to the strategic bomber campaign. At a time when Coastal Command lacked the resources to fight U-boats, when in North Africa and the Mediterranean Britain was hopelessly outclassed by the quality and quantity of German aircraft, and while in Malaya and Singapore aircraft as deficient as Brewster Buffaloes were used to combat the Mitsubishi Zero, all Britain could do was build more and more bombers to continue missing their targets in Germany. As one admiral commented, 'If only some of the hundreds of bombers who fly over Germany (and often fail to do anything because of the weather) had been torpedo aircraft and divebombers the Old Empire would be in a better condition than it is now.' Director of Military Operations, Sir John Kennedy, was of the same opinion: 'I should like to take 50 per cent of the bomber effort off Germany even at this late hour, and distribute it in the Atlantic, and in the Middle East and Indian theatres. The price we pay at sea and on land for our present bombing policy is high indeed.'

Everyone seemed aware that the bombing campaign was wasteful and ineffective. So why did it go on? It grew into a kind of Frankenstein 's monster which took up all British resources in its aim to kill Germans irrespective of their military significance. Ships, tanks and guns were overlooked in the urge to build planes. Tactical aircraft were neglected in the endless demand for more and more strategic bombers. Why did Winston Churchill allow this imbalance to continue? The answer lay in the influence of his *éminence grise*, Lord Cherwell.

The future of strategic bombing policy now became part of the long-standing feud between two of Britain's leading scientists, Sir Henry Tizard of Imperial College and Professor Lindemann (Lord Cherwell). Tizard wanted part of the resources spent on bombing Germany to be used to improve Britain's air strength in other areas, notably Coastal Command's campaign against the U-boats. The bitterness of the Tizard–Cherwell feud stemmed from their post-graduate research years in Berlin, where they had been friends, but the friendship had waned as Tizard, 'the balanced, extrovert Englishman' found less and less to like or admire in the 'faintly Teutonic' and 'monastic' Lindemann. Churchill was to find in Lindemann something Tizard had missed, the ruthlessness and the passion for winning the war that did not come easily to many leading Englishmen of the day. With the future of the strategic bombing campaign in the balance after the Butt Report, Cherwell suddenly threw his considerable intellectual weight behind Bomber Command. On 30 March 1942, he sent a memorandum to Churchill containing apocalyptic predictions and statistics of what the bombing of Germany would achieve. It was a formula for genocide.

It was what Portal had been waiting for, an intellectual heavyweight providing the ammunition to shoot down his opponents. Sir Archibald Sinclair, Secretary of State for Air, stood right behind him, as did the new head of Bomber Command, Arthur Harris. Tizard, on the other hand, found Lindemann's statistics incredible, at least five times too high. The argument swayed one way and the other. The 'new boy' Harris now provided the clinching argument – the 'one thousand bomber' raid on Cologne – which was a triumph that offered Churchill a vision of things to come. If one thousand bombers could set Cologne ablaze, what would the four thousand that Harris requested do? Churchill was won over; Cherwell, Portal, Sinclair and, most of all, Harris would have their way. Instead of distributing resources throughout the air services, Bomber Command would have most of the cake. In return Bomber Command was given the 'go-ahead' to 'area-bomb' Germany into the Stone Age. In recognition of the fact that the bombers could not hit precise military targets they would kill Germans instead and destroy their homes. It was

The German city of Cologne after Arthur Harris's 'Thousand Bomber Raid' in 1942. This was Bomber Command's first real success over Germany and proved a turning-point in the air war.

Not only were these bombs often unsuited to the task for which they were used because of their general characteristics…, but they were also relatively inefficient and all too often defective weapons. Their charge-weight ratio was only about twenty-seven per cent as compared with the fifty per cent ratio of the corresponding German bombs. The explosives with which they were charged were relatively ineffective and large numbers of the bombs failed to explode.

SIR CHARLES WEBSTER, OFFICIAL HISTORY

The Germans used Triolin in their superior bombs. Britain rejected the aluminium additive, which improved explosive power by 80-100 per cent, on grounds of cost. Many Bomber Command missions were a waste of time – and lives – as the bombs carried were defective. After Dunkirk, Barnes Wallis proved the feasibility of the ten-ton bomb, which could have gone into production once the Lancaster was available to carry it. It took the Air Ministry three years to accept the ten-ton bomb, even though its effectiveness in urban bombing could have been truly horrifying.

to be genocide waged against the German people, and it took years for this realization to dawn on the Prime Minister and cause him to commit a crime of a different kind - the shunning of Bomber Command at the end of the war.

TAME BOARS AND SLANTING MUSIC

The strategic air campaign conducted over Germany by Britain's Bomber Command between 1942 and 1945 was a see-saw of triumph and disaster. The year 1943 saw much triumph for the British; but the following year brought some comfort for the German defenders. While the British public were elated to hear of the first 'One thousand bomber raid' on Cologne and the success of 'Operation Gomorrah' over Hamburg, far less was heard about the terrible setback Bomber command suffered on the night of 30/31 March 1944, during the raid on Nuremberg.

The concept of 'area bombing' will always be associated in the mind of the public with the person of Sir Arthur Harris, who became head of Bomber Command on 22 February 1942. Harris became to the Second World War what Field Marshal Haig had been to the First, a controversial figure who provided victories that confronted armchair strategists with the realities of total war. In 1942 Britain lacked the means to carry the war to the Germans. Harris provided the means through his strategy of 'area bombing'. It may have seemed unheroic – except for the performances by the aircrews – but it was effective. Or was it? Certainly it brought the realities of war home to the German civilians and cut through Nazi propaganda that the British could offer no threat to the German homeland; but what else did it achieve?

RAF bombing raids between 1939 and 1941 had produced disappointing results (see p.113). They were still aimed at specific targets, the destruction of which was thought would diminish German military potential. But photographic evidence revealed that the bombers were scoring few hits on important targets and causing minimal damage. The findings of the Butt Report (see p.116) – that bombing raids were inaccurate and ineffective – suggested that it was pointless for Britain to squander lives and aircraft over Germany. Yet if the bombers could not hit specific targets was there any other way in which British four-engine strategic bombers could damage the enemy? If not, then there was nothing Britain could contribute to the fight against Fascism until Russia and the United States had assembled overwhelming superiority in men and equipment. If Britain played no part in the defeat of Nazism in Germany, then who would listen to her voice in world affairs after the war? And so Britain had few options in 1942 but to listen to the theories of Marshal of the RAF, Lord Trenchard, Professor Lindemann (Lord Cherwell) and the new head of Bomber Command, Arthur Harris. To these men it did not matter what you hit as long as it was German and it hurt the German people. If the bombers could not hit the ball-bearing factory or the aircraft plant, then they should hit the town instead and hopefully kill the workers. The aim should be to destroy the local administration, the homes of the workers and all the things that enabled life to continue.

So it began – Britain's contribution to the destruction of Hitler's regime. In a war against an enemy as unredeemably evil as Nazi Germany it was inevitable that any opponent, however righteous his cause, would find himself compelled to resort to methods of which in other circumstances he would be forced to dis-approve. Although Britain wished to maintain possession of the moral high ground, victory over evil could not be achieved without employing some of the weapons that were used by the other side. This was an inevitable moral dilemma for those involved in a 'Just War'. To Winston Churchill, as well as to the vast numbers of ordinary people who supported him, the greater immorality for Britain was to risk defeat by Germany or be forced to a negotiated peace with Nazism. This was certainly the view of the Church, as well as of most politicians. However, how far could one get drawn into the evil of war before becoming tainted with the very qualities one had set out to destroy? Britain's professed aim to liberate the oppressed peoples of Europe was a thoroughly laudable one, but was not a strategy of civilian bombing, aimed specifically against the lives and property of the German people rather than the military potential of Nazi Germany, running very close to genocide? While Britain's American allies concentrated entirely on military targets, Bomber Command under the leadership of Arthur Harris - and with the tacit agreement of the Prime Minister - preferred area bombing to precision bombing. By doing so Britain committed both a moral blunder - in exchanging terror for terror with the Nazis - and a military blunder, in failing to use Britain's principal military weapon (the heavy bomber) against the enemy's military weak points.

Harris's strategy was as negative and attritional as Haig's had been in the First World War and – according to the Americans – as pointless. Albert Speer later questioned Allied tactics, pointing out that an assault on Germany's power stations – let alone the oil refineries (see p.148) – would have halted Germany's industrial capacity to conduct a war faster than any other single tactic. The problem was that by 1944, Harris seemed to be hypnotized by what he was doing and was tied into a system of killing for its own sake. German accusations of 'terror bombing' are accurate in terms of the intention by the British to destroy morale rather than war industry. The controversy that surrounds 'area bombing' has not gone away and centres more than anything on the destruction of Dresden (see p.127) in 1945.

Yet it must be remembered that Harris was not alone in favouring a policy of destroying Germany's civilian infrastructure. Voices other than his were influencing Winston Churchill into making area bombing Britain's preferred strategic option. Lord Cherwell regarded himself as an expert on the German people and, as such, on the question of German morale. Just as their morale had cracked in 1918 (admittedly after four years of British naval blockade) he thought it would crack again if the German frontline soldiers heard of the destruction of their families and homes. So great was Cherwell's influence that there were few willing to remind him of the need for Britain to maintain herself on the moral high ground. In the depths of wartime, and with British cities – notably London – having suffered heavy and indiscriminate bombing of civilian areas, few people were willing to voice the moral argument. In a sense, there was a more effective one available. The morale of the British people had stood up well to the bombing, why did Cherwell assume it would be any different in Germany? But Churchill was grasping at this offer of a cheap – cheap in terms of British lives at least – way of winning the war. At that time Britain was currently turning out a large fleet of four-engine bombers. If these were not used to raid Germany, what were they to be used for? And why had they been built in preference to the hundreds of escort vessels that were needed in the Atlantic

No sir, only military targets are being bombed.

SIR ARCHIBALD SINCLAIR, SECRETARY OF STATE FOR AIR, IN THE HOUSE OF COMMONS, 1943

This was an example of a minister misleading Parliament. Sinclair was a strong supporter of 'area bombing', and he knew that civilian areas were being targeted.

against the U-boat, or the heavy warships needed in the Mediterranean, or the tanks that would one day be needed if Europe was ever to be liberated? Cherwell had used 'lies, damned lies and statistics' to win the argument. The figures he proposed for German casualties as a result of a bombing campaign were, according to the later US Strategic Bombing Survey, exaggerated by a power of ten. Cherwell and Harris had won the day in 1942 and for the next two years they held the ear of Winston Churchill. Area bombing or 'terror bombing'? Fundamentally it meant the same thing.

While Bomber Command sowed the wind over Germany in 1943, they were to reap the whirlwind over Nuremberg the following year. Harris's boast that he could wreck Berlin from end to end, and that he could force Germany to surrender by bombing alone came back to haunt him and all the advocates of 'area bombing'.

Defeat teaches more lessons than victory and the disaster of the Hamburg raids, beginning on 24 July 1943, during which Bomber Command had first used Window (aluminium strips dropped from planes to blind German radar) as a blocking device, led to improvements in the German night defences. By far the most significant for the Nuremberg raid was the scheme of a junior officer in the Luftwaffe, Oberst Hajo Hermann, for what was nicknamed 'Wild Sow' and 'Tame Sow'. For 'Wild Sow', Hermann advised making a virtue out of necessity. Germany had a surplus of bomber pilots unoccupied and a number of day fighters that had no radar sets aboard. If the British use of Window was going to 'blind' the night fighters, why not send the single-engined day fighters aloft, piloted by the ex-bomber pilots, and let them attack the British bombers purely visually. They would have no guidance from ground controllers but neither would they be blinded by Window. And, moreover, they would be free to make up their own minds who to attack, hence they would fly 'wild'. If groups of these day fighters were kept near the main cities they could attack the enemy bombers as soon as they approached. Admittedly the limited fuel capacity of the

The Avro Lancaster was the most successful bomber of the Second World War. Its reliability and its enormous bombload enabled Arthur Harris to carry the war into Germany more than two years before Britain landed troops on the continent. However, its very success may have blinded Harris to the arguments in favour of precision bombing.

day fighters could lead to congestion on the landing fields as they came down to refuel, but any losses there would be more than justified by the damage they would inflict on the enemy bombers. In some ways this was a desperate measure which cost Germany the lives of experienced pilots, but at the time it was the best short-term answer to the blinding effects of Window. On the other hand, 'Tame Sow' became the keystone of Germany's future night defences. By this alternative system nightfighters could be vectored in from bases over Holland so that they flew within the British bomber-stream, shooting down the Lancasters and Halifaxes as they were on the outward journey towards their targets.

While junior officers were supplying the good ideas, Germany's leader Adolf Hitler was doing what he could to lose the war through sheer ineptitude. During 1941 the Luftwaffe had been using Ju 88s as 'intruders' to patrol near British airfields and try to attack bomber formations as they took off or before they had left British air space. However, in October 1941 Hitler insisted that such aircraft must in future remain near to German cities so that their victories could be seen by the German public. Hitler believed this was essential to maintain morale. On these dubious grounds the Führer removed one of the Luftwaffe's main defenses against Bomber Command and allowed it to operate only on the European mainland. It may have helped Goebbels' propaganda to display the wrecks of RAF aircraft that had crashed in Germany. However, it would have been more effective militarily if the wrecks had been in England or in the sea where they could do no harm. Many of the RAF's losses were suffered as they planes flew home after dropping their bombs.

But the Germans did have one new and deadly weapon. In the words of Louis Armstrong, 'Now you has jazz.' The Germans translated jazz as 'schräge Musik' - or 'slanting music'. It was an obscure allusion, but in simple terms it applied to the night fighter's new capacity to fly under a bomber and fire diagonally upwards at the undefended underside of the plane. Unlike the main American bombers, few of the British planes had protection in this area. Ironically, the Mark 2 Lancasters had such a turret, but this had been generally removed to increase speed and allow a heavier bombload. Bomber Command Group 6 at Knaresborough – the Canadians under C.M. McEwen – moved against the tide by keeping this turret, which may have saved them casualties over Nuremberg, but other groups took the risk of removing it, to their cost.

The choice of Nuremberg as a target to raid was a curious one. Although it had the historical buildings and churches that Harris loved to burn – Lübeck and Rostock had made a lovely blaze, with all those wooden buildings and ornamental beamwork – it was not of vital importance to Germany's war production. More than likely the target was selected for reasons of propaganda rather than strategy. It was, of course, 'a political target of the first importance and one of the Holy Cities of the Nazi creed'. It had held the great Nazi rallies of the 1930s, had given its name to the anti-Semitic laws of 1935 and would be in the forefront of Hitler's proposed 'Thousand-year Reich' should that ever be established. More than any other city, Nuremberg was the heart of National Socialism. Its destruction had symbolic importance. What Nuremberg did not really have was any significance for the German armaments industry, particularly not for aircraft or tanks. Above all, it was not one of the main targets of the 'Pointblank Programme', which Britain had agreed with the Americans.

Furthermore, Nuremberg was a difficult city to reach, three times as far into Germany as the Ruhr and more difficult even than a raid on Berlin, for little of

Lübeck was built more like a fire-lighter than a human habitation … The main object of the attack was to learn to what extent a first wave of aircraft could guide a second wave to the aiming-point by starting a conflagration; I ordered a half-an-hour interval between the two waves in order to allow the fires to get a good hold.

SIR ARTHUR HARRIS, 1942

'Bomber Harris' has been accused of 'war crimes' and 'terrorism', but such charges have to be balanced against the sort of war that was being fought. Nazi Germany complained about attacks on 'cultural' targets as if the war between Britain and Germany should be conducted according to different rules from those that applied on the Eastern Front. Was there no culture in Poland and Russia? The problem seems to have been that Harris did not behave in a way that Germans expected of a British gentleman.

the flight could be made over the North Sea. As a result, the bombers would be vulnerable to enemy attack for as long if not longer than any raid ever undertaken by Bomber Command. Moreover, on the night chosen for the attack, the moon did not set until 01.48. Unless the forecast cloud was unusually punctual there was a danger that it might offer little protection to the bombers, which would have to make most of the journey illuminated by moonlight – an open invitation to German fighter planes. Another major consideration was the choice of route, which should have by-passed known areas of anti-aircraft defences and night fighters. This meant that the Ruhr and the area around Frankfurt had to be be avoided. This did not happen.

When the details of the plan were eventually issued on the afternoon before the attack they created uproar, aircrews reacting to news of the operation with agonized cries of 'Jeezus'. Some of them could barely believe what they were seeing. The choice of a 'long leg' between Charleroi in Belgium and Fulda in Germany – a distance of 265 miles or about an hour's flying – before the turn south towards Nuremberg, was bound to be dangerous. Without the usual feints and diversions the bomber-stream would be flying on the same course for too long; in addition, the route elected went straight through the 'Cologne gap', which the Germans had chosen to defend by erecting a nightfighter beacon at Bonn. The Pathfinder pilots, who would lead the way, immediately complained to Air Vice-Marshal Bennett and pressed him to support their idea for a revised plan with four legs instead of two. The matter was referred to the heads of the five bomber groups but they stuck by the original plan. Their philosophy was that the 'shortest way out and the quickest way back' was always best, regardless of the risks entailed. Of course, they were not flying with the bombers. Oddly enough they believed that the lack of feints and diversions would bluff the Germans, who would not expect such a direct approach. Ominously, when the route was revealed to the air crews it was likened in shape to an axe. One comedian brought the house down by calling out, 'Chop! Chop!' But there was nothing to laugh about. 'Chop' was RAF slang for the destruction of a plane. As someone was later to say, this was going to be the 'biggest chop night ever for Bomber Command'.

To make matters worse, a Mosquito on meteorological reconnaissance reported back to Harris's deputy, Air Vice-Marshal Sir Robert Saundby, that the outward flight of the bombers was unlikely to have cloud cover as had been hoped, and would now be in bright moonlight for much of the way. Furthermore, the area around Nuremberg was likely to have enough cloud cover to prevent the Pathfinders from marking the targets accurately. It was bad news on both fronts – no moonlight when it was needed to mark the targets, but enough to enable the German defenders to see the British bombers in the sky. This news should have been enough to bring about the cancellation of the operation. When Saundby showed the weather-report to Harris he expected him to call off the raid. To his surprise, Harris simply nodded as if he had expected it, and the raid went on. Saundby later wondered whether there was some political imperative behind Harris's decision. As far as one can tell there was not: the decision was his own.

Many voices then – and later – were raised against the route chosen. One of the leading Mosquito pilots insisted that the bombers would be flying very close to a visual beacon known to be an assembly point for German night fighters, which was insane. But when he contacted Bomber Command HQ he was told that there would be no change of route. This was another instance of clear evidence warning against the mission being ignored. It was as if Bomber Command had a death-wish. In fact, the truth later emerged that Bomber Command knew about the beacon but had decided that no route could always be perfectly safe and that risks had to be taken.

Take-off for so many bombers took the best part of an hour in the late evening of 11 March, but soon the bomber-stream had assembled over the North Sea. Once the bombers crossed the Belgian coast the hoped-for thick cloud cover disappeared. It was to be bright moonlight all the way from now onwards. As the bomber stream reached Cologne – 712 bombers flew across the Rhine – it was apparent that much was going wrong. In the first place, there was no element of surprise. It seemed as if every fighter in Germany was waiting for them (200–250 nightfighters reached the battle area, the greatest number for any bomber raid). Secondly, there was no radar jamming, so the German nightfighters knew the direction in which the British bombers were flying. And, if that was not enough, a new and completely unexpected factor was making the job of the nightfighters easier than ever. Because of the weather, condensation had created vapour trails behind each plane. Long white lines of cloud pointed the way to their targets for each German pilot. Even worse, the German fighters were going to introduce 'a touch of jazz' to the night skies over Germany. With full fuel tanks and at least two hours' flying time, the nightfighters could take things steadily and pick their targets. Never before had so many British bombers presented themselves like sheep for the slaughter.

The discipline of the bomber-stream had been the strength of Bomber Command in previous actions. Unity was strength and the massed gunfire of the heavy bombers' turrets formed their best defense against the nightfighters. But this time, with the vapour trails creating a long white line in the night sky, the stream had become a trap, providing the German fighters with an unmissable target. They did not even have to search for targets, every RAF plane was specially illuminated for them. The bombers who broke away from the stream and made their own way to Nuremberg were the ones who survived. Meanwhile, the slanting music of the nightfighters was a shock to the Lancaster pilots. They had never previously encountered planes that could fire vertically upward, cutting the huge bombers in half without warning. With no fighter escorts and without turrets on their undersides, they were totally defenceless.

Nevertheless, so huge was the bomber-stream that those flying at the front were hardly aware of the disaster that was striking those flying further back. The Pathfinders and the first of the five waves of Lancasters and Halifaxes had escaped almost unscathed, while those at the rear had time to react to the chaos ahead. It was the second, third and fourth waves that suffered most of the losses at this stage. By the time the second leg of the journey was completed 59 bombers had been destroyed (41 Lancasters and 18 Halifaxes). The carnage had taken just 60 minutes. In terms of aerial warfare it stands alongside 1 July 1916 for the British Army, as the greatest and most concentrated slaughter that any air force has ever suffered. And the carnage had claimed the lives of air crew as greedily as that of the aircraft in which they flew. Few men escaped from their damaged planes. In fact, in the case of only one stricken aircraft had the whole crew survived. Parachutes had been available, but were generally found to be too bulky and were rarely worn. Moreover, the suddenness of the slanting attacks gave little time for the crew to save themselves.

An ultimatum is going to be presented to the English and Americans. If they do not stop the air war immediately, retaliation will be made the subject of another speech.

GERMAN JOKE, 1944

This significant joke shows two things. First, that morale in Germany had not cracked in spite of British bombing. Second, that the German people realized the inadequacies of the Nazi regime but could do nothing to overthrow it – except laugh.

The short leg of the journey, from a point in the Thuringian Forest to Nuremberg, was hardly any better in terms of casualties. On this last part of the approach, ten more British bombers were shot down. Nevertheless, terrible as the casualties had been so far, four out of five of the aircraft that had left Britain – 643 bombers – had reached the environs of Nuremberg and were ready to follow the Pathfinders' markers over the city. Unfortunately, the second stage of the night's mishaps was about to occur. As the weather-reconnaissance Mosquito had reported, a thick layer of cloud between 1500 and 11,000 feet thick – a veritable blanket through which the bombardiers would have to aim their bombs – was in position, masking Nuremberg. It was bad luck that of all places it should be so thick over the very city being targeted that night. And yet the British had been warned. The marking planes dropped their flares as best they could, but although many were near Nuremberg, many more were dropped ten miles away at the small town of Lauf.

At 01.10 the main group of of 559 bombers should have been attacking the principal target. Instead, of the 47 planes expected to drop their bombs each minute, just three turned up in the first minute and after a full five minutes only thirty more. Where were the rest of them? They were scattered all over the place, with the heaviest concentration following the flares towards Lauf. The cloud was so thick over Nuremberg that the target flares gave off little light. Thus most pilots assumed that the real target was in the vicinity of the small town, where the markers were much brighter. The people of Lauf were about to suffer an inexplicable attack from hundreds of British bombers believing they were over Nuremberg. So complete had been the British error of targeting that fire engines were even rushed from Nuremberg to the blazing town. The bombers also mistakenly destroyed a prisoner-of-war camp, killing an unknown number of Russian prisoners, giving Goebbels and his propaganda machine a field day. As one senior officer commented, 'It was without doubt the worst night that I can ever remember and I could not recall when the RAF was thrown into so much confusion resulting, of course, in bombs being scattered anywhere.' The general conclusion from those pilots who returned was that the whole affair was a shambles.

Other bombers had lost their way or had left the bomber-stream intending to rejoin it later. These were blown off course by heavy winds and found themselves without realizing it some 55 miles from Nuremberg, over Schweinfurt instead. They dropped their bombs on that city by mistake, but at least it was a better target than Lauf. Most tragic of the blunders perpetrated that night was the attack on Ostend by two Lancasters. In view of the severe difficulties which prevented them reaching Nuremberg, the pilots had been offered 'last resort' targets to save wasting bombs. Why Ostend was chosen as such an option is difficult to understand. Suffice it to say that the only worthwhile target would have been the docks. Both planes missed these and instead bombed a densely populated civilian area, containing no German military posts or barracks. Thirty-six Belgian civilians died – including old people and a baby of six months – and a square mile of the city was devastated, with hundreds of houses destroyed.

The German fighters kept up their pursuit of the bombers as they turned for home and more casualties were inflicted. Yet so many British bombers were carrying damage that the Germans could safely leave the wind and the distance to whittle their numbers away on the return flight. On a night on which 95 British bombers had been lost over occupied Europe and Germany, it may seem strange to single out one plane for consideration, but for sheer courage coupled with incredible bad luck, it is impossible to disregard the story of the Halifax from 578 squadron piloted by Cyril Barton. Barton's bad luck began when still 70 miles from Nuremberg, when his plane was attacked by a Junkers 88 night-fighter, which wrecked his intercom system and damaged the Halifax quite severely. One of his engines was then put out of action by an Me-210. With all of his turrets out of action, Barton's plane was helpless but he flew on, deter-mined to deliver his payload. Unable to communicate with his crew by inter-com, Barton tried to make do with shouts and gestures. One of these gestures was completely misunderstood by his men, three of whom – navigator, bom-bardier and wireless operator – promptly baled out, leaving him with just three men aboard. In view of the fact that he would have to navigate himself home he might have been excused for dropping his bombs and returning home at once. Instead, he gritted his teeth and flew on to Nuremberg before jettisoning his payload. As he turned for home one of his propellers was blown off and two of his fuel tanks were found to be leaking. Incredibly, Barton held his route to England, with no navigator to guide him nor a wireless operator to 'get a fix', and still unable to communicate with what was left of his crew. After an epic flight and very short on fuel as a result of his leaking tanks, he reached the coast of England far north of where he had intended, and looked for somewhere to land. Ordering his crew to prepare for a crash landing, he came in with just one engine running. He crashed into a field, dying at the controls but saving the lives of the three remaining crew, for which heroism he received a posthumous Victoria Cross.

The returning pilots could not convince the intelligence officers just how great the disaster of the night before had been. One New Zealander was asked how many bombers he had seen crash and when he replied 'approximately thir-ty', he was met with disbelief. The officer eventually decided to report just eight. Angrily the Kiwi told him that the previous night had been probably the worst in the history of Bomber Command. He was right. Elsewhere, station commanders angrily quashed rumours of eighty or ninety planes lost. Even the rumours were underestimates. Many crews were unwilling to admit they had

Sir Arthur Harris, head of Bomber Command, was the most controversial military leader on the Allied side during the Second World War. He presented political leaders with the full consequences of 'Total War' and was forced by Churchill in 1945 to carry the burden of guilt for Germany's civilian dead.

been so far off target that they had bombed Schweinfurt. They did not think they could have missed Nuremberg by so far – but they had.

The British did not meet their returning heroes with flags flying. It would hardly have been appropriate. Yet some crews received little to remind them what they were fighting for. Those who had landed in the south in damaged planes had to make their way back to their airfields in the north by train, if they could afford the fare. Several were ordered off trains because they were travelling without tickets. One air crew crossed London by tube, complete with parachutes. When they reached Beverley in Yorkshire, after a long train journey, they asked the station master if they could use his phone to ring the airfield at Leconfield for some transport. He refused. The seven men then found they had not got two pence between them to use a public phone.

In terms of casualties it had been a sensational night for the Germans. In Nuremberg itself just 40 Germans and 12 foreign workers had died, almost as few as had been killed in Ostend by mistake. In the 107 British bombers destroyed before or during the raid, 545 men of Bomber Command died. It was indeed the worst night of the war for Bomber Command and it had all been unnecessary. The flightpath had been wrong in the first place and flying conditions had been just about as bad as they could be. In view of the fact that Harris and his colleagues had clear and accurate meteorological information there was no justification whatsoever for ordering the raid to continue. The lives of air crew and the valuable planes they flew in had been squandered in a way that called the judgment of Arthur Harris into question. As we now know, even had the raid succeeded in turning Nuremberg into a fireball like Hamburg it would not have shortened the war by a single day. Ironically, the bombers that lost their way and bombed Schweinfurt by mistake contributed more to the Allied war effort than any amount of bombers over Nuremberg.

Inside Germany the authorities puzzled over this latest example of the insanity of the English. Why had 800 heavy bombers been sent to bomb the tiny town of Lauf, when Nuremberg had been so close by? Many Germans were convinced that the intention had been to commit an atrocity in the shape of the eradication of a whole community. The village of Schönberg, close to Lauf, had been hit by hundreds of tons of bombs. In the village farmyards burned carcasses of pigs mimicked the aroma of charred human flesh – a ghoulish reminder for the villagers of what might have been. Elsewhere in the village, a man had been killed when a heavy beam fell on him while he was clearing his barn.

The disaster had not come about simply because of the inappropriate weather conditions, the bright moonlight, the heavy winds, and the choice of the wrong flightpath. Any of these factors would have been enough to cause the cancellation of any previous raid but 'Bomber' Harris had disregarded them all in attacking Nuremberg, a city that was not even on his official list of targets. Why did he go ahead with so much against him? The answer lies in human fallibility. Harris was responsible for committing his bomber force night after night. Any commander, fighting so many battles, was bound to make mistakes once in a while. In Harris's case, however, the failure rate had been growing steadily during his assaults on Berlin – he had lost over a thousand bombers during the five-month campaign. The Nuremberg disaster was the final straw. Had the attention not shifted to the D-Day invasion of Normandy, Harris was in danger of so losing his grip that he might have lost Bomber Command's offensive capacity over Germany and given the defenders a morale-boosting victory through the success of their 'Wild Sow' and – particularly – 'Tame Sow' tactics. It was a military blunder – and all that jazz!

OPERATION THUNDERCLAP

By the autumn of 1944 the military situation in Europe suggested to the Anglo-American ground commanders that the war could be brought to an end within months. This was certainly the view of General Montgomery and helps to explain the thinking behind Operation Market Garden (see p.137) – the failed attempt to seize the Rhine bridges. However, if Montgomery had succeeded and a swift Allied drive across northern Germany towards Berlin had accelerated the strategic collapse of the Nazis, there were some in RAF Bomber Command who felt that Montgomery would have stolen their thunder. For several years Sir Arthur Harris had believed that an enormous air operation, lasting for virtually 96 hours non-stop would have destroyed Berlin and cracked German morale completely. Now, with the Russians advancing into eastern Germany, was the opportunity to mount 'Thunderclap', the name originally given to the plan to destroy Berlin. This was a political rather than a military decision. The Russians did not need Harris to level German cities for them, particularly those from which they hoped to benefit in the long run. On the other hand, Harris – and Churchill – wanted to demonstrate to Stalin that the military capacity of Great Britain would still be a potent force in the postwar world. Hence, the destruction of Dresden was more a demonstration of strategic bombing at its most effective rather than a purely military operation.

In Bomber Command's cold logic, the destruction of German morale was best achieved by killing people. The Director of Bombing Operations, Air Commodore Bufton, presented the following argument to Harris in favour of 'Thunderclap': 'If we assume that the day-time population of the area attacked is 300,000, we may expect 220,000 casualties. Fifty per cent of these, or 110,000, may expect to be killed . . . Such an attack, resulting in so many deaths, cannot help but have a shattering effect on political and civilian morale all over Germany.'

For the moment though, 'Thunderclap' was shelved until a propitious moment should occur. This was to be the Yalta Conference on 26 January 1945, at which Churchill and Roosevelt would meet Soviet leader Joseph Stalin. Churchill was eager to be seen to be helping the Russian advance on the ground and called on Bomber Command to hit the cities to which retreating German troops were heading. These included Leipzig, Chemnitz and Dresden. In fact, it was understood that Dresden was already crammed with refugees who had fled before the Russian advance, but this did not change its status as an 'especially attractive target', in the prime minister's own words.

Bomber Command's briefing notes on Dresden referred to it being the largest unbombed area left in Germany. Its population of 600,000 had probably been doubled by refugees and prisoners-of-war. Yet, it had little strategic significance except, perhaps, that the Russians would have liked to have seen it bombed. Sir Arthur Harris scornfully referred to 'sentimental views' of Dresden prevalent among some senior RAF commanders: 'The feeling, such as there is, over Dresden, could be easily explained by any psychiatrist. It is connected with

The bombs fell indiscriminately on Nazis and anti-Nazis, on women and children and works of art, on dogs and pet canaries ... Those wanton, quite impersonal killings ... did not so much breed fear and a desire to bow before the storm, but rather a certain fatalistic cussedness, a dogged determination to survive and, if possible, to help others to survive, whatever their politics, whatever their creed.

CHRISTABEL BIELENBERG, 1944

This quotation is by an Englishwoman who married a German and lived through the horrors of British bombing. It shows clearly that, contrary to the expectations of Bomber Command, their raids did not weaken morale, rather they strengthened it. Christabel Bielenberg shows that it unites people in shared suffering against a distant, anonymous and relentless foe.

The German people are bearing these raids like a chastisement of God.

GENERAL GALLAND, 1944

Galland was perhaps the most realistic of all Luftwaffe commanders. He was a courageous and efficient German airman, who followed orders but hated the Nazis for their decadence and their inefficiency. Here he is speaking for the 'old' and the 'new' Germany, which is aware of the crimes that have been committed in its name and cannot be purged of them without punishment.

German bands and Dresden shepherdesses. Actually Dresden was a mass of munition works...' Harris was wrong. It housed hardly any munitions. Did Harris believe his own lies? The Americans were not convinced by them. Their later assessment of the effectiveness of the Dresden Raid was that it had 'caused serious damage to the cigar and cigarette industry.'

What do you tell professional airmen about a target, when your intention is to massacre women and children, and refugees? Do you expect them to obey their orders without question? If so, why do you need to tell them anything? Bomber Command's leaders must have regarded the Dresden raid as something unusual, because they chose to lie to their men. The various group leaders explained the purpose of the raid with these *canards*. In No.1 Group aircrew were told that Dresden was being bombed because it was a vital railway centre. No.3 Group were led to believe that Dresden was a German Army headquarters. No.6 Group learned that Dresden was an important industrial area, producing electric motors, precision instruments, chemicals and munitions (strange that it had not been attacked before then!). It got worse at squadron level. Dresden soon became the hub of all German resistance – indeed a 'fortress city' – and a production centre for poison gas. Incidentally, in passing, it was also Gestapo headquarters. These were simply lies. Dresden was, in fact, one of the architectural jewels of Eastern Europe which had suffered just one raid – by 30 American planes – in the whole war. It was presumed by the inhabitants that – like Florence and Venice – it was being spared because even in wartime men did not stoop so low as to destroy beauty for its own sake. If the people of Dresden thought that they had learned nothing of Sir Arthur Harris's war against German culture. Viewing the historical areas of German cities as the best place to drop the incendiaries because the old buildings burned so well, Harris, it was said (unkindly?), made the cathedrals the first bomb marker in any city.

Bomber Command attacked Dresden on the night of 13 February 1945, in two waves, three hours apart. The aim of the first attack by 245 bombers was to stoke up a 'good fire' in the old city along the lines of the Hamburg firestorm, and when the fire-fighters were in the streets trying to control the flames a second strike by 529 Lancasters would drop high explosives to kill the firemen as well as more incendiaries to try to provide the draught to keep the firestorm burning. In case British bombers were shot down over Russian lines – the Russians were just 80 miles from Dresden – every crewman was equipped with a Union Jack embroidered with 'I am an Englishman' in Russian.

Nobody who bombed Dresden ever forgot the sight. Some likened it to a sea of fire or the crater of a volcano filled with molten lava. Pilots spoke of feeling the heat in their cockpits thousands of feet above the city. Against 1400 heavy bombers of Bomber Command flying over Germany that night, Dresden was protected by just 27 fighters. In the old city of Dresden the temperatures were reaching 1000 degrees centigrade. Nobody could survive that, irrespective of what shelter they found.

At midday on 14 February, the incredible happened: 400 American 'Flying Fortress' bombers also hit Dresden, dropping bombs on the ashes below, while Mustang fighters machine-gunned the survivors who picked their way among the debris. Even the assembly-point for children who had lived through the previous night's raid and who now stood helplessly together in the park was strafed by American fighters. Still the Americans could not leave Dresden alone, raiding it three more times.

The German city of Dresden after 'Operation Thunderclap' in February 1945. The great firestorms left buildings standing but whole areas completely devoid of human life. Accurate casualty figures will never be known.

In one night Bomber Command destroyed all nineteen permanent hospitals in Dresden, killing not only so many civilians that nobody will ever know the true number but also slaughtering their own prisoners-of-war and the prisoners from other nations at war with Germany. So many rings and other items of jewellery were collected from the bodies of the dead at Dresden that it horribly aped the desecration of the bodies of the Jews in the extermination camps. The dead of Dresden yielded up a million pounds to Nazi Party funds.

How many died? It should matter. Individual lives should not lose their meaning by absorption into a mountain of statistics, nor should they become footballs for revisionist historians or official apologists to kick about. On the night of the attack Dresden was full to overflowing with a population – including refugees – of about 1,200,000. Bomber Command, slowly realizing that this kind of mass slaughter was no longer to the public taste, tried to minimize the figures. Opponents of the 'Area Bombing' campaign tried to exaggerate them.

Realistically, a figure of between 100,000 and 150,000 dead should be accepted in view of the dreadful firestorm that was stoked up. Such figures brought no tears to the eyes of Germany's leader. To Hitler, it was the start of Germany's immolation. The German people had failed him and it was best that they should succumb in this way.

But world public opinion was quick to denounce the British pilots as 'child killers' and 'terror flyers'. Churchill seemed suddenly to have lost his taste for Bomber Command's methods. Dresden was its greatest success and yet Sir Arthur Harris received in reward a stinging response from Churchill in a memorandum which read: 'It seems to me that the moment has come when the question of bombing German cities simply for the sake of increasing the terror, though under other pretexts, should be reviewed . . . The destruction of Dresden remains a serious query against the conduct of Allied bombing . . . I feel the need for more precise concentration upon military objectives, such as oil and communications behind the immediate battle-zone, rather than on mere acts of terror and wanton destruction, however impressive.'

Harris must have found Churchill's accusations crushing. The Prime Minister was agreeing with Goebbels in referring to 'acts of terror and wanton destruction' by Bomber Command. Was the Dresden raid the 'raid too far'? Almost certainly it was. The war was coming to an end; there really was no need to talk of breaking civilian morale any more. And Churchill's reference to 'pretexts' indicates that he had suspected that Bomber Command had been covering their terror raids by giving them a bogus military significance. Had Churchill suspected this for very long he should have dismissed Harris and called on Bomber Command to cooperate with the Americans in their precision raids. The fact that he did not means that he used Bomber Command's area tactics while it suited him, but quickly shifted from it to precision bombing once he realized that Harris might stand accused of war crimes. Ironically, at the end of the war the Soviet Union wanted the bombing of civilian populations to be made a war crime at the Nuremberg Trials. They were successfully blocked by the British. In May 1943, the Nazis had published a list of 1100 schools, 600 churches and 300 hospitals, not to mention innumerable sites of architectural or historical importance, that had been destroyed by the RAF. The world would not listen. The Germans had done as much themselves. Were they not reaping the whirlwind? Moreover, Air Secretary Sir Archibald Sinclair claimed at the same time, 'the targets of Bomber Command are always military, but night-bombing of military objectives necessarily involves bombing in the area in which they are situated.'

Sir Arthur Harris had been very useful when there was no alternative to him. Now, men like 'Bomber' Harris would be inconvenient in the postwar world. Harris was bitter at his fall from favour, but his viewpoint was never one that could fit into the myth of Bomber Command, of the Lancasters and the Halifaxes carrying British heroes through the flak night after night to attack German railway networks, munition factories, rocket sites, heavy water plants and dams with 'bouncing bombs'. The myth has no place in the context of the firestorms of Hamburg and Dresden and the casualties for the latter, which are now generally declared to have exceeded those of the nuclear holocausts at Hiroshima and Nagasaki.

And so Churchill committed a great crime against the men of Bomber Command who had followed orders and taken the war to Germany while no other British servicemen were bearing the main weight of the enemy's strength

Germany must collapse before this programme which is more than half completed already has proceeded much further . . . We can wreck Berlin from end to end, if the USAF will come in on it. It will cost between 400–500 aircraft. It will cost Germany the war.

SIR ARTHUR HARRIS TO
WINSTON CHURCHILL,
3 NOVEMBER 1943

This quotation came back to haunt Harris during 1944 and 1945 when he nearly broke the strength of Bomber Command by trying to destroy Berlin. But cities – particularly capital cities – are not merely bricks and mortar, they are ideas. Bomber Command could not destroy Berlin until Germans stopped believing in it. Nor could Harris defeat Germany by bombing. A nation can only be defeated by land-based forces occupying the territory and being seen by the enemy.

as they did. In the victory celebrations as the war ended there was no campaign medal for Bomber Command, nor did its commanders share in the glories heaped on Fighter Command and Coastal Command. It was as if Bomber Command represented the dark side of man's nature, vital to victory and yet embarrassing to reveal in the light of day.

Allied Airborne Operations

SCATTERED TO THE FOUR WINDS

Airborne troops have always been among the élite in modern armies. They are often called upon to risk their lives before even encountering an enemy, leaping out of a plane and falling – perhaps in pitch darkness – thousands of feet to the ground, swinging helplessly for minutes below their parachutes at the mercy of an enemy who can pick them off at his leisure. Such men deserve at least the assurance that, should death find them early, it will at least not have been at the hands of one of their own comrades. The Allied airborne operation over Sicily in July 1943, deprived thousands of such élite soldiers of even this comfort. Their numbers were laid waste by their own colleagues, their own pilots and those of their allies. Their dismal end comprises the most disgraceful example of all aerial amicides. Their murderers – for no other word adequately describes what happened during this airborne operation – were legion. The mass hysteria that cost them their lives called into question the professionalism of US servicemen of all ranks.

During the preparations for Operation Husky – the Anglo-American invasion of Sicily from North Africa under Montgomery and Patton – the planners envisaged four separate strikes by airborne troops, arriving in Sicily at night either by parachute or by glider. The first wave was to be spearheaded by the British 1st Air Landing Brigade under Brigadier Hicks, which would land in Sicily from Waco and Horsa gliders towed almost entirely by American C-47 'Dakota' transports. Once they had landed they were to secure a strategic bridge and hold it until British ground troops could move out of their beachhead. Next, US paratroops from Colonel James Gavin's 505th Regiment would be brought in by 266 C-47s and dropped on four zones north of Gela. Their job was to hold any German counter-attacks developing against General Patton's 7th Army on its beachhead. The following evening the third and fourth strikes would be made. First, more C-47s would bring in Colonel Reuben Tucker's 504th Regiment to reinforce Gavin's men at Gela, while the final strike would be by the most experienced part of the allied airborne troops, the British 1st Parachute Brigade, led by Brigadier Lathbury, whose task was to capture the vital Primasole Bridge.

Both British and American airborne commanders considered that this operation carried an additional danger from friendly fire. Their flight paths into Sicily were to be directly over the invasion fleet, as well as along the invasion beaches. It would take only one gunner to lose his nerve and the C-47 transports and the gliders slowly passing over could be blasted out of the air by the naval gunners. General Matthew Ridgway, commander of the US airborne troops, tried to gain an assurance from the navy that there was no chance of this happening.

Ground crews loading a jeep through the nose of a glider during preparations for the airborne invasion of Sicily in 1943. Both glider-borne troops and para-troops of American and British airborne divisions suffered appalling losses from friendly fire during 'Operation Husky'.

Britain's Admiral Cunningham refused to give any assurance. As he pointed out, no warship could allow planes to come close enough to be identified. By the time an enemy was identified it might already be too late. Having fought through the vicious naval war in the Mediterranean, the British admiral was not going to take any chances now. If planes flew too near his fleet he would shoot them down – and apologize later. Disappointed at this refusal, Ridgway pressed for a rethink of the flight paths of the airborne troops. There was a chance that as things stood there could be a disaster. Ridgway warned that unless he could get a guarantee of safety he would advise calling off the airborne assaults altogether. His threat seemed to have an effect. General George Patton, commander of the US 7th Army, told Ridgway that the navy would be prepared to cooperate, but only if the gliders and their troop transports altered their flight path and flew no closer than seven miles from the ships. Ridgway was relieved though it is difficult to see why. There was no way that Admiral Cunningham could guarantee that all of his gunners would keep their nerve. Moreover, it might have been more likely if the gunners themselves had been told what to expect. Possibly from administrative muddle or – more likely – through some junior officer's obsession with secrecy, most of the American naval gunners as well as those manning guns on the merchant ships in the invasion fleet were not told that there was going to be an airborne invasion at all, and so nobody was prepared to see friendly planes flying overhead. As an illustration of the muddle, even Admiral Hewitt, commanding the American naval forces, only found out about the airborne attack on the day it was due to take place. It was hardly surprising that the gunners were the last to learn.

As the African sun set in Tunisia on 9 July 1943 the British 1st Air Landing Brigade took off from six airfields around Kairouan. They were travelling in gliders piloted by men from the 1st battalion of the Glider Pilot Regiment. The gliders were being towed by American C-47s of Colonel Ray Dunn's 51st

Troop Carrier Wing. Dunn's men, for all their skill and bluster were, in the main, pilots from civil aviation. Few if any had seen any action or flown through flak. It was a gamble – one might even say a blunder – to entrust such élite British troops to such uncertain pilots. In the event, as the gliders came into sight of Sicily everything began to go wrong. The flak, an inevitable feature of air warfare, seemed to take the American C-47 pilots by surprise. They did not like it and were soon showing in no uncertain manner that they were not prepared to face it. They began to take violent evasive action with the result that the gliders were dragged and tossed around in the high winds. To make matters worse, the allied fleet travelling to Sicily far below, opened fire on the C-47s. The result of this was sheer panic on the part of the American tow-pilots. Many reached a decision that was to cause the deaths of hundreds of British troops. They detached the gliders at least five miles from the shore. The reason for this change of plan was obvious: the American pilots would not have to face the continuous flak and could turn away and fly back to Africa. The result was that many men of the 1st Air Landing Brigade drowned off the coast of Sicily that night. Other tow–pilots simply turned tail and flew back to Tunisia without even releasing the gliders. Soon the whole brigade was scattered to the four winds.

Gliders were soon diving into the sea, miles from the shore line. The glider carrying General Hopkinson, commander of the 1st Airborne Division was one of those to ditch in the sea. However, as a result of a curious coincidence the General's 'luck was in'. He had managed to get clear of the wrecked glider and had found a piece of wreckage on which to cling. Even so he was probably at his last gasp when he was spotted by a British destroyer, commanded by an old school chum whom he had not seen for twenty years since they had rowed together for Cambridge in the Boat Race. A plate of eggs and bacon and a change of clothes aboard the destroyer soon revitalized the general, though the task that now faced him, of finding the rest of his men, would prove an impossible one.

In fact, the 1st Air Landing Brigade had been destroyed and it was obvious who was to blame – Colonel Dunn's tow-pilots. Later evidence shows that of the 147 gliders that had left Tunisia the previous evening, 69 had crashed into the sea, drowning 326 of the British paratroopers. Of the others, just two had been shot down by friend or foe, several had been towed back to Tunisia and 59 had landed somewhere in Sicily, though they were spread out across an area of 25 square miles. Resentment against the American tow-pilots was so strong that when they got back to Tunisia, British troops there had to be confined to camp to prevent a lynching.

Two gliders even landed on different islands, one in Sardinia and another in Malta. It has been said that the British sense of humour flourishes at times when it seems most inappropriate, and the disaster of the airborne troops over Sicily bears this out, as the British soon saw the funny side of their predicament. The fate of one glider crew was farcical. Expecting to land on a rocky coastal area in Sicily, the men found themselves instead on a broad, sandy beach. Far from encountering Italian troops – or even German ones – the paratroopers were amazed to find that their whole invasion force had been preceded to Sicily by a British mobile bath unit that passed them by on the road. Then the truth dawned on them. They were not in Sicily at all; they had landed back in North Africa – and nobody had even told them . . .

Another glider had a close encounter with a large, shadowy ship, which appeared to be anchored off the shore. The paratroopers extricated themselves from the wreck of their glider and swam over to the ship, climbing up the anchor chain and onto the deserted deck. Suddenly, a sailor emerged on deck carrying a slop bucket. As he saw the commandos he called for help and soon the twelve paratroopers were being attacked by sailors - British ones. Only with some difficulty could the twelve explain that they were not enemy saboteurs but glider troops, somewhat off target.

The most comic of all the landings was by the glider that reached Malta. Unaware of their detour the airborne troops readied themselves for action and prepared to move off towards their rendezvous point. At this moment a jeep drew up with two occupants who wanted to know what the Red Devils thought they were doing there. The young lieutenant leading the commandos replied that he was heading for his assigned landing zone at Syracuse. A surprised voice replied from the jeep, 'We are sorry to inform you that you are not in Sicily, but on the main airstrip at Malta, and what's more, you are blocking one of the runways and the fighters cannot take off. So please take the jeep and pull not only the trailer but also that bloody glider 200 yards in that direction.' Consternation and collapse of stout party.

But any laughter had a bitter tone. The truth was that hundreds of British lives had been needlessly thrown away by the incompetence or cowardice of the American tow-pilots. There was nothing accidental about what had happened: mass hysteria on the part of inexperienced pilots had resulted in the ditching of gliders into the sea at night, miles from the shore and far from any chance of rescue.

Meanwhile, Colonel James Gavin and the 505th Regimental Combat Team was already in the skies above the Anglo-American invasion fleet. Gavin, with fingers crossed, was praying that none of the naval gunners lost his nerve and opened fire on the hundreds of C-47s. However, some of the American C-47 pilots panicked in the face of the heavy flak. As a result, some US paratroopers were scattered over an area of a thousand square miles, many dropped at too low an altitude so that their parachutes failed to open and they were killed outright or broke bones. The American paratroopers who fell into the British sector of the landing beaches in the early hours of 10 July found that the British troops, not expecting to see Americans there, opened fire on them. Nobody had given the Americans the British passwords.

General Ridgway, from his floating headquarters with the invasion fleet, could only wince as news of the Gavin fiasco was added to the sorry tale of the gliders. None of the American troops landed where they were supposed to, many being up to sixty miles from their landing zones. Some had not even landed in Sicily at all, but were in Sardinia, Malta or even – in a few tragic cases – in the mountains of Southern Italy, where their bodies lay undiscovered for many years.

Gavin's disaster – though bad enough in its own right – was by way of being a mere *intermezzo* between two yet more tragic acts. A more dismal fate than that which had overtaken the British gliders was about to hit Colonel Reuben Tucker's 504th Regiment. With the airborne operation already in tatters, Patton ordered Ridgway to bring in the third wave of paratroops. But the danger of 'friendly fire' – the danger that Ridgway had feared all along – was greater now than even he realized. The invasion fleet had been under attack all day from German bombers and the anti-aircaft gunners were so tired that they were liable to fire at anything that flew over. The sirens from the Stuka dive-bombers had shaken everyone and the gunners were itching to hit back at the Germans who had just sunk a hospital ship near the coast. It was into this cauldron of emotion that the C-47s carrying the American paratroopers would soon fly. Ridgway still believed that the naval commanders would stop their gunners firing, but nobody could guarantee that the gun crews on the ships and along 35 miles of invasion beaches would all stick to their orders. When Ridgway checked around the AA battery commanders he found, to his horror, that many had been told nothing at all about the order not to fire.

With better weather than the previous night, and much lower wind, and with Gavin's 505th already – presumably – in position, Colonel Tucker saw his men's role as simply that of a back-up. As the coast of Sicily came into sight, the paratroopers aboard the leading C-47s were preparing for the drop. Behind them the mass of the regiment were being brought in at 700 feet over the massed ships, landing craft and land troops of the American Seventh Army. Suddenly the sound of a single machine gun was heard, firing up at one of the passing Dakotas. It was the sound that every American knew, the moment in the western film when the bad guys spring the ambush. It was followed by a few more desultory rounds from other guns and then by a cacophonous roar as hundreds of guns began firing into the sky. The impossible had happened – Tucker's 504th Regiment was being ambushed by Patton's Seventh Army.

The pilots of the C-47s desperately fired recognition flares, but the only answer they got was an even heavier barrage of bullets, shells and rockets. Afterwards, when the gunners were asked to explain why they had fired, most claimed that they thought the low-flying transports were German bombers and that they had taken so much punishment during the day that they were looking to get their own back. Some of the more inexperienced men even admitted that they could not distinguish a C-47 from a German bomber, while others claimed that they thought the planes were dropping German paratroopers onto the beaches. One and all agreed that they knew nothing about the flight of American paratroopers over the fleet.

On the ground the mood was one of mass hysteria. So high was the tension on the Gela beaches that a single incident could make a hundred – a thousand – men act as one, without rational thought. With the C-47s flying at just 700 feet it was almost impossible for the gunners to miss. Aboard the transports paratroopers were killed in their seats, either shot by machine-gun bullets or ripped apart by shrapnel. Below, watching the slaughter, Ridgway and Patton stood staring in horror – Ridgway, in tears for the massacre of his fine division, Patton simply repeating 'Oh, my God! Oh, my God!' But Tucker's men were beyond help. Planes were crashing into the sea, or onto the beaches. For days afterwards the bodies of US paratroopers were washed up at Gela.

Colonel Tucker was one of the fortunate ones who landed at the correct dropping point, but he must have wondered if he had landed in a tableau from Dante's Inferno. As he touched down he found that not far away a group of turret-gunners in Sherman tanks were firing wildly into the sky at the passing planes and cheering hysterically as they saw a plane going down in flames. He rushed towards the tankers screaming for them to stop firing, but as they turned towards him he was shocked to see the blood-lust written on their faces. For the record, when the plane that transported Tucker got back to Tunisia it was found to have been holed over a thousand times by bullets and shrapnel, all of which was fired by American guns. Along the Gela beachhead American troops were allowing their frenzy to drive them unwittingly into atrocity. The naval gunners, exhilarated by the massacre of what they believed to be German planes, now began killing the parachutists as they floated helplessly down, many of them leaping only to escape from the burning C-47s. The night sky was lit up by burning planes and parachutes, and by the tracer fire arcing upwards. With the grimmest of all grim humour, one of the C-47 pilots commented later: 'Evidently the only safe place for us over Sicily tonight is over enemy territory.'

By dawn the full extent of the catastrophe was clear. Of a total of 5307 paratroopers who had flown in the first three strikes, less than 2000 were still fit for combat and over 1200 of them had died from 'friendly fire'. The élite troops of the American 82nd Airborne Division and the 1st British Airborne Division had been frittered away in what came to be known as the 'Sicily Disaster'. Eisenhower furiously wrote to Patton, 'If the cited report is true, the incident could only have been occasioned by inexcusable carelessness and negligence on the part of someone.' How could Eisenhower possibly account for the loss of so many Allied lives when the enemy had not even been involved?

As the search for scapegoats began, the last phase of the ill-fated airborne assault reached Sicily: the British 1st Parachute Brigade under Brigadier Lathbury. Chaos was still the order of the day. The American pilots were no better by daylight than by night. Colonel Pearson had to force his pilot to fly on through the flak by threatening to shoot him and by holding a revolver in his back. Of sixteen gliders that took off with Lathbury's flight, four were shot down by friendly fire and most of the others succumbed to enemy guns. Of Lathbury's paratroops, most went the same way that Gavin's men had gone, scattered to the winds, some ending up on the Italian mainland but far too many others not reaching land at all and perishing in the sea. One group even landed on Mount Etna, though as many as 30 per cent were taken straight back to Tunisia. Faced with the full strength of two German regiments, complete with Tiger tanks, Lathbury found himself at the dropping zone with just 295 men out of his total force of 1856.

When just about everything goes wrong with an operation scapegoats are available everywhere. But what could be learned from dismissing or demoting a few middle rank men? Ridgway had more or less predicted what would happen if allied transports and gliders flew over an invasion fleet and were funnelled over an invasion beach bristling with anti-aircraft gunners. He had asked for guarantees, but he had been refused. Perhaps he should have had the moral courage to cancel the operation. When Eisenhower received the final report from Patton the facts were so disgraceful that he decided the whole fiasco must be hushed up. There were just too many reputations at stake.

SEEING THINGS AT ARNHEM

The great Anglo-American airborne operation called 'Market Garden' was one of the most severely flawed of all major operations in World War Two. Its inadequacies were numerous, each one qualifying it – particularly the Arnhem component – to be included in a book of aerial blunders. Selection has therefore been necessary and I have decided to look at three aspects of the Arnhem fiasco: photo reconnaissance, choice of landing areas and radio communications.

The story of intelligence officer Major Brian Urquhart's 'spiriting away' by a medical officer virtually on the eve of the operation has been made famous by Cornelius Ryan's book, *A Bridge Too Far*, as well as the film of the same name. It is an episode that strikes one as more suited to fiction than to a work of history. Nevertheless, incredible as it may seem, it is true. Several times in previous books in this series I have had to refer to a lack of moral courage on the part of some military commander or other. Yet rarely can this have taken so blatant a form as it did in the case of Lieutenant-General F.M. Browning. Confronted with photographic evidence that contradicted completely the assumption about the presence of German troops in the area, he rejected the truth and took measures to 'silence' the man who had presented it to him. Such actions by a commanding officer should be viewed in the strictest possible way. The airborne troops, had they been informed that they would be facing tanks, would at least have been able to take more anti-tank weapons with them.

Major Brian Urquhart, an Intelligence Officer on Browning's staff, had collated evidence from a number of sources that cast real doubt on the likely success of Operation 'Market Garden'. The plan had been based on the assumption of the airborne troops meeting slight opposition around Arnhem, but Urquhart was convinced that two Panzer divisions – 9th and 10th – were resting and reforming near Arnhem. Unknown to Browning, Ultra had already deciphered German signals confirming this. It was therefore known in high circles, higher even than Browning for example, that British airborne troops at Arnhem would meet armoured resistance. Unable to convince Browning of this danger, Urquhart ordered a photo reconnaissance over the area and on 15 September he got what he wanted – photographic evidence. Modern German tanks were just eight miles from the landing area selected for the 1st Airborne. Urquhart rushed to show Browning but was received with gentle irritation and treated 'as a nervous child suffering from a nightmare'. What happened afterwards was certainly decisive but not quite in the way Urquhart had expected. Instead of putting the evidence up to General Montgomery with a recommendation to call the whole thing off, Browning asked the senior medical officer to see Urquhart and arrange for him to be sent on sick leave due to his 'nervous strain and exhaustion'. The doctor followed orders but was unhappily aware that he was involved in some kind of cover-up. The problem was that too much was riding on 'Market Garden' for it to be cancelled at this stage, whatever intelligence might come up with to cast doubt on its wisdom. If a man as senior as Browning could be left out of the Ultra secret, then it was clear that even his recommendation to call off the show might have been received by Montgomery and Eisenhower with a stubborn refusal.

A CROWDED MARKET AND NO GARDEN

I f a worse plan for an airborne operation has been conceived than that for Operation 'Market Garden' then fortunately it has not come to the attention of this author. It hardly needed a military strategist of great intellect to appreciate that the requirements for any such operation involving paratroopers and glider troops are secrecy and/or proximity to the objective. Uncluttered by heavy equipment, paratroops should be used to 'seize and hold'. They should not be dropped eight miles from the bridge they are supposed to capture, in the middle of a swarm of enemy troops and heavy armour and left to fight their way through to the target, then left to hold it for three times as long as planned, completely without air support and unable to communicate with their disparate parts through radio insufficiency. For all this – and more – to have happened to the British airborne troops at Arnhem speaks volumes for the deplorable planning that went into the whole operation.

The first problem that influenced everything else was that there were not enough American transport aircraft available to shift the entire British airborne contingent in one day – not in two days either, but in three. This being the case, the operation should have been cancelled forthwith. If there was a need for that many troops in the first place, they should be taken there in the first place, not in 'dribs and drabs'. The American airborne divisions were both being delivered in one day – the 101st at Eindhoven and the 82nd at Nijmegen – but the delivery of the British and Poles to Arnhem would take three days.

Secondly, not only would the British arrive in three drops but they could not be dropped near their objective – the bridge at Arnhem. This ran counter to the most important tenet of airborne warfare: the need for the paratroops to land in and around their target and with complete surprise. The Germans were hardly likely to be surprised by the third day to see the Polish paratroopers landing. The American General James Gavin summed up the problem by saying that it was better to take casualties at the start in landing at the right objective than to have to fight your way towards the target. Never was this truer than at Arnhem.

Major-General Urquhart – no relation of the Intelligence Officer (above) – was a new appointment to the command of the 1st Airborne Division and Arnhem was to be his first airborne operation. Had he had more experience he might have complained more forcefully about the dropping zones allocated to his troops. The zones had been chosen by Air Vice-Marshal Hollinghurst, who believed the area to the south of Arnhem to be very low-lying and marshy, quite unsuitable to glider-landings though excellent for parachute drops. The best area for drops was, in Hollinghurst's opinion, in wooded area to the north of the city. Unfortunately, these dropping zones would be between five and eight miles away from the Rhine bridges. Urquhart was thoroughly unhappy about the three drops on separate days and the distance from the target. He approached his superiors requesting two drops on the first day, but he was refused. Next he tried to get the dropping zones changed only to be blocked by Hollinghurst, who did not want the aerial plans to be changed.

Urquhart was in danger of becoming the 'fall guy' for a completely botched operation. If only half his division could go on the first day, then half of those would have to guard the dropping areas for the next day, leaving him with just a third of his division to actually fight their way through to the bridges. The Polish Brigade was allocated a dropping ground to the south of the river, because it was expected that the fighting would be all over by the time they arrived and they would be able to cross the main Arnhem bridge which Urquhart would by then have captured.

There was too much politicking going on for Urquhart's taste. He was a fighting soldier and felt he should get on and follow orders rather than rock the boat by demanding too many changes. In this he was wrong. He was not to learn until much later that Browning had consulted Major-General Gale, then

Major-General R.E. Urquhart, D.S.O. and Bar, Commander of the British 1st Airborne Division during Operation 'Market Garden'. Urquhart's failure to question the aerial planning resulted in the British blunders in and around Arnhem in 1944.

commanding the 6th Airborne Division, about the air plan. Gale had told him that he would resign rather than accept what Urquhart was being asked to do. He would have insisted on a drop by a whole brigade directly onto the Arnhem road bridge, so that he could guarantee to hold it while the rest of the division moved up. But although Browning accepted what he said, he asked him not to express that view to Urquhart. Browning believed that everything had gone too far to turn back. Significantly, the Polish commander, General Sosabowski, was highly critical of the air plan himself and believed it would fail because the British were abandoning surprise in favour of feeding in troops in 'packets', giving the Germans the chance to destroy them in detail. The operation should have been a *coup de main*, instead the effort was being dissipated.

Blunders that occur in the comfort of headquarters in Britain are always less forgivable than those that occur in the heat of battle. And so one finds it difficult to understand how the British troops at Arnhem were allowed to leave Britain with such inadequate communications equipment. Montgomery may have been in a hurry to cross the Rhine and end the war early, but how would a disaster at Arnhem – however heroic – justify botched preparation and planning? Many British lives were lost because of decisions taken without due thought and attention. The subject of radios requires some explanation.

GOOSE EGGS AT ARNHEM

One section of the British airborne troops due to take part in the landings did not share the general state of euphoria, and they were the Divisional Signals. They knew something that nobody else seemed to realize: the goose egg (the name given to the oval drawn on the map round all airborne units in an operation) drawn around 1st Airborne's dropping zones was too wide for the radios to provide proper communications. Certainly in the first stage of the action, just when things were at their most urgent and potentially confusing, separate units would not be able to communicate with each other. This unhappy situation was the result of inadequate radios.

At that stage of the war Britain's airborne troops operated three different radio strengths. The standard unit set was known as the '19', which had a range of twelve miles, but which was heavy and required a jeep for transport as well as a mobile battery charger. The '22' was smaller, though still requiring a jeep and a battery charger, and had a range of just six miles. The smallest set, the '68' was portable, had replaceable dry batteries, but had a range of just three miles. Obviously size being a priority, most of the sets with 1st Airborne were the '68s'. And provided that the dropping area was a relatively small goose-egg, and weather conditions were good, then the '68s' might do. However, if – as at Arnhem – the drops had created a very large goose-egg indeed, none of the '68s' or indeed the larger '22s' would be of much use at all. Hollinghurst's dropping plan had – inadvertently – overlooked this danger with the result that the separate parts of 1st Airborne were almost totally cut off from each other.

Major Tony Deane-Drummond, second-in-command of Divisional Signals, realized this problem as soon as he saw the goose-egg for the Arnhem plan. He immediately took up the matter with his CO, Lieutenant-Colonel Stephenson. Deane-Drummond explained that he had never been happy with the '68', only accepting it in the first place because he was told that the division's goose-egg would never be larger than three miles. Moreover, all plans had been based on the assumption that drops would always be astride or adjacent to the target. However, with the Arnhem air plan, the light radios could not function until all

British gliders landing airborne troops at Arnhem in 1944. The British landing zones were far too scattered and too far from the vital bridge that was their target. Inadequate radios meant that the scattered groups could not communicate with one another.

units of the division had reached Arnhem. Should some units be cut off by enemy forces they would be out of contact with divisional headquarters. Only the '19s' would have been any use and for those one would have needed more jeeps, and therefore more transport planes to carry them.

Even before the 1st Airborne Division left Britain it was known – or should have been – that there would be a virtual communications blackout for much of the first day, or even longer if units met heavy opposition or failed to assemble quickly. Yet apparently this problem was airily dismissed by officers who were eager to get on with the mission, having suffered cancellations in the past. For this blunder, General Urquhart must take the blame. Communications being so vital in an operation of this kind, it was not a subject that could be left to chance. Had Deane-Drummond been consulted before 1st Airborne left Britain, the whole operation must have fallen into doubt.

Reputations were riding on the success of this operation and it seems that, whatever the deficiencies of the forces to be used, and whatever evidence there was that Arnhem was an ill-judged target, it was going to take place anyway. If 'Market' was already revealing itself to be flawed, 'Garden' was also a hare-brained scheme, though its consideration is not a part of this book. Above all, the fault lies with General Montgomery, whose sweeping vision of a quick end to the war overlooked the numerous flaws in the plan and condemned it to failure. His final comment that 'Market Garden' had been nine-tenths a success overlooks completely the destruction of the British 1st Airborne Division at Arnhem. Of the 11,920 British and Polish airborne troops who landed at Arnhem, 1485 died and 6525 were taken prisoner. Casualties of 67 per cent are not usually grounds for celebration.

War in the Pacific

SLEEPY LAGOON

The Japanese attack on Pearl Harbor has a place in history as perhaps the best example of the surprise attack or, in today's parlance, the pre-emptive strike. Yet, as has been demonstrated by numerous historians since 1941, it should not have come as a surprise to the Americans. The fact that it did and thereby caught the American defenders almost literally 'napping' reveals the deep complacency that prevailed among the American military leadership.

The Pacific Fleet in Pearl Harbor was protected by the latest radar – as one might expect from such an affluent economy as that of the United States – yet in its operation this radar was hardly as useful as a telescope, in that the men who operated it on Sunday 7 December 1941, were not prepared to believe what they saw. The old adage 'Better safe than sorry' never seems to have occurred to Lieutenant Kermit Tyler, to whom fell the responsibility for missing the significance of the Japanese blips on the screen and uttering the immortal words, 'Well, don't worry about it.'

It could have been a scene from Rodgers and Hammerstein's *South Pacific*. It was a quiet Sunday morning and at the Army's Opana radar station on the northern tip of the island of Oahu two private soldiers, Joseph Lockard and George Elliott were completing the 4.00 a.m. to 7.00 a.m.. watch and dreaming of dames, or possibly of their breakfast. Opana was the most remote of five mobile radar units set up around the island. It was a cosy posting, looking out over the blue waters of the Pacific and dreaming of Bali Hai. It was hard sometimes to take it seriously. Lockard and Elliott were supposed to have a third man with them but, well it was a Sunday and, what the heck? They were guarding the US Pacific Fleet but how the heck do you protect all those battlewagons with a Colt .45 pistol and seven bullets, which was all they had with them in case the Japanese came ashore from a submarine? They were linked to an information centre at Fort Shafter, which tracked the plots they reported. Theoretically they could pick up planes up to 150 miles away which should give the island as much as 60 minutes' notice of incoming enemy aircraft. But all this was theoretical, because the radar units were often on the blink.

At the information centre that Sunday morning Lieutenant Kermit Tyler was the only officer on duty. He was as relaxed and preoccupied as the two soldiers out on the point. Nothing was happening and Tyler was pleased at that. He did not really know what he was meant to do if it did happen. He had only once before drawn this duty and the other time he had had assistance. This time he was alone, except for enlisted men at the plotting table and a telephonist.

About 06.10 a station phoned in with a report of planes north of Oahu – about 130 miles away. Tyler noted the arrows pushed out onto the board. He was unconcerned. Soon it would be time for breakfast and the unit would be closed down at 07.00. Seven o'clock came and the enlisted men packed up and went, leaving Tyler, whose duty did not officially end until 08.00 alone in the room. While Tyler doodled, Lockard and Elliott at Opana did not switch off their radar until the truck arrived to take them to breakfast. It was late and so Elliott continued operating the unit, trying to get the hang of it. Suddenly at 07.02 a large blip flashed on the screen, the biggest contact that either of the men had ever seen. Was it a fault? Lockard, the more experienced operator, took over and soon verified that there was nothing wrong with the set; it was a huge flight of planes, about 137 miles to the north-east. Elliott tried to contact the Information Centre. The first line was dead. He tried a different line and got Private Joseph McDonald, who told him everyone had gone. Elliott excitedly told him of the sighting. McDonald reiterated that there was nobody there so he wrote down the message on a pad. Then he spotted Tyler. McDonald called out to the officer that there was 'an awful big flight' of planes and this was the first time he had ever received anything like this. Tyler was unimpressed and seemed preoccupied. On his own initiative McDonald rang Opana back and spoke this time to Lockard. What was happening now? The blips were travelling towards Oahu at 180 mph. By 07.15 they were just 92 miles away.

Lockard asked for instructions. McDonald told him that Tyler had said everything was all right. Lockard asked to speak to Tyler. Then Tyler remembered that the aircraft carriers were currently at sea and probably this was just a flight of Navy planes. On the other hand, they could be the B-17s that were expected from the West coast. In either case it hardly mattered – the blips must be one or the other – they were friendly aircraft. When Lockard tried to argue Tyler silenced him with, 'Well, don't worry about it.'

At that moment, with the Japanese still 30 minutes' flight away, there was time to scramble the fighters and get the navy gunners in position. If it was left any longer it would be too late. Tyler had had his chance of making history and he flunked it.

Elliott and Lockard continued to track the planes as they came closer. By 07.39 they were just 22 miles from the island. It was too late now to do anything but pray. Then the truck arrived to take them to breakfast and they closed up the unit and left at 07.45. Back at the Information Centre McDonald was uneasy. He asked Tyler what he really thought of the blips. Tyler reassuringly told him, 'It's nothing.' All was well, at least in the mind of Kermit Tyler. He had just fifteen minutes to go to the end of his duty and in one respect he had been right, twelve B-17s were approaching Pearl Harbor from the north-east.

'Out of the mouths of babes and sucklings' – well, in this case, not quite a babe, instead a thirteen-year-old boy named James B. Mann Junior – came the first alert that Japanese planes were about to attack Pearl Harbor. Where the radar screens had failed, Junior's keen eyes saw that there was something wrong with the hundred or more planes arriving over the island. As he told his less eagle-eyed father: 'They've changed the colour of our planes.' Before Mr. Mann Snr, could raise the alarm the Japanese did it for him by bombing and strafing Wheeler Field, where 62 of the Army's brand-new P-40s were neatly lined up. Soon they were all smoking wrecks.

The Second World War had started for America. Japan had chosen to wake a sleeping giant. And whose was the greater blunder, America's for sleeping or Japan's for waking her?

Pearl Harbor after the Japanese attack on 7 December, 1941. The incompetence of American radar operators combined with the general apathy of senior political and military leaders both in Hawaii and the United States to allow the Japanese carrier-based aircraft freedom of the skies over America's Pacific Fleet.

GHOST RIDERS IN THE SKY

The American-built Brewster Buffalo fighter may have been a public relations triumph for the Brewster sales force, but as a warplane it was one of the worst in history. Like its namesake, the woolly quadruped, it was destined to suffer serious depletion of its numbers. In the words of one of the Americans who had flown the Buffalo, 'The Brewster fighter turned out to be a perfect dud.' But that was not what the salesmen had said on the publicity sheets, and when Britain chose to buy hundreds of Buffaloes to patrol the skies over her Far Eastern empire it was because it was believed that compared with what the Japanese might have, the Brewster was a world-beater. The Americans had already spread the word among their pilots, based on what kind of intelligence reports it is difficult to imagine: 'The Japs will be flying antiquated junk over China. Many of your kills will be unarmed transports. I suppose you know that the Japanese are renowned for their inability to fly. And they all wear corrective glasses.' Even the prestigious *Aircraft* magazine joined the fray, defeating the Japanese with the volume rather than the accuracy of their newsprint: 'America's aviation experts can say without hesitation that the chief military airplanes of Japan are either outdated already, or are becoming outdated.' In fact, the Brewster Buffalo was going to find itself up against probably the best fighter in the world, the Mitsubishi A6M2 Zero-Sen – ever afterwards known as the 'Zero' – flown by pilots both rigorously trained and confident from their experience in war conditions over China. A comparison of specifications between the Buffalo and the Zero is illuminating. The Zero had a top speed of 330 mph, a range of 1900 miles and an armament of two 20mm cannon, as well as two 7.7mm machine-guns. The Buffalo was a ton heavier, 50 or 60 miles an hour slower, had less than half the range, less than half the firepower and was difficult to manoeuvre. At a time when the Zero might have been too powerful for a Spitfire or an Me109, it was reminiscent of 'ghost riders in the sky' every time a Buffalo encountered one of the Japanese fighters.

The problem was not a new one; it was a product of ethnocentrism. Both the British and the Americans underestimated their Asiatic opponents, convincing themselves that whatever was produced in Europe or America must be better than anything made in Japan. Even on its trials the Buffalo performed far less well than its specifications. It could not reach within 25 mph of its expected speed and was so heavy that when it tried to land on an aircraft carrier the landing gear simply collapsed. The Brewster company promptly blamed the navy pilots. The truth, apparently, was sabotage within the Brewster factory. The US Navy – for whom the plane had originally been intended – secretly suppressed the reports of the plane's failures and sold the first batch to the Finns, who were soon to be engaged in war with Russia. Surprisingly, orders for the Buffalo flooded in from other European states. The British, as soon as they tested it, realized they had bought a dud which could not possibly face the Messerschmitt Me-109. So they were all sent to Malaya where, it was hoped, they would not be recognized for the failures that they were. However, the Buffalos were sensitive beasts and did not respond well to the heat and humidity of Southeast Asia. More significantly, every time a Buffalo actually got into the air to encounter the Japanese fighters it was shot down. The British began with 154 Buffaloes in Malaya and Singapore on the day Japan declared war. Within weeks there was only one Buffalo in the whole of Southeast Asia – the

Japanese had captured it and wanted to return it Japan to keep as a trophy.

Ironically, the Finns made good use of their Buffaloes in their 'Winter War' with the Soviet Union. Admittedly they were facing Russian aircraft inferior to the Japanese Zero fighter, but the Finns were neither as arrogant nor as racist as the Anglo-Americans, and were content to fight their enemy with whatever weapons they had. As a result, in the Russo-Finnish War of 1939-40, the Finnish Buffaloes enjoyed one of the best 'kill-to-loss' ratios of any fighter plane in the Second World War. Yet this is scant comfort for the RAF pilots who died in their hundreds flying Buffalo fighters on what were little more than suicide missions against the Japanese.

ZERO AND OUT

Their encounters with the Mitsubishi Zero fighter came as a great shock to the British and Americans in the Pacific War, yet this is merely an indication of the grossest deficiencies in Anglo-American military intelligence. Just as the British in 1939 waited for London to be blitzed by German heavy bombers that did not exist, so no American observers seem to have noticed that this Japanese super-plane had been in action over China eighteen months before Pearl Harbor. It was unforgivable for the British particularly – who possessed in the Spitfire a fighter that could match the Zero – to leave their Eastern empire under the protection of such feeble aircraft as the Buffalo (see p. 144). As a result, for more than two years the Zero ruled the skies until finally challenged successfully by new American fighters like the Lightning and the Corsair.

However, just as the British and Americans blundered at the outset, so the Japanese rested on their laurels and did not prepare themselves for the inevitable reaction from their enemies. Having gained a great lead with the Zero, the Japanese became complacent and neglected to improve the Zero, even failing to

The deck of the Japanese aircraft carrier Soryu *is crowded with Zero-Sen fighter aircraft preparing to attack Allied shipping in the South Java Sea. Only months after his success at Pearl Harbor, Admiral Nagumo was to prove fallible himself at the battle of Midway and the* Soryu, *along with Japan's three other large fleet carriers, were to be sunk by American dive-bombers.*

The fortunes of war had turned on Nagumo's muddle over rearming his planes. Had they been aloft when the Americans arrived they would have offered air cover, as well as threatening the American carriers with complete destruction. Nagumo's blunder, to try to continue a bombing mission over Midway when their were enemy ships in the area, was unforgivable.

American Precision Bombing

OIL STRIKE

German dependence on Rumanian oil made the Ploesti oil fields a major Allied target during 1943. Once North Africa was firmly in Allied hands it was possible to make the 2700-mile round trip to Ploesti from airfields in Libya, crossing the Mediterranean and flying over the Balkans. Although this was preferable to flying from bases in England, the raid that took place on 1 August, 1943 still turned out to be one of the most disastrous ever carried out by the US Air Force. The reason for this is not hard to find: too many men were giving orders and too few were taking any notice.

Operation 'Statesman', as the mission to Ploesti was called, began when three groups of VIII Bomber Command in England flew to North Africa, where they came under the control of IX Bomber Command, led by Major-General Lewis Brereton. These B-24 Liberators were being prepared for a low-level mission in daylight against what was hoped would be light flak defences and limited fighter cover. The emphasis was on 'low-level' and, as we shall see, this meant virtually ground level, the sort of height where people on the ground dive for cover. That it would be dangerous was an understatement. Brereton did not quite hand out the wreaths before the raid, but he can hardly have improved morale by telling the pilots, 'We expect our losses to be fifty per cent but even though we should lose everything we've sent, but hit the target, it will be well worth it.' Those who were about to die just about continued to salute him. It was rare – virtually unknown, in fact – for suicide missions to be planned in democratic armies.

The plan for the bombing of Ploesti's nine oil refineries had been prepared by Brigadier-General Uzal G. Ent, who for some unknown reason believed that the refineries were scantily defended and could be destroyed by bombers approaching at 'tree-top' level. Unfortunately, Ent was totally misguided. Even as he was planning the operation, the Germans were equipping the Ploesti fields with some of the heaviest anti-aircraft defences in the world, as well as 120 German fighters with top pilots. In addition to misjudging the defences, Ent had authorized the use of time fuses on the bombs. This meant that the most precise timing was called for as chaos would result if some aircraft were to be delayed. They might arrive over the target at 'tree-top' level just as the fused bombs exploded.

At dawn on 1 August, the lines of B-24s took off from Benina Airfield at Benghazi. Immediately one of the Liberators crashed, and another burst into flames. It was an ominous start. Within minutes of take-off eleven of the bombers had turned back with mechanical problems. Then the plane carrying one of the mission's senior navigators crashed into the sea. This plane had been the 'lead' aircraft for many of the B-24s, and a good deal of confusion ensued. Nevertheless, by midday the aerial fleet had reached Albania. Here it encountered heavy cloud that made navigation even more difficult. The two lead groups crossed into Rumania on schedule and made their first turn towards Pitesti, 60 miles to the west of Ploesti. However, the three groups following lost their way, circled for a while over the Danube and then set off towards Ploesti 20 minutes behind the others. From now on the planes came down to almost ground level, flying just over the top of the houses. Scattering peasants working in the fields threw their pitchforks at the American planes. One Liberator flew so low that corn stalks were found in cracks in the bottom of the fuselage when it returned to base.

An operation of this kind needed the most accurate navigation as well as the most skilful piloting. Nobody could criticize the pilots who were taking 'low-flying' to mean 'brushing the thatched cottage roofs'. Unfortunately, the navigation also 'plumbed the depths' rather than 'reaching the heights'. Passing Pitesti, the Liberators were due to fly east past the town of Targoviste, before turning southeast and following the railway to Ploesti and approaching the oil fields from the north. Each crew had its assigned target and intelligence had provided ample photographs of the area so that nobody could have any excuses for not knowing his target. At least that was the general idea.

However, crashes and mechanical errors had already depleted the air fleet and now confusion was to set in as the commanding officer, General Ent, revealed he could not tell north from south. When the two leading groups reached Targoviste, they encountered a railway running south. The lead plane, carrying General Ent as well as Colonel Compton, the group leader, decided that this was the railway they must follow to Ploesti. The plane's navigator, a junior officer, pointed out that this was the wrong track, since it led away from Ploesti not towards it. In this dispute there was only ever going to be one winner: gold braid. The navigator was silenced by rank and Ent ordered the 60 bombers with him to follow the track which in fact led towards the Rumanian capital of Bucharest, and not the oil facilities at Ploesti. The Germans – and the Rumanians – were baffled by this American flightpath. Bucharest was an historic city with no military importance whatsoever. If the Americans wanted to behave like Vandals then Bucharest was a suitable place, otherwise it was a complete waste of time. Why did they not attack Ploesti instead?

As the B-24s flew over castles and church spires, Ent had the feeling he had made a mistake. Perhaps he should have listened to the guy with the map. Now he broke radio silence and informed the planes with him that they would have to turn about and fly back to Ploesti, approaching the oil installations from the south. The problem was that weeks of preparation were wasted as everyone had been briefed for an approach from the north.

Meanwhile, the three groups that had fallen behind Ent's command plane had followed the maps correctly and were approaching Ploesti from the north as planned. To the chaos that the Americans had already caused for themselves, the anti-aircraft guns now added an unexpectedly heavy and accurate fire. In the skies above Rumania two large masses of American B-24s were flying towards each other from opposite directions, with a combined speed of 600 mph. Irresistible force and the immovable object were about to slug it out.

Confusion was already general around Ploesti, with heavy anti-aircraft fire shooting down plane after plane. The 93rd Group, which had flown with Compton and Ent, dropped their bombs randomly, far from the oil facilities, before breaking away. Compton, with the 376th Group, had circled round Ploesti to try to pick up his correct approach path. When he was unable to do so Ent realized that the whole affair was in danger of dissolving in chaos so he radioed to the planes to pick their own targets and act individually. As the three groups approaching from the north arrived over Ploesti, they found the area shrouded in smoke and American planes attacking their targets but approaching from the south. Pandemonium ensued, with bombers narrowly missing each other and criss-crossing the oil plant as they tried desperately to avoid collisions. The northern groups found some of their targets already attacked and could do nothing but drop their bombs into the flames. Many of the oil tanks were left untouched, while in other places two groups of bombers continually hit the same target.

Meanwhile, one American group had been ordered to attack the Steaua Romana oil refinery some distance away, at Campina. This should have been relatively straightforward, particularly in view of the attention that was being devoted to the raid on Ploesti. But what looked easy on a map turned out to be very different in reality. The Liberators had to fly down a valley and, incredibly, so low was their approach run that at times the German machine-gunners on the side of the valley were actually firing down on the planes as they flew towards the target. Losses were understandably heavy.

Only now did the mixed units of German and Rumanian fighters intervene. It was an amazing sight, as German Me-109s and Focke-Wulfs flew into action alongside Rumanian Gloster Gladiator biplanes, bought from Britain in 1935. Slow as the Gladiators were they enjoyed one of their best days, flying above the American Liberators and dropping clusters of bombs on them. To make matters worse, on the return journey the Americans were also attacked by 200 Italian fighters. While they had managed to stay low the B-24s were relatively safe from the fighters, but as they had to raise their ceiling to pass over the mountains they were pounced on and shot down in their dozens. Few of the B-24s had enough fuel to return to their bases in North Africa and most of the survivors sought refuge in British bases in the Mediterranean such as Cyprus. Some were interned in neutral Turkey. Of the 179 Liberators that took part in the raid, 66 were lost and most of the others lost an engine and were so badly damaged that they never flew again. Of the crews, 440 men died, 220 became prisoners of war or were interned, and many of the survivors were injured.

How does one assess the Ploesti Raid? Certainly it was a disaster, but need it have been? The planning had been good but the execution was at fault. Admittedly the defences had been stronger than expected, particularly the highly effective anti-aircraft fire, but the raid had failed not because of the enemy but because the navigators on the Liberators had made a hash of the approach flights. In their defence, the biggest mistake had been made when two senior officers – Compton and Ent – had pulled rank on a young lieutenant who was navigating Compton's lead plane. If they had listened to him the whole operation might have gone differently. At least all the American planes would have been flying in the same direction and, presumably, able to concentrate on the targets that had been allocated to them. The intervention of General Ent on that occasion, and later when he radioed that everyone should attack whatever target they could regardless of their orders, was at best unhelpful and at worst a

The subject of morale had been dropped, and I was now required to proceed with a joint Anglo-American bombing offensive for the general disorganization of German industry … which gave me a wide range of choice and allowed me to attack pretty well any German industrial city of 100,000 inhabitants and above … the new instructions therefore made no difference.

SIR ARTHUR HARRIS ON THE CASABLANCA CONFERENCE, 1943

Harris was never convinced of the value of precision-bombing military installations, as practised by the Americans. As this quote shows, he 'twisted' his orders, notably those to attack German 'oil installations', so that he could continue his assault on the morale of the German people. Even after he was shown to be wrong, he never lost faith in 'area bombing'. But his resolution – so valuable when things were tough – became obsessional when the need for saturation bombing of German cities was no longer vital to victory.

While RAF Bomber Command continued its strategic bombing of German cities, the Americans preferred to concentrate on precision bombing of industrial and military targets. Here a B-24 Liberator flies over a smoking oil installation at Ploesti in Rumania. American losses in the Ploesti raid in 1943 were their heaviest of the war.

sign of panic. It was Ent who lacked discipline on this raid, not the younger officers. Any operation which mixes so many senior men - one general and at least five full colonels - with so many junior officers who, as navigators, should have the final word was asking for trouble. Perhaps there were just too many chiefs and not enough Indians.

FOR FLETCHER'S AMERICAN CHEESE

Switzerland's claim to neutrality in wartime is one of that nation's defining characteristics which, like cuckoo clocks and illegal bank accounts, has generally endeared her to her neighbours. However, never before have these less fortunate lands stretched Swiss patience so much as during the spring and summer of 1944. No less a power than the United States appeared to be at war with the small Alpine state.

On April Fool's Day 1944, the Swiss town of Schaffhausen was shaken by the impact of exploding bombs. Amazing to relate, the town was under attack from American aircraft overhead. One is reminded of how one America survivor of the Japanese attack on Pearl Harbor had summed up his feelings: 'I didn't even know they were mad at us.' Many Swiss must have shared this sentiment. They were neutral: why were the Americans bombing them? The truth seemed too incredible to be true. The American navigators were so incompetent that they thought they were flying over Germany and believed they were bombing the correct targets. Admittedly the weather could be difficult over the mountainous terrain of the Swiss–German border, but were the Americans unable to follow their maps or operate their instruments no better than that? And if there was doubt about their location why did they drop their bombs at all, causing so many 'friendly casualties'? US air chiefs already had enough on their minds without being pestered by neutral states, standing on their dignity and asserting their territorial rights. These things happened in wartime. But the Swiss were not prepared to accept that as an explanation. American bombing of their territory was an act of war and unless it ceased the Swiss would retaliate. They informed the Americans that single aircraft violating Swiss airspace would be escorted to a landing field and forced to land there, while formations of two or more bombers would be attacked without warning. Soon after the Schaffhausen raid – as it came to be known – Swiss aircraft, acting on this policy, shot down an American bomber and impounded another. The Swiss might have expected the Americans to take notice, but compared with the titanic struggle going on in Northern Europe the Swiss response was no more than a pinprick for them. In fact, in the aftermath of the Swiss action, 'friendly fire' incidents actually seemed to increase.

Politically the Americans felt embarrassed by this open display of their aerial incompetence, but the air commanders could find no way of preventing a certain number of navigational errors which involved their crews overflying Swiss airspace. The American ambassador in Switzerland, Leland Harrison, bore the brunt of Swiss fury. Even as he tried to apologize for the Schaffhausen raid, offering to pay compensation to the victims, the Swiss foreign minister described the incident as a 'deliberate attack' in which 50 American planes had inflicted civilian casualties of over a hundred dead and wounded. The use of the word 'deliberate' shook the Americans. Clearly the Swiss were not looking for explanations or excuses. They expected the bombing to stop – or else. In fact, the Americans had not even been aware of just how inaccurate their bombing often was. It was not until the commander of the US Strategic Air Force in Europe, Carl A. Spaatz, collected together all the evidence that the truth was revealed. Spaatz had begun by hoping that the Schaffhausen Raid was a 'one-off', the sort of blunder that was inseparable from modern war on such a scale. He was prepared to apologize to the Swiss, though he and his senior officers had a lot more important things to think about than minor mishaps in Switzerland, not least the imminent D-Day landings in France. In any case, some American air chiefs were of the opinion that the Swiss military was dominated by pro-Nazis anyway and that they deserved everything that was coming to them. Anglo-American raids over Germany involving 500-1000 bombers at a time were bound to suffer from a few planes blown off course by adverse winds.

Unfortunately the views of the American air force commanders were leaked to the press and there was an immediate outcry in Switzerland, which grew in intensity when meteorological evidence showed that weather conditions over Schaffhausen on 1 April had been excellent, with near perfect visibility. In

Germany, Goebbels and the Nazi propaganda machine accused the Americans of 'war crimes'. It was a public relations disaster for the US. The Americans carried out their own investigation, which revealed that on 1 April things might have been clear in Switzerland but that there had been adverse conditions over France, with heavy cloud and strong winds, which had broken up the bomber formations, scattering the planes over a wide area. The original target had been the German town of Ludwigshafen am Rhein, but when gaps in the cloud allowed the Americans to identify a city on the east bank of the Rhine some of them did not realize that they had been blown across the Swiss border and were, in fact, 50 miles from their target, flying over Schaffhausen. Even now the disaster should have been avoided if pilots had followed standard American procedure forbidding the bombing of targets within 50 miles of Germany's borders unless a positive identification could be made. And the lack of two important targets in the German city—the benzol storage plant and the butadiene factory—should have shown the pilots that they were not over Ludwigshafen. So the bombs should not have been dropped – but they were – and over a hundred casualties were inflicted. To understand why the Americans dropped their bombs we need to consider the state of mind of bomber crews who had flown half-way across Europe to deliver their payload and, finding themselves off course, faced the prospect of flying back to England with all their bombs aboard. Pumped up with adrenalin, they would be sorely tempted to find somewhere to dump their bombs. Any doubts as to the advisability of this course of action would be suppressed on the dangerous – if human – assumption that one German city is as good as another. After that gravity takes over . . .

While the American commanders were grappling with the Schaffhausen problem the Swiss hit them with news of more such bombing incidents. Faced with a growing problem the Swiss air force fought fire with fire. On 13 April, Swiss fighters shot down a damaged American bomber, killing six crewmen. Now it was the turn of the Americans to protest. In the space of three days in July 1944 a total of 23 American bombers were forced to land by Swiss fighters. The problem was escalating towards the unthinkable – war between the United States and Switzerland. While the politicians fumed at the diplomatic embarrassment, and the Nazis laughed at the moral crusaders with egg on their faces, American pilots did everything they could to carry the war across the Swiss border. One plane even collided with the castle of Weyden, home of the president of the International Red Cross, a damaged US bomber, abandoned by her crew, scoring a direct hit as if radio-controlled.

The Americans tried to cover their embarrassment by putting the blame on the Nazis, claiming that German pilots were flying captured and repaired American planes over Switzerland in an attempt to score propaganda points. Whoever was responsible for this theory was simply blinding himself to the dozens of cases of American friendly fire achieved without any German cooperation. For example, on 29 October 1944, American bombers attacked the railway junction at Noirmont, even though Swiss flags were painted on a number of the village roofs and were quite unmissable in the good visibility that day. Were American pilots even aware of Swiss neutrality and did they care who they hit as long as they got rid of their bombs?

Even Christmas Day brought no relief for the hard-pressed neutrals. Santa Claus's gift for the Swiss town of Thyngen was a basketful of high explosives courtesy of the bombers of the US 1st Tactical Air Force, who thought they were attacking the Singen railway bridge in Germany. New Year brought no new resolutions on the part of American pilots: the bombing of Switzerland continued and seemed even to gather pace. In the early days of 1945 US bombers attacked Chiasso and the hydro-electric plant at Brúsio in the Puschlav valley in southern Switzerland.

While the military were trying to wreck Swiss–American relations on a permanent basis, the politicians were dusting off their 'doves of peace' and looking for an amicable solution. On 22 February President Roosevelt sent a special representative, Laughlan Currie, to Switzerland to apologize for the serious violations of Swiss airspace. He could hardly have known or suspected that, as he prepared to draw on a lifetime's experience in the art of diplomacy, he was about to be upstaged in a most dramatic and undiplomatic way. At a special ceremony held in Schaffhausen, he was in the process of laying a wreath on the graves of the civilians killed by American bombs, when the dull rumble of bomb blasts was heard amid the silence of that solemn occasion. As he was honoring the dead in Schaffhausen the American bombers were at it again, just ten miles away. It was the biggest raid so far on Swiss territory, with thirteen separate incidents. At Stein-am-Rhein seven civilians were killed and some sixteen injured. And as the sun beat down on Currie's embarrassed face he knew that this time it was quite impossible to blame adverse weather conditions. There was nothing left for Currie but to take out his nation's cheque book and agree to pay for breakages.

In the early months of 1945, with the war in Europe drawing to a close, it seemed that the American forces could do nothing right. 'Friendly fire' cases might be infinitesimal in comparison with the enormous amount of successful American air activity but they were getting all the headlines. In London, Eisenhower might feel himself the most powerful man on earth, ordering and directing the lives of millions of men on the ground and in the air, but he seemed quite incapable of controlling those rogue American flyers who appeared to take a special delight in annoying the Swiss. There was nothing for it: there had to be a public admission of guilt. When, in early March, six US B-24s dropped twelve tons of explosives on Zurich, while others hit Basel with more than sixteen tons, the reputation of the American Air Force was on the line. Now matters were taken out of Eisenhower's hands. In Washington, General Marshall ordered Ike to send General Spaatz – the most senior American air commander in Europe – to Switzerland in person to explain why his pilots could not fly straight or bomb the right targets.

It was an amazing decision to uproot General Spaatz – SHAEF Air commander – from his office in England when the war with Germany was still undecided. Soon Spaatz, kitted out in civilian clothes and with a Tyrolean hat for disguise, was in the small French town of Annemasse in Savoie, to meet the Swiss representatives. It was like a scene from a Broadway show. In fact, it *was* a scene from a Broadway show. A war between the United States and Switzerland had been fought once before – in George and Ira Gershwin's 1927 hit musical *Strike Up the Band*. And the good ol' US of A had fought the Swiss to uphold the integrity of Fletcher's American Cheese. Whether Spaatz's aides apprised him of this precedent for war is unknown. It would have been of doubtful use as the Swiss were not smiling or showing the sort of hospitality the Swiss maids had shown in Gershwin's show. Resisting whatever blandishments Spaatz could offer, their delegates presented him with a full list of grievances and it was a very long list at that. Their demand for compensation was readily accepted by the American delegation and Spaatz agreed to prohibit bombing within 150 miles of the Swiss border. The compensation finally paid to Switzerland for bomb damage amounted to some $18 million, settled in October 1949.

But one puzzle was never cleared up. Why was it that so many American pilots mistook their targets over so long a period? The bombing of Zurich in March 1945 was inexplicable. The city was situated on a substantial body of water – the lake of Zurich – and was clearly identifiable. Moreover, to attack Zurich the American bombers had to fly deep into Swiss territory, and no sort of navigational error or adverse weather conditions could account for this. In fact, the Zurich fiasco did lead to a court martial. On 1 June 1945, the pilot and navigator of the lead aircraft in the squadron that bombed Zurich were tried by court martial at Horsham St Faith in England. As it happened the presiding officer on that occasion was none other than the future Hollywood star James Stewart, then a US colonel. In the event, both men were acquitted; their equipment had been at fault. Although the final decision to drop the bombs had been theirs it was decided to overlook human failings and, in the spirit of the Broadway show, allow everything to end happily. Yet as the Americans struck up the band and marched off home, many of the Swiss extras were still apparently 'playing dead'.

SCREWING UP ON OPERATION COBRA

Most handymen would agree that there are better ways of driving in a screw than by using a hammer. Apart from the fact that it is the wrong tool for the job, a hammer is all crushing force, a screwdriver lean precision. As such the different tools symbolize the opposing sides in the dispute that broke out over the conduct of Allied military policy in the weeks following the Normandy landings of 6 June 1944.

The problem was that the Anglo-American forces had half-expected the Nazi hold on Europe to crack once they gained a foothold in France. Instead, German resistance stiffened and they exploited the difficult Normandy terrain, notably the thick hedgerows known as the *bocage*, to prevent the Allied breakout from the beachheads. The enthusiasm that had accompanied the great invasion began to wane as it became obvious that the landing was not the first step in a war-winning drive through France and across the Rhine but merely the first stage of a terrible, attritional battle that would occasionally bring reminders of the Western Front fighting of 1914–18. What was needed by the Americans was a massive bombardment of the forward German positions which would enable them to achieve a decisive breakthrough into the open countryside. How could this saturation bombardment be achieved at short notice? Was it possible, for example, for the heavy bombers of the US Eighth Air Force to suspend their assault on Germany's cities for long enough to lend their efforts to the men on the ground? Herein lay a problem. The heavy bomber had never been designed for ground support. In the eyes of the air commanders heavy bombers were just not suited to precision-bombing. Their capacity to carpetbomb was not in question, but their capacity to bomb precisely at a time when friendly troops were within range was a very different matter. As Supreme Allied Commander, General Eisenhower was under pressure to use every

Air Marshal Sir Trafford Leigh-Mallory, K.C.B., D.S.O., was Allied Air Commander at SHAEF in 1944 and reported directly to General Eisenhower. During Operation 'Cobra' he was frequently at odds with other American and British air chiefs who felt he was incompetent to hold such an influential position.

means available to get his ground troops moving again and if heavy bombers could assist then he was prepared to use them. But in doing so Eisenhower was planning to use the wrong tool for the job.

Opinion among the air commanders was divided. Eisenhower's air chief, the British airman Trafford Leigh-Malory was all for going ahead with the heavy bombers in a ground-support role. Against him was Eisenhower's deputy, Arthur Tedder and the leading American airman, Carl Spaatz, who regarded Eisenhower's proposal to carpet-bomb an area in which friendly forces were operating as little short of madness. At this stage of the war personalities played a significant part in the squabbles that ensued, as well as bruised egos. Tedder and Spaatz both doubted Leigh-Mallory's strategic grasp of the war and Spaatz in particular was no admirer of the British airman's judgment. Nevertheless, Leigh-Mallory retained Eisenhower's confidence and he continued with his plans for carpet-bombing to precede an allied breakout from the Normandy bridgeheads, even threatening to resign if Tedder or Spaatz tried to obstruct him. Time favoured Leigh-Mallory in that ground operations had virtually come to a halt. Something was needed to regain the impetus of the Anglo-American invasion and he offered to provide it. The result of this impatience was Operation 'Cobra'.

The planned bombing was to take place near the town of St Lô, where General Omar Bradley's US First Army was being held up. Bradley was all in favour of the operation, but as an infantryman with no experience of air operations he credited the bombers with a flexibility they simply did not possess. In fact, he was asking for something that had never been tried before: the sort of saturation of the enemy front in 60 minutes that would take heavy artillery weeks to achieve. The bombers would concentrate on an area five miles wide and one mile deep, using light bombs to achieve minimum cratering and maximum anti-personnel effect. It was expected that the concentrated effects of the bombing would knock the resistance out of the German defenders for long enough to allow the American tanks to achieve their breakthrough.

Tedder and Spaatz were astounded when they heard what was being proposed. Bombing so close to the Allied front line was just asking for trouble. Bradley did not understand what he was requesting. Instead the air chiefs demanded a safety zone of at least 3000 yards, though even this was scarcely enough to guarantee that there would be no mishaps. But the 3000-yard safety zone was ridiculous in Bradley's eyes. What was the use of pounding the enemy until he was dazed and then holding your assault troops so far back that by the time they had crossed the safety zone the Germans had recovered and were ready to repel the assault? To Bradley a distance of 800 yards was the maximum he would ask his men to fall back. To the airmen this was tantamount to suicide. After much wrangling a compromise was reached which satisfied neither side. Bradley would order his men to fall back 1500 yards and the airmen would try to operate within these constraints. It was a decision Bradley was to live to regret.

The next question was how should the bombers approach the bombing zone? Bradley insisted that they should come in along the road that ran from St.Lô to Pèriers, parallel to his front line, so that they did not overfly his own ground troops. On the map in his headquarters this road was the most important and the most obvious feature of the area. But from 15,000 feet and with smoke shrouding the battlefield the road was all but invisible. In any case the airmen pointed out that there were simply too many bombers – 1500 or so heavies – to fly in over an area only one mile wide within a time limit of just 60 minutes. Again Bradley was asking the impossible. The air chiefs insisted that only a north–south approach, using the Normandy coastline for reference and the St.Lô–Pèriers highway as a sighter for the bombardiers, was possible. Bradley was furious. He was not going to allow all those bombers to fly over American positions. It was a parallel approach to the road or nothing. But Bradley had not won his point, even though he may have thought he had. At a meeting at Stanmore, Bradley and Leigh-Mallory argued their case against the air chiefs and Bradley left assuming that the airmen agreed with him. They did not, but Leigh-Mallory led him to believe that he would get his own way in the end.

Plans were speeded up and the date for Operation 'Cobra' was set, though bad weather was to force several postponements. The ground troops were told to expect minimal resistance after the bombers had done their job, on the assumption that those Germans left alive after the bombing would be just a shattered remnant with no stomach for a fight. (British troops who had been given similar assurances on the Somme in the summer of 1916 might have had something to say about that . . .) However, the bomber crews were receiving instructions that would have alarmed Bradley had he heard them. They were being warned about the danger of bombing short 'because the penetration route is directly over friendly troops'. The air plan was for 1586 heavy bombers to take the direct route across the English Channel and the Normandy coast before attacking the target area in three waves, each lasting fifteen minutes, with a five-minute interval between waves. The German positions would be hit by 50,000 general purpose and fragmentation bombs. Formations of twelve to fourteen bombers would follow the example of a lead aircraft and drop their bombs in line with the lead bombardier. It was a massive display of American aerial power, but with any operation on this scale many things could go wrong.

Bad weather led to a postponement of the operation on 23 July and should have done so again the following day. However, by the time Leigh-Mallory decided to call the whole show off on 24 July, it was already too late to prevent many of Eighth Air Force's heavy bombers from taking off. The 2nd Bomber Division managed to abort their own attack as heavy cloud cover over the target area made identification impossible. The 3rd Bomber Division also failed to locate the target, though perhaps 40 of its planes did drop their bombs in the vicinity. The real problems began when the 1st Bomber Division arrived over France and found that the weather was improving. Although some of these aircraft did receive the recall signals most did not and as many as 317 heavy bombers dropped a total of 10,000 high-explosive bombs. In the confusion some of these bombs fell short. In one case a lead bombardier had a faulty bomb release mechanism and, to make things worse, he also dropped his bombs short of the target. He was then followed by a further twelve or fourteen planes which took their lead from him. These bombs all fell on American troops, men from the US 30th Division who were forced to dive into ditches for cover. Within seconds 25 soldiers were killed and a further 131 wounded.

General Omar Bradley could not believe his ears when the news reached him. It was exactly what he had feared all along. Why had the bombers flown in on a perpendicular line rather than the parallel one on which he insisted? The airmen must have lied to him. He asked Leigh-Mallory for an explanation. Leigh-Mallory promised to get one from Eighth Air Force. But was Leigh-Mallory deceiving Bradley? After all, he already knew that the bombers were going to overfly the American troops rather than follow Bradley's plan for an approach along the road.

Meanwhile, Leigh-Mallory had decided to try again the next day, 25 July, when the meteorologists promised him better weather. But first he had to persuade Bradley to accept another perpendicular approach by the heavy bombers. As he pointed out, it was now far too late to change Eighth Air Force's mind about the time needed for a parallel run, and so – uneasily - Bradley accepted.

The next morning the weather had improved but there was still cloud cover at 14,000 feet, forcing the bombers to fly at a lower altitude than planned and necessitating the bombardiers to recalculate their bombing data. In addition, a wind coming from the south was blowing a huge column of smoke from the target zone – which had just been hit by Ninth Air Force's fighter-bombers – northwards, directly into the path of the heavy bombers. It was proving difficult for navigators and bombardiers to pick out landmarks, for the whole area was covered by immense clouds of smoke, dust and red marker flares. Eventually, 4000 tons of bombs were dropped in and around the target area, but human error resulted in heavy casualties among the American ground troops. Two lead bombardiers released their bombs without first achieving correct identification and were then followed by their entire units. The results on the ground were catastrophic. The 30th Infantry Division, which had suffered casualties the previous day, was again in the forefront with 61 men killed and 374 wounded. A further 64 men were listed as missing and 164 suffered total nervous collapse as a result of shell shock or 'combat fatigue'. Throughout VII Corps there were many other losses, including in the final list of 111 fatalities General Leslie McNair, the most senior American officer lost during the entire war. McNair had been in a forward position—despite warnings that he should stay at the rear—observing the effects of the saturation bombing. He died when his bunker suffered a direct hit. Bradley was horrified when he received the news. 'Oh Christ,' he said, 'not another short drop'. Something of an understatement for what had been a massacre.

Many American soldiers had cheered as the seemingly endless lines of B-17s and B-24s flew towards them. Suddenly there came the awful realization that, just as they had yesterday, these bombers were going to drop short over American lines. As one man wrote afterwards, 'My outfit was decimated, our anti-tank guns blown apart. I saw one of our truck drivers, Jesse Ivy, lying split down the middle. Captain Bell was buried in a crater with only his head visible. He suffocated before we could reach him.' The bitterness of the GIs towards the airmen who killed them knew no bounds and many of them fired their rifles impotently into the skies at their tormentors.

Nevertheless, in spite of the appalling casualties to friendly forces the bombing went on and was at once followed up by American infantry assaults on the German front. Disappointingly, the first waves of American troops found the Germans, apparently unruffled by their ordeal, waiting for them. (Again one is reminded of the Somme in 1916, when German machine-gunners weathered the British artillery storm deep in their dug-outs, emerging to wreak terrible havoc on the advancing troops.) It turned out that German losses had been only slightly heavier than those of the Americans – 700 to 601 – a good advertisement for the effectiveness of German tunnelling. Unlike the Americans, few of whom had dug foxholes, the Germans had been thoroughly prepared for anything less than the Day of Judgment.

German resistance on the afternoon of 25 July was unexpectedly strong. The previous day's abortive strike had prepared the Germans for what might come next. Although German forward positions were destroyed, reserves had been held back beyond the target area and were quickly rushed to the front once the bombing had stopped. As a result, American progress was slow and when 1st Army failed to achieve the expected breakout, the search began for scapegoats. Incredibly, the army blamed General Doolittle's Eighth Air Force for 'lacking enthusiasm for ground support'. But the air chiefs replied by blaming Bradley. Heavy bombers had never previously been asked to make precision raids. The decision to use them like that was his and Eisenhower's. But this did not convince Omar Bradley. Why had the airmen insisted on flying directly over his troops? His conclusion was bitter, even slanderous. 'It was duplicity,' Bradley wrote later. But this was unfair as well as untrue. He had been told repeatedly that 60 minutes was far too short a time for 1500 heavy bombers to carry out the operation if they approached parallel to the St.Lô to Pèriers highway. Nor was it certain, even if they had approached in that way, that there would have been no friendly casualties. A safety margin of 3000 yards was the minimum the airmen thought advisable, and Bradley was being unrealistic by attempting to reduce it to 800, or even the 1500 yards that was the final unwilling compromise. Bradley simply did not understand (and was apparently unwilling to try to understand) the problems of the strategic bomber asked to become a tactical bomber for a 'one-off' mission.

In terms of blame, Bradley did not stand alone. Air Chief Marshal Trafford Leigh-Mallory failed as coordinator of ground and air units during Operation 'Cobra'. His own experience had been with single-engine fighters and he really knew little and understood less of the problems of the heavy bomber. In his liaison capacity between the British and the Americans Leigh-Mallory was a failure; a British officer at SHAEF wrote him off as having a reputation for incompetence and 'a pompous, arrogant attitude'. As well as misleading Bradley as to the route to be taken by the bombers, he also made a personal decision that contributed to the fiasco. When he overruled the meteorologists and allowed the bombers to set off on 24 July, before later recalling them, it was too late to stop some of them dropping their bombs on American troops. It also meant that the American troops who had abandoned the safety zone on 24 July had to fight to regain the territory when news came that the operation had been postponed.

Ironically, Operation 'Cobra' was counted a success. It did contribute to an American breakout and in the context of the war as a whole the 'friendly fire' losses, though enormous, were hushed up and soon absorbed into the overall casualty figures. The blunders by Leigh-Mallory did not prevent his knighthood, nor those by Omar Bradley his elevation to five-star general. And Eisenhower – the man who could not tell a hammer from a screwdriver – rose to become president of the United States.

Goering and the Luftwaffe

Hermann Goering's leadership of the Luftwaffe served to diminish the work of the numerous professional officers who served Germany during the Second World War. It was Germany's misfortune to have decisions made by this decadent Nazi which frequently placed her pilots at a grave disadvantage, particularly in the long, attritional struggle against the RAF, whose professional leaders were subject to the controls of a democratic system. Goering's blunders contributed in no small way to Germany's defeat in 1945.

THE IRON MAN

It has been said that those whom the gods wish to destroy they first make mad. Rarely can this have been more true than in the case of Nazi Germany and the Luftwaffe. On four or more occasions during the Second World War the fate of Britain – and, one is tempted to add, the fate of Europe and of the civilized world – hung on the slenderest of threads: the judgment of Hermann Goering. And on each occasion his decision was so disastrously wrong that one might almost have supposed that he was secretly in the pay of the British. In the aftermath of the Second World War, a German historian observed that in 1939 Germany had 'the Navy of Imperial Germany, the Army of eighteenth-century Prussia and the Air Force of National Socialism'. It was not meant as a compliment to the Nazis. In the mind of most Germans, it was the Luftwaffe that had lost the war for Germany, allowing the British and American bombers to rove far and wide destroying their homeland while the man who should have been stopping them was resting on a perfumed couch like some Turkish pasha, enjoying the delights of Europe's art galleries pillaged in the name of National Socialism.

As one of Baron Manfred von Richthofen's Flying Circus during the First World War – in fact as the man who succeeded to command on the death of the Red Baron – Hermann Goering had the sort of reputation that was almost self-recommending when he first met Adolf Hitler in 1922. At that stage the young ex-corporal may even have looked up to Goering. At any rate, he realized that Goering, as an ace flyer and a holder of the *Pour le Mérite*, Germany's highest military award, would add enormous prestige to his struggling party. It did not take long, however, for the sly but easy-going Goering to fall completely under the spell of Hitler's personality and when the latter became Chancellor of Germany in 1933, Goering's sycophancy enabled him to accumulate ranks and titles and offices like a medieval pluralist. As well as Reichskommissioner of Aviation, he also became Reichsminister of Forestry and Reichsminister of Hunting. As head of the German air force – the Luftwaffe – his appetite for hard work was enormous and during the mid-30s this 'Cinderella' service began to develop into a threat to all Europe. For a while Goering became known as the 'Iron Man' of Nazi Germany, the driving force behind German rearmament. But corrosion soon set in. The problem was that from the start he had wanted every aspect of the Luftwaffe to be under his personal control and refused to admit that anyone – except Hitler – might know better than himself. As a result the Luftwaffe became his own personal air force and he treated everyone in it, even men like his deputies Ernst Udet and Erhard Milch, as his personal servants. Goering sometimes displayed shows of temper. On one occasion he received a report that stressed the very high qualities of the latest British fighters – Hawker Hurricanes and Supermarine Spitfires – illogically, Goering became so enraged that he threatened to have Udet shot if the report turned out to be true. Like many dictators – and with the Luftwaffe that was how he saw himself – he insisted on hearing only good news. In this way he developed a misguided and wholly inaccurate view of the strength of his air force. Numbers were juggled to a point where, at one moment during the Battle of Britain, his simple arithmetic led him to believe that the British had virtually run out of planes altogether. He completely overlooked the fact that British factories were turning out new fighters at twice the rate of German factories (see p.97). He firmly believed in the invincibility of the Luftwaffe and made matters worse by so exaggerating its achievements that Hitler was profoundly disappointed at anything less than miracles.

My name is not Goering if an enemy aircraft is ever seen over Germany. You can call me Meyer.

HERMANN GOERING ON BRITISH BOMBING OF GERMANY, 1940

As head of the Luftwaffe, Goering boasted that Britain would be impotent in air warfare. This quote later returned to haunt him after the RAF raid on Hamburg in 1943.

URALBOMBER

Soon after the Nazis came to power and Goering assumed command of the Luftwaffe, the question of a four-engined, long-range strategic bomber came under consideration. Anyone who had read *Mein Kampf* had to be aware that war between Germany and the Soviet Union was a long-term aim of National Socialism and in view of this Germany would need strategic aircraft rather than simply tactical, battlefield planes. As a result, the four-engined machine was nicknamed the 'Uralbomber', indicating in the clearest possible way where it was eventually intended to be used. The design was strongly supported by senior figures in the Air Force like the Chief of Air Command, Generalleutnant Walther Wever. At a time when other major powers were still confined to two-engined medium bombers, the Uralbomber would have given Germany the means to make Douhet's theories of massive aerial bombardment a reality. By 1936, two companies had prepared prototypes – Junkers and Dornier – and although they were concerned over the relatively weak engines available, the two bombers (Ju-89 and Do-19) were both ready for testing. Significantly, the Air Ministry in Britain – lagging behind as usual – was in the process of calling for designs for a four-engine heavy bomber (see pp.66-8). Had the Uralbomber been built Germany would have had at least three year's start on Britain and London could really have faced aerial destruction in 1939 or 1940. However, at this critical juncture Hermann Goering made the first of his dramatic interventions by cancelling the four-engined bomber project.

In putting an end to the Uralbomber, Goering was removing Germany's potential to conduct a global war. As a result, he was limiting Hitler's ability to conduct foreign policy. Whether Hitler understood this is doubtful, and this circumscription of his power to strike at distant enemies – of which Russia was bound to be the main one – would suggest that he was not well-advised on his future strategic needs. Once again short-termism and opportunism were to be the bane of German rearmament. As has been said, a nation that does not have the army appropriate to its policies, must have policies appropriate to its army. In this case one can substitute 'air force' for 'army'.

Many able men in the Luftwaffe fought to save the Uralbomber and Goering's cancellation did not go unchallenged. He was told that the performance of the four-engine aircraft would be superior to all two-engine machines and would be the air-weapon of the future. The bomber's range would have been extraordinary, its ceiling sufficient to keep it out of danger from anti-aircraft guns and its bomb loads prodigious. In addition, it would be faster than existing bombers and – more to the point – fighters. In reply Goering insisted that Germany could probably build no more than a thousand of these four-engine bombers, as against more than twice as many medium bombers. And what was the point of a ceiling of 30,000 feet when at that height there was always heavy cloud cover so that there was no chance of seeing or hitting the target? General Deichmann, frustrated at having to argue with such a narrow-minded commander, lost his temper. What was the point of ten thousand medium bombers which would probably be shot down by the enemy before they reached their target when compared with one thousand of the heavy-bombers which would be too fast, too strong and would fly too high to be intercepted? Goering, unconvinced, was not for moving. The four-engine bomber plan was dropped in 1937. The world breathed a sigh of relief.

What did Germany lose by Goering's stupidity? Probably the war-winning weapon of 1940. The heavy bomber would probably have won the Battle of Britain for Germany. Such bombers could have operated the length and breadth of Britain, flying too high for the anti-aircraft defenses and needing fewer – if any – German fighters for escort. Thus more Me-109s would have been available to fight the Spitfires and Hurricanes on even terms. Furthermore, Operation 'Barbarossa', Hitler's invasion of Russia in 1941, would have gone much better for the Germans, as they would have the means to strike at factories beyond the Urals, thus preventing Russia's miraculous recovery. Even more than the war in the Soviet Union, Germany's struggle against Britain in

We don't need the expensive heavy bomber; it demands an excessive amount of material by comparison with the two-engined dive-bomber.

Ernst Udet, 1940

Germany's failure to build heavy bombers was one of her greatest errors. Udet was a First World War 'fighter ace', second only to the 'Red Baron', but the damage he inflicted on Germany by his inadequate work at the Luftwaffe – reflected in this sort of advice – was incalculable.

North Africa and the Mediterranean would have been simplified by the possession of long-range bombers. The ability to use Italian airfields would have enabled German bombers to attack Gibraltar, Malta and Cairo, perhaps with a decisive effect. The case is unanswerable: Goering's blunder was absolute.

THE RUBBER LION

The comforts that came with power were Goering's undoing. He became preoccupied with furnishing his palace at Karinhall with superb art treasures and living the life of some petty princeling of eighteenth-century Germany. Most of the work was done by his deputies, notably General Milch, while Goering himself took longer and longer siestas. Milch warned him, 'You're ruining the air force this way. Somebody has to be in charge of everything. If I don't do it, then you'll have to . . . but you won't!' Goering pretended to be concerned – for a few days – but soon he had slipped back into his old ways. He spent a lot of time playing with his miniature railway system which took up an entire upper floor at Karinhall and had miniature planes attached to wires which could bomb the tracks. He also designed himself ever grander uniforms to encase his ever expanding bulk. With war threatening in Europe by the late 1930s, Goering was all bluster. The Luftwaffe had done well enough in Spain. Perhaps all would be well. But he had no interest in a hard-fought war. He had grown too accustomed to soft living to wish to risk losing it. Far more than Hitler, Goering realized the personal consequences of defeat. As he told a colleague in September 1939: 'If we lose this war, then heaven have mercy on our souls!' Essentially Micawber-like, Goering was rarely depressed for long and believed that something would turn up to save him – and Germany – from the consequences of his actions.

Once war began Goering was elated by the ease with which the Luftwaffe overwhelmed the Polish Air force and supported the Wehrmacht's armoured forces. He was immensely popular with his men and some of the distance that had grown between himself and Hitler lessened. The Führer still treated Goering well, but he was aware of his limitations and no longer believed everything he was told about the Luftwaffe's success. Sensing this, Goering strove to regain Hitler's trust. During the campaign in the West, he took an active part in directing operations and it was his eagerness to win the Führer's approval that caused him to make a disastrous error of judgement. This blunder was the product of two conflicting pressures: one was his desire to impress Hitler and retain his trust and the second was to continue enjoying the good life of hunting on his estates in East Prussia. Incredibly, Goering often tried to brief his air staff during stag hunts at Romintern and dictated letters between shots. According to one biographer, 'Among the dark Satanic forests of pine, beech and oak, Goering felt like a Teutonic knight of old. He would carry a spear' and be dressed in 'red top boots of Russian leather with golden spurs, in floor length coats like a French emperor, in silk blouses with puffy sleeves.'

Even before the invasion of France in May 1940 Goering had made a fundamental error of judgment. On 7 February 1940 he ordered aircraft development work to stop. Anything that could not be used on the battlefield in the next twelve months was regarded as irrelevant. He decided that the war would be over by 1941 and future plans had to be short term only. As a result experimental work on jets and rocket-propelled aircraft was officially stopped, though the air manufacturers carried on a minimal programme in secret. Work on jet fighters were already quite advanced in Germany and, but for Goering's decree, the Luftwaffe would have had such planes in operation probably by 1943, with all that that might have entailed for the Anglo-American strategic bombing campaign.

MISSING THE BOAT AT DUNKIRK

Goering's next – and most controversial – blunder was his appeal to Hitler to allow him to use the Luftwaffe to destroy the British forces in and around Dunkirk. It is likely that Hitler had got cold feet about the enormity of his victory so far and feared to lose his tanks in the low, marshy area into which the British were retreating. Moreover, he feared that if he committed his tanks to an encircling operation of the Anglo-French forces at Dunkirk, he might be struck a heavy blow by unbroken French armies to the south. He found Goering's offer to finish the British from the air – militarily unsound as it was – a godsend. If the Luftwaffe succeeded then all would be well and the army could concentrate on completing the victory over France. If they failed, it would be Goering's fault and not his.

However, Goering had been badly misled by the performance of the RAF in the Battle of France. The German pilots had met few Spitfires so far, most of which had been held back for the defence of Britain. Once the British army faced complete annihilation it became necessary for more Spitfires to be sent to cover the retreat from Dunkirk. For the first time, the Me-109 pilots found themselves up against the best the British had, and in large numbers.

The Stuka dive-bombers which had triumphed in the campaign against France and which Goering assumed would be equally successful against the British troops in Dunkirk or the ships evacuating them, were an easy prey for fast-moving British fighters. The all-conquering Stuka was quite unable to defend itself against the Hurricane and Spitfire, and for the first time the Luftwaffe was forced back on the defensive. Goering soon found that in promising Hitler a virtually bloodless victory for the Luftwaffe he had overextended himself. He had claimed that dive-bombing a helpless rabble of troops was the Luftwaffe's speciality. It may have been, but the British troops – even during evacuation – were never reduced to a rabble.

Goering infuriated his pilots by his casual 'small talk'. They knew the desperate struggles that they were having against the British fighters, yet their commander seemed to make light of it. At one briefing a squadron commander lost his temper when he heard Goering tell his pilots not to panic if they heard a Spitfire coming up on their tail. 'I wanted the ground to open up and swallow me!' he said, '*Donnerwetter*, the ignorance! In a plane's cockpit you can't even hear your own machine guns.' Goering's World War One experience was not helping much now. Still, he always had his private world of hunting. At the height of the crisis around Dunkirk, Goering ordered a stag to be brought from Karinhall so that he could stage a staghunt in a nearby forest. Donning his hunting costume, Goering left his Luftwaffe generals poring over maps of the battlefield. He returned later in a bad mood. He had fallen asleep, missed the stag and by now his dinner was cold. He took consolation in his acquisition of nineteen

Flemish 'Old Masters', including works by Rubens, Rembrandt, Breughel and Cranach which he had transported to his palace at Karinhall. These were soon followed by medieval wood carvings and Leonardo's great painting 'Leda and the Swan'. Goering's conduct of the air war was also affected by his propensity for malingering. On more than one occasion, men of the seniority of Milch and Galland received their orders over the phone from Goering's nurse, Christa Gormanns. From time to time nine different doctors attended the 'Iron Man' administering medicines, or more often simply pandering to his drug addiction. Hitler should have recognized the liability that Goering was becoming.

Hitler's decision to halt his tanks on the outskirts of Dunkirk has always been considered one of the German leader's most significant mistakes. He had defeated the British army in France, but he needed to emphasize this to the British people by driving their soldiers into the sea, or rounding them up in their tens of thousands and transporting them to prison camps in Germany. The British would not make peace with him without having suffered a defeat from which there was no coming back – and this had to be a defeat on the ground in which German soldiers were seen to capture British troops. The sight of columns of broken 'Tommies' winding their way to captivity, humbled by defeat, might even have broken Winston Churchill's resolve and caused him to fall from power. Victory from the air could never be so complete. Bombs might fall and kill those unfortunate enough to be in range, but most of the men on the Dunkirk beaches would find cover in the sand dunes which took the bulk of the bomb's blast, allowing them to emerge unhurt once the Stuka had flown off. A dive-bomber could sink a boat or explode a tank, but it could do little against men scattering in all directions, invulnerable as a swarm of ants under a heavy heel. What Goering was promising to do was impossible. Churchill was willing to sacrifice the army's equipment: what he wanted was the quarter of a million British soldiers. With these he could build for a future when they would be rearmed with better guns and tanks than those they were leaving in France. Without the returning troops, no amount of patriotic speeches could have hidden the enormity of the disaster.

When Goering challenged the British in the air, he was unknowingly challeng-

A view of the Dunkirk beaches, with oil tanks burning in the background. Goering's boast to Hitler that his Luftwaffe could destroy the British forces at Dunkirk gave the Royal Navy the opportunity to evacuate the vast majority of the troops trapped on the beaches. Goering's blunder marked a turning-point in the war.

ing them to fight a battle they were bound to win, a defensive battle over the English Channel and the South coast of England for which they had been preparing (see p.96). The Germans, supremely capable in the land battles prior to Dunkirk, abandoned their advantage and attacked Britain's strength, her modern front line fighters with early warning radar. Against the Spitfires and Hurricanes, operating from bases in Southern England, Goering's bombers had to fly to Dunkirk from bases far from the action, some of them even in Germany. It was a typically rash and thoughtless action by Goering, based not on clear military thinking but on personal whim. It may have struck Hitler as a convenient way to finish the British, but it should have been resisted at all costs. Until the aerial battle over Dunkirk everything had gone right for the Germans, but after Goering's intervention the victorious mould was cracked. It would still take five years of grim fighting before the war culminated in Hitler's suicide in the Berlin bunker, but from June 1940 Hitler was fighting a war he could never win.

Goering also failed to draw the right lesson from the air battle over Dunkirk. Concerned only with the failure of the Luftwaffe, he never for a moment considered the strength of the RAF. Had he done so he might have resisted the temptation to continue the struggle during the Battle of Britain. Germany did not need to endanger her aerial power by ramming her head against such a strong adversary. Hitler was not committed to an invasion of Britain, which was bound to produce a struggle to the death against the RAF and either a defeat or at best a highly damaging victory. With his real interest in an invasion of Russia, he needed the Luftwaffe intact for action in the east, not frittered away in a battle that Britain was obliged to win in the interests of national survival, but which for Hitler was of subsidiary interest.

At Dunkirk Goering had promised more than he could deliver and the reputation of the Luftwaffe was never as high again. The loss of prestige tarnished the great campaign against France. A closer investigation of the way the fight over Dunkirk was conducted shows Goering for the sheer opportunist that he was. Little planning had gone into the battle. One wing of Ju88 bombers involved in the battle were stationed in Holland and had to fly along the English Channel to reach Dunkirk, all the time at the mercy of British fighters. So impressive was the first appearance of the Spitfires that for a day they gained aerial supremacy over Dunkirk, even getting the better of the Me-109s and taking a heavy toll of the slower Me-110s and the German bombers. In addition, fog over Northern France limited the contribution by the German VIII Air corps, which was the unit best equipped and trained for dive bombing. For three days this group was unable to operate, yet never for a moment did Goering's conviction leave him that air power alone could crush the British. As a result by 4 June the British had succeeded in getting 338,226 British and French soldiers – minus their equipment – off the Dunkirk beaches under the eyes of the all-conquering Luftwaffe. It was one of the greatest disasters suffered by the Germans in the war, in some ways more terrible for them than the loss of von Paulus' VIth Army at Stalingrad in 1943. Goering's blundering had let the enemy escape to fight another day. Churchill was able to turn defeat into the peculiar kind of victory that seems to mean so much to the British, one that is achieved when all hope has gone and one which is therefore transformed into something miraculous. Victory in defeat went to the British, defeat in victory to the Germans. Invigorated, the British felt more purposeful now that they stood alone against Hitler. The complexities of foreign alliances were removed and the issues simplified: it was now a matter of national survival. Defeat, in the minds of the British in 1940, meant an invasion by Germany and the loss of an independence held for a thousand years. It was unthinkable and therefore unacceptable. Against this determination Goering could offer nothing but bluster and faulty strategy.

GOERING'S BLIND SPOT

Goering failed to learn anything from the fighter battles over Dunkirk, and the Luftwaffe stumbled into the Battle of Britain without clear directives. This paved the way for Goering's next blunder as head of the Luftwaffe. Although Germany had a lead over Britain in radar technology, she was much slower in adapting this to a military purpose. Britain had already based her national defence on a combination of radar and modern fighter aircraft. Even when the Chamberlain government was still mired in a policy of appeasement towards Nazi Germany in 1937-8, fundamental decisions were being taken which would stand the nation in good stead should war become unavoidable. One of the decisions was the construction of a chain of twenty radar stations – at a cost of a million pounds – along the south and east coasts of England. This was to provide early warning of German attacks.

The radar stations were so obviously the eyes of the British defence plan, one would suppose the Luftwaffe would have made their destruction a number one priority. And, in fact, one would be right. In order to facilitate the invasion of England – Operation 'Sealion' – set for sometime in September 1940, Goering designated the two weeks leading up to the invasion 'Adlerangriff' (Eagle Attack), during which one of the main targets for attack would be the radar stations. Every station from Portland Bill to the Thames Estuary was to be eliminated by low-level bombing attack, while the coastal airfields were wrecked. It must be conceded that the destruction of radar stations had never been attempted before in wartime and nobody could be quite certain how easy or how difficult it would be to put them out of action, and for how long they would stay inoperable. Luftwaffe pilots assumed that the masts and tall towers would be simple to destroy, but what about the unassuming buildings below?

The first attack – on 12 August 1940 – on the radar system was led by one of Germany's ace flyers, Hauptmann Walter Rubensdoerffer. He was surprised to meet no opposition from British fighters and no anti-aircraft fire. First Pevensey, then Dover, Rye and Dunkirk (Kent) stations were attacked and hit. The devastation seemed complete, with every hut destroyed. Goering was delighted at the news. It seemed now that when he launched his final destructive attack on Britain the RAF would be blind and unable to respond. Meanwhile, the key radar station at Ventnor on the Isle of Wight was also destroyed – or so it seemed – with virtually every building on the site left in flames. The Germans believed it would be months before it was operational again. The British must be blind by now. Yet, incredibly, within three days Ventnor was operating again thanks to a mobile unit erected nearby. Evidence of the swift recovery of the radar stations had a remarkable effect on Goering. After just a week of attacks on these vital points in the British defences he decided on 19 August that they were unprofitable. Clearly they could be reconstituted easily and he wanted to use his bombers against a more satisfying target.

Hermann Goering lecturing Luftwaffe pilots about to attack England in September 1940. Although himself an ace from the First World War, Goering was not abreast of the latest developments in air warfare and frequently made embarrassing 'gaffes'. His dismissal of the importance of the British radar stations was vital to the outcome of the Battle of Britain.

Had Fighter Command read of this decision they would have been convinced that the gods had indeed made Goering mad.

London had been 'off limits' to the Luftwaffe since the start of the war. Hitler did not believe in indiscriminate civilian bombing nor in the destruction of national morale. In that sense he was wiser than many of his opponents in Britain who were fervently to support the idea of strategic or 'area' bombing in an attempt to break German morale. However, as a dictator, he was dependent more on public opinion than a democratic leader. Having assured the German people that the war was almost over he could not easily accept even the slightest suggestion that what he was saying was not true. He knew that if he attacked London there would be two immediate results: firstly, the British would – however weakly – respond by attacking Berlin, and secondly, they would resist his peace overtures if they had suffered significant civilian casualties. Thus London was, for the moment, safe.

However, the Luftwaffe's attacks on the RAF airfields and radar stations, as well as oil storages, took them closer and closer to London. It would only take a mistake by a single pilot and Hitler's ruling would be broken. And that is just what happened. On 24 August two German bombers (the names of the pilots have been expunged from the Luftwaffe lists) lost their way and in panic dropped their bombs blind. They fell variously over Islington, Tottenham, Finchley, Stepney and Bethnal Green, killing a number of people leaving pubs at closing time. One bomb landed at Cripplegate, destroying St Giles's Church and smashing a statue of Milton nearby. When he heard of the attack Goering was shocked, and ordered the pilots posted to infantry regiments. It was a propaganda gift to Churchill, who would make the most of it to win American opinion to the British cause. Furthermore, it triggered the response all the Germans feared: Churchill ordered the bombing of Berlin. A few bombs fell on the German capital, causing only minor casualties. But the impossible had been seen to happen. The Nazis had promised that Berlin was inviolate. But the British bombers had got through. Was Hitler telling the truth when he told the Germans that the British were beaten?

Hitler responded as only he knew how: with demonic fury. He addressed a meeting at the Sportpalast in Berlin with the question: 'When will England be invaded?' He told his audience that the English keep asking, 'Why doesn't he come?' Then he raised his voice into a shout: 'Be calm! Be calm! He's coming, he's coming!' And the bombing of Berlin? Hitler shrieked, 'When the British Air Force drops three or four thousand kilograms of bombs, then we will in one night drop 200, 300 or 400,000 kilograms. When they declare that they will increase their attacks on our cities, then we will raze their cities to the ground.'

Hermann Goering had boldly promised the German people that no British bombers would appear over the Fatherland or his name was Meyer (equivalent to the British 'or I'm a Dutchman'). Already as he appeared in public he could hear voices whispering 'Meyer'. In time the voices would be angrily shouting 'Meyer' and reminding him of the broomstick he had promised to eat if British bombs fell.

Goering left Karinhall by his special train and travelled to France. He was going to take personal control of the Battle of Britain, and with Hitler's permission the Luftwaffe had a new target. No longer were targets with tactical significance the aim – airfields, radar stations, aeronautical factories – now it was to be the strategic bombing of London. The Nazis had been worked into a corner from which they could not escape except with a grand gesture. The Luftwaffe generals shrugged their shoulders in despair. London was the target, but had the Luftwaffe been created with urban bombing in mind? What use would the Stuka dive-bombers be in such an attritional struggle? Hitler and Goering were taking on an enemy that could not be beaten. When Goering arrived in France and announced from the cliffs of Cap Blanc Nez, overlooking the Channel, that he was aiming 'a stroke straight to the enemy's heart', he was opening a Pandora's Box. The evils it released would eventually fall on German cities - Lübeck, Rostock, Kappel, Essen, Cologne, Hamburg, Berlin . . . and Dresden.

COLLAPSE OF STOUT PARTY

In spite – or perhaps because of – their long friendship, Goering stood in awe of Hitler. As he once told the banker Hjalmar Schacht, 'Do you know, Mr Schacht, I always make up my mind to tell Hitler certain things and then the minute I enter his office my courage invariably deserts me.' Goering was by no means alone in feeling this way, but as Germany's Number Two and head of the Luftwaffe his weakness vis-à-vis Hitler was dangerous, particularly so in cases where the Führer's judgement was flawed. The question of jet planes is a case in point. By weakly accepting Hitler's impossible requirements, Goering was losing Germany's last possible chance at staving off defeat and achieving a negotiated peace.

By 1943 American fighters were filling the skies over Germany, specifically seeking combat against the Luftwaffe's declining fighter force. The once-excellent Messerschmitt 109 was unable to match the specifications of the best new American and British fighters. It seemed that only a miracle could save Germany. But as many German scientists realized, they still might have some surprises for the enemy. One of these was the jet fighter, in the development of which Germany was in advance of the rest of the world.

Germany had tested a jet fighter – the He-178 – even before the war broke out in 1939 and Heinkel continued to develop the plane in the early years of the war. Willy Messerschmitt was also active in the field, and his Me-262 soon overtook Heinkel's research. It seemed that the future lay with Willy's machine. Unfortunately, this view was not shared by Goering's chief advisers, Udet and Milch. Frustrated, Messerschmitt warned them in 1941 that Britain was also working on such a plane and if they got theirs – the Gloster Meteor – out first it might spell disaster for Germany.

Undeterred, Messerschmitt continued with his trials of the Me-262 and even persuaded General Galland to fly the plane on 22 May 1943. Galland was overjoyed, calling the jet plane a tremendous stroke of luck for Germany and offering the Luftwaffe the chance to outperform all existing allied planes. He recommended that the development of other fighters should be scrapped to provide capacity to develop the Me-262. Galland told Goering that if 4000 fighters were built each month, a quarter of them must be jets. Goering was disturbed and felt Hitler would never agree, but Galland demanded that the matter be put to the Führer. Incredibly, Hitler imposed a condition on the plane's development that proved quite impossible. He had been excited by news of what the jets could do, but was unwilling to see them develop purely as fighters. Even though every day the cities of Germany were being pounded by Anglo-American bombers, he did not support the idea of a fighter that could have given his tortured people some relief. All he could think of was to make his enemies suffer as much as he had. If the Me-262 was to be developed it must carry bombs. It must become a fighter-bomber.

Goering was quite aware of the fatal mistake that was being made. If the jet programme was suspended or forced to adapt itself to a new set of criteria then the war would be lost before jets could ever be used in combat. Goering should have threatened resignation to keep the jet fighter programme intact, but he had never had any moral courage when dealing with Hitler and was a mere shadow of the former 'Iron Man'. He feebly gave way and lost Germany's final chance of saving something from the war. He told his generals that henceforth the Me-262 would be described as a 'superspeed bomber' and would be used against the expected Anglo-American invasion of France. But the capacity of such a fighter-bomber would have been tiny in the context of the D-Day operation. It would have delivered mere pinpricks, whereas as a fighter the Me-262 might have seriously diminished the strategic bombing of German industry. As it was, the the new bomber-variant was not ready for D-Day and the Me-262 played a minor part in the rest of the war. Goering allowed Hitler to waste Germany's lead over Britain in jet technology, and had to bear the frustration of learning that the British jet – the Gloster Meteor – had already come into action against the V.1. programme.

At this stage of the war Hermann Goering was but a pitiful shadow of the man who had led von Richthofen's Circus in the First World War and won the 'Blue Max' for gallantry. The 'Iron Man' who had built the Luftwaffe to a level that overawed Germany's neighbours was now a degenerate, spending most of his time at Karinhall, dressed in silk pantaloons, red slippers, diamond-studded belt, green silk shirt, violet-coloured stockings, with peroxided hair and rouged cheeks.

As the Russians closed in on his private kingdom in East Prussia he sent train-loads of his art treasures south for safety, including 739 of the world's most valuable paintings and priceless treasures pillaged from museums, art galleries and monasteries from every part of Europe – except Britain, the rock on which Goering's Luftwaffe dashed itself and was destroyed.

THE FORTRESS OF KÖPENICK

In 1906 a shoemaker in Prussia perpetrated a hoax on the burghers of the town of Köpenick. He obtained a secondhand Prussian captain's uniform and, having donned it, he ordered a squad of soldiers to follow him and arrest the local Bürgermeister and take possession of the municipal treasury. The shoemaker was not named Hermann Goering – but he might have been, as Goering demonstrated in his defeat of the American 'raid' on the fortress of Köpenick in 1943.

In fact the Americans were raiding Düren in the Rhineland, rather than Köpenick, but they were flying above heavy cloud and were protected by 'Window'. Observing the way that the German radar screens were blocked by the Window Goering decided that it was the moment to take control himself. He decided that as the Window appeared to be drifting eastwards the Americans must be intending to raid Schweinfurt, the centre of the ballbearings industry. He called up his nightfighters and ordered them to fly to Schweinfurt.

When he began to receive reports of planes heading towards Schweinfurt, Goering congratulated himself on guessing the Americans' every move. But when the German nightfighters reached Schweinfurt they found no sign of American bombers. Thinking quickly, Goering decided that the American raid must be aimed at Leipzig. The nightfighters now flew towards Leipzig, while the radar crews picked up the signals from planes approaching the Leuna Works at Leipzig. But when the fighters arrived at Leipzig there were still no Americans. Goering, by now thoroughly rattled, told the fighters to fly to the Skoda works at Pilsen, in Czechoslovakia. They were bound to find the Americans there. But they did not. The pfennig dropped. The nightfighters had been chasing their own radar blips.

Goering, by now in tears of laughter, admitted that he had blundered. He sent out a congratulatory telegram to himself and thanked the fighter pilots for having successfully defeated an attack on the fortress of Köpenick. How many of his pilots were laughing after this night's 'entertainment' is not recorded.

THE KOMET: ME-163B

O n several occasions just before and during the Second World War, Germany had opportunities to make such technological leaps in the field of aviation that the outcome of the war and even the future of mankind could have been affected. These leaps, fortunately never made by the ever-conservative Nazi leadership, generally involved research into jet propulsion for planes and rockets. Even though the British designer Sir Frank Whittle had designed an early working jet engine, the Germans had been much quicker to see its military potential. Although the jet-powered Gloster Meteor flew before the end of the war in Europe, even entering the fray against the V-weapons, Willy Messerschmitt tested an early rocket plane in January 1939. With the subsequent Me-163 Germany appeared to have taken a quantum leap in military aviation. Instead, it ended by wasting money and costing the lives of many experienced pilots to no obvious military advantage. The Me-163 – cruelly nicknamed the 'Devil's Sled' – was a luxury that Germany could not afford.

In 1939, with war imminent, Professor Lippisch, technical director of the Rhön Glider company and an expert on Delta wings and rocket propulsion, transferred his team of experts to Messerschmitt's factory in Augsburg. Although he was not aware of it at first, Lippisch would soon be working on a prototype for the first German rocket plane. The plane was to be known as the Me-163A Experimental. When one of Goering's Luftwaffe generals, Ernst Udet, saw the plans at Augsburg, he was mesmerized. The plane was so incredibly fast that he knew he must have it. It was the first step in the creation of the rocket plane. Soon, with an advanced engine fitted, the Me-163 could achieve speeds approaching a thousand k/h (625 mph). The speed, close to that of sound, was fantastic for that date. It was so superior to the top speeds of existing fighters that if the Me-163 became available in large num-

The German rocket-plane, the Me 163B, known as 'the Komet'. Although the Germans were far in advance of the Allies with their jet and liquid fuelled-rocket planes, not all of them were practical, as was the case with the Komet, which killed more German pilots than it did Allied aircrew. By 1944 Hitler was looking for new kinds of bombers and was unimpressed with Messerschmitt's fast fighters, like the Me-262.

bers it would have the potential to sweep the skies clear of enemy aircraft. Udet insisted that a fully-armed fighter version should be developed. By April 1942, the Me-163B Komet was ready for testing. In the meantime, special training courses had been set up, on which pilots could gain experience by flying the prototype Me-163As. Never had pilots been through a more rigorous or dangerous selection procedure. In fact, the course was Darwinian in the worst sense – only the fittest (luckiest) survived. On the training course wartime privations were waived. For men who were about to die the very best food was available. In every other respect, however, the prospective pilots were subjected to intense hardships. The Komet could climb to 40,000 feet, but the drawback was that the pilot's cabin was unpressurized. The pilots were therefore trained to withstand extreme atmospheric pressure and bitter cold. Many men died training in low-compression chambers, while others froze to death.

The Komet could only have been developed in a totalitarian state. It was far too dangerous to be a viable weapon, yet its potential seemed exciting to the deranged minds of scientists absolved of responsibility for the human suffering they caused. In laymen's terms, the Komet amounted to little more than a freakish trip to hell and – sometimes - back. It was powered by immensely volatile chemicals that were allowed to interact. The unfortunate pilot sat more or less on top of the subsequent explosion. The motor – the first liquid-fuelled rocket in the world – used C-stoff (a solution of 30 per cent hydrazine hydrate in menthol) and T-stoff (concentration of 80 per cent hydrogen peroxide solution mixed with hydrocarbon stabilizers). There was no ignition, merely explosive propulsion. During the early stages of the work on the rocket, several technicians were literally blown through the roof by their own volatile liquids.

And while the chemists worked on the rocket, ever tougher efforts were made to condition the pilots for what they would experience in the Komet. But the training was cruel and ultimately pointless. So terrible were the conditions inside the rocket plane that nobody could ever get used to them. Each trip would be as terrifying and as damaging as the previous one. Survival alone was the aim. One pilot who did survive, Mano Ziegler, later wrote of his experiences with the Komet. And he described how most of his friends died, literally torn to pieces as the rocket-plane exploded on landing. The problem was that the fuel was simply too volatile. Even when it did not blow the plane and pilot to smithereens, it usually flooded the cockpit with steam, so that the pilot could see nothing and was in danger of being burned to death rather than blown to kingdom come. Landing was an experience in itself. The engine often cut out, leaving the plane to cartwheel across the runway. If the plane did not explode the T-stoff tanks often leaked onto the pilot, who – horrifying to relate – was literally dissolved by the chemicals. It is hard not to admire the courage of these young men who not only sacrificed their lives for their country but accepted so terrible a death.

As a fighter-interceptor the Me-163 was a fiasco. Its twin cannon were slow to fire and often jammed. And the Komet was so fast that it was past the American bombers before it could even fire a couple of shells. American gunners simply gulped and waved as the rocket-plane shot harmlessly by them.

The Germans next adapted the Me-163 as a 'dive-fighter'. The rocket climbed several thousand feet above the American planes and then dived down on them. Again it was too fast, flying headlong downwards and often straight

I am not interested in this plane as a fighter. Does it carry bombs? I order this plane to be built as a bomber!

ADOLF HITLER ON THE NEW ME-262 JET FIGHTER, 1944

A decisive moment in the entire war. The Me-262, if mass produced as a fighter, could have had a considerable effect on Anglo-American air superiority. However, by this stage of the war Hitler's strategy was geared to grand gestures and irrational attacks. He wanted the Me-262 to bomb the Allied troops as they came ashore on the Normandy beaches. Redesigning the Me-262 as a dive-bomber ensured that it hardly saw any service at all in the Luftwaffe.

into the ground. The tremendous speed of these rockets used up all their fuel in a matter of minutes and few of them ever had enough to make a second attack or a safe landing. Incredibly, the Me-163 had enough fuel for just two and a half minutes of flight. They often fell victim to American Mustang fighters as they were slowly ascending to their dive positions. If they had reached their ceiling too quickly – thereby using up their fuel – they would have fallen like a stone from a height of perhaps 30,000 feet.

It is doubtful if bomber crews over Germany in 1944 found much to laugh about. However, the antics of these originally feared rocket-planes might have provided an exception to the rule. Few of them were actually shot down by the Allies – there was usually no need. The Me-163 proved to be the suicide plane *par excellence*. Far more of them self-destructed than were destroyed by enemy action. They were an example of untrammelled technological progress – a good idea in principle but best forgotten after a good night's sleep. One innovation of Messerschmitt's boffins is worth recording. It involved the installation of air-to-air rockets in the Komet's wings, guided by photo-electric cells. The idea was that when the Komet flew under a bomber the shadow of the plane would trigger the rocket. The process actually worked on one occasion. Unfortunately, the explosion shattered the Komet and the stricken American bomber fell on top of it. It was also found that the shadows cast by clouds triggered the rockets. Thus the Komets flew around the skies of Germany intercepting stratocumulus formations like some crazed meteorologist armed with air-to-air missiles.

Only a few hundred of the Komets ever saw service with the Luftwaffe and the best products of the German rocket-scientists were either destroyed by the Allied bombing campaign or were captured by the Soviets and put to their own use.

PART FOUR:
POST-1945

WHEN IS A WAR NOT A WAR?

The suspicion that Britain was no longer a great power remained simply a suspicion until, in 1956, Sir Anthony Eden chose to make it a demonstrable fact by occupying the Suez Canal with all the force that he could command. The French, who had lost their claim to greatness in 1940, joined Britain in this tawdry adventure, eager to make room for their old enemy on the bench reserved for superannuated ex-colonial powers. Once the Royal Air Force had bestirred itself to command Egyptian air space, the question arose: what next? And what came next was one of Britain's most dismal displays of air power.

On 26 July 1956 President Nasser nationalized the Suez Canal, endangering Britain's traditional lifeline with her eastern empire. Britain's wartime foreign secretary, Sir Anthony Eden, was now prime minister, and as determined to resist the dictator Nasser as Britain had once appeased another dictator, Adolf Hitler, during the 1930s. As a result, Britain's ageing military machine was cranked into action. The chiefs of staff were ordered to draw up a plan for regaining the canal, but whether this would take the form of Sir Garnet Wolesley's Victorian expedition in 1882 which culminated in a full colonial set-piece battle at Tel el-Kebir or by a modern *coup de main*, involving airborne troops, nobody seemed certain. In fact, the option for a *coup de main* did not really exist. Although this was the likeliest to have succeeded – Britain had something of a reputation for her airborne operations and probably world opinion would have minded less if the thing had been done quickly and relatively cleanly – neither Britain nor France had parachute troops available or anything like a quick-reaction force. In any case, Operation 'Market Garden' in 1944 (see p.137) had put paid to any chance that Britain would risk using paratroopers without a massive military back-up, and so the planning for seizing the canal was based on a six-week build-up. This was inevitable once British planners opted to use sixty squadrons of British and French planes, including a large fleet and a French battleship! It was to be a Victorian operation after all.

The slow build-up was the outcome of Treasury cutbacks in British military strength. For example, the Royal Air Force had just five squadrons of troop-carrying Hastings and Valetta aircraft, which – at a push and a squeeze – might have carried one parachute battalion. Moreover, the pre-war Hastings did not have the capacity to carry the army's Champ motor vehicle. As a result, an effort was made to retrace the jeeps that had been sold to Arabs as the British had withdrawn from the area. As many as possible were repurchased, painted and deemed ready for use.

Britain's aerial strike against Egypt would begin by neutralizing President Nasser's air force, after which a programme of psychological warfare would break the morale of Egypt's people. Like the famous 'Confetti War' carried out by Bomber Command in 1939-40, this was to cause great unease among

Britain's service chiefs. Moreover, this time Britain decided that bombing with leaflets alone – rather than bombs – might break the resolve of Egypt's fellahin. As most of them could not read the leaflets, pictures and cartoons were used to convey Britain's message. Most of all, however, Britain wanted to avoid memories of her 'area bombing' of Germany, and civilian casualties were to be avoided at all costs. The French thought this was a waste of time – which it was – when every day more countries joined the call in the United Nations for Britain and France to get out of Egypt.

The work of the Director of Psychological Warfare, Bernard Ferguson, might have been dreamed up by Evelyn Waugh and used in his novel, *Black Mischief*. Ferguson and his 24 assistants first occupied a broadcasting station in Cyprus to broadcast to Cairo. They also set up a printing press to prepare the leaflets which they hoped the RAF would drop for them. These leaflets, in bundles, were supposed to be 'exploded' at a thousand feet above the ground, so that the message of the 'great white queen' could gently fall upon the heads of the righteous. Unfortunately, the device which 'exploded' the bundles did not work properly, and many of them only exploded at head height, injuring people, while some bundles fell like bricks from the blue sky above, injuring even more. To the Egyptians they were every bit as dangerous as anything else which might fall from a clear blue sky. The leaflets were clearly dangerous and should be avoided at all costs.

Ferguson had a regular 'box of tricks', including his infamous 'voice-aircraft', which had served in Kenya against the Mau-Mau, and which flew over Egypt spreading the politico-economic arguments for Britain's possession of the Suez Canal to a baffled Arab people. In addition, the '24' prepared themselves to drive round in trucks equipped with loud-hailers, chanting 'Nasser out' and other memorable slogans. This aural assault on the enemy suffered a setback when, during a refuelling stopover at Aden, somebody stole the 'voice aircraft's' voice'. A further whimsicality concerned the anti-Nasser broadcasts that were being broadcast from Cyprus. Ferguson had chosen Palestinians to make the broadcasts, but to Egyptians their voices were suspiciously like those of Jews. The word soon spread among the Egyptians that Britain was employing Jews to abuse the name of their leader, Gamel Abdul Nasser, which finally put paid to the efforts of the 'psycho-warriors'.

In the last days of October 1956, Sir Anthony Eden was looking for a fig-leaf. He had nothing else to preserve his modesty after he had committed himself to reoccupying the canal. How could he do it without offending world opinion? The answer he came up with was a travesty of British 'honest diplomacy'. A secret meeting had taken place at Sèvres, outside Paris, between Britain, France and Israel, at which a plan had been concocted. Eden would claim to be concerned only with the safety of the canal which might be endangered if Israel invaded Egypt, which is exactly what Israel agreed to do if Britain promised to eliminate the Egyptian air force. Eden would publicly demand that both Egyptian and Israeli troops keep clear of the Suez Canal, which Britain would occupy to preserve it intact. If President Nasser refused to evacuate his troops from the Canal zone, which he was certain to do, Britain would then have a *casus belli*, and would then proceed to destroy Egypt's air force - and the world would look on and applaud. The French never believed a word of it, but were content to go along with Eden's search for decency.

On 29 October 1956 Israel crossed into Sinai, and Eden issued his ultimatum. Supported by Russia and the Eastern bloc, President Nasser refused to evacuate his troops from the Canal Zone. Britain now faced 'war-war' instead of 'jaw-jaw'. Her assessment of Egypt's strength – as just slightly less than the whole of Nazi Germany – was hopelessly unrealistic. One of Israel's senior commanders, General Moshe Dayan, later laughed at the enormity of Britain's preparations: 'Who did Britain think she was invading? The Soviet Union?' Events were soon to prove that Britain had grossly overestimated Egyptian strength and was indulging in overkill. Meanwhile, world support for Egypt was reaching overwhelming proportions at the United Nations.

Britain, with memories of the need to bomb Germany at night to counter the strength of German nightfighters and flak, decided to adopt the same approach against Egypt, on the assumption that the danger in the desert was much the same as over the Ruhr. The French were stupefied by Britain's caution. Meanwhile, Britain prepared to bomb Egypt's airfields. In spite of the fact that it was obvious to any informed source that Egypt's anti-aircraft defences were feeble, it was decided that Britain's Canberra bombers would operate by night. Incredibly, Britain allocated 48 hours to the destruction of the Egyptian air force and used 44 squadrons to destroy 260 aircraft on the ground. In the 1967 war, Israel was to destroy 300 Egyptian planes on the ground in just three hours. A joke at that time was that the Egyptian planes would be obsolescent before the British got round to attacking them. Perhaps that is what the British were hoping.

Apart from moving very slowly and acting under cover of night, the RAF now decided that bombs must be limited to 1000 pounds in weight, to reduce the risk of injury to civilians. Furthermore, to reduce casualties to an absolute minimum, it was decided to tell the Egyptians when the raids would be carried out. This was taking things a little too far, but was in keeping with the surreal atmosphere of the whole operation. Was Britain at war with Egypt? Apparently not, said the Prime Minister. But if Egyptians died in the ensuing raids had they been murdered, killed in action or what? The British never did make up their minds, so that captured British soldiers were later treated as murderers rather than legitimate prisoners-of-war.

Informing the enemy of the time you are going to attack their air bases could have been very costly, had the Egyptian flak defences been anywhere near as strong as was feared by the British commanders. Instead, the Egyptians responded with suitable discretion, many of their MIG fighters escaping to airfields in Syria and Saudi Arabia. An attempt by the British to bomb one of the Ilyushin bombers bases at Cairo West was called off because American civilians were being evacuated nearby. The British Canberras and Valiants were carrying small bombs and releasing them from a great height: it was more a demonstration on how to miss than to hit, with the airfields bearing the brunt of the attack rather than the enemy aircraft. Furthermore, with the British propaganda war in tatters – RAF crews refused to risk their lives carrying leaflets – the decision was taken not to bomb Radio Cairo, in case someone got hurt. As a result, the airwaves were filled with Islamic invective aimed against Britain, with stories of atrocities and mass civilian deaths. It was not for a couple of days that the British realized that radio Cairo was not in the middle of the city but fifteen miles away in the desert. It was promptly bombed and silenced, but by that time the damage was done.

This shambles of an air campaign eroded British morale to the extent that

British servicemen lost confidence in their reason for being in Egypt and wanted to return home. It hardly helped to hear that the Soviet Union was threatening to bombard London with missiles. In Britain, the health of the Prime Minister broke down and it was to relief all around, particularly to the aircrews of the RAF, that the decision was taken to pull out of Egypt. The air campaign had been a disaster. Most of all it was uncertain in purpose. Was the aim to keep Egypt and Israel from damaging the Canal, to help to overthrow Nasser, to defend the invasion fleet or to defend Israel from Russian bombers? Nobody – least of all the commanders – really knew. Although they had to destroy the Egyptian Air Force it had to be done without causing any casualties. In addition, Ferguson's Propaganda Unit had to destroy Egyptian morale by talking to a peasant community that had only just gained its colonial freedom from Britain and trusted the British even less than the Jews. If any of the air marshals in London had been able to find his way through this maze, he would have found himself facing one last and terrible decision: was Britain actually strong enough to defeat an Arab state equipped with Soviet arms? For some reason Britain believed Egypt to be a powerful military state with eastern-bloc advisers and perhaps even Soviet pilots. There was no evidence for any of these fears. Air intelligence must have been deplorable indeed if this was not known. After all, Britain had been responsible for training the Egyptian pilots and it was well known how poorly many of them performed.

The Israelis, though they needed the threat of Britain's aerial might rather than its reality, were amused by the ponderous approach Britain had adopted towards the whole affair. The British were prisoners of their Second World War experiences. They feared Egypt as they had once feared Germany. They refused to use airborne troops for a swift assault on the Canal because they were afraid of enduring another Arnhem. How they believed the Egyptians would provide the same kind of resistance as German panzer troops is a matter of some conjecture. Moshe Dayan, tongue in cheek, described the Allied operation: 'After a lengthy incubation, two chicks had finally burst through.'

SECRET AGENTS IN VIETNAM

Although the air war in Vietnam occasionally witnessed classic 'dog-fights' between Russian-made Mig fighters and the latest American fighters, equipped with state-of-the-art weaponry, it was fundamentally different from that which had taken place over Korea in the early 1950s. Never before had the quantitative and qualitative advantages enjoyed by one combatant been so minimized by the terrain. Ground support became intensely difficult and helicopter gunships took over much of this role from the jets. Meanwhile, the strategic bombers – B-52s – adopted 'area bombing' in a way that would have pleased Sir Arthur Harris. Unable to strike at heavy urban concentrations, they bombed the jungle with napalm in an attempt to destroy much of the environment in which Communist troops operated, but which was alien territory to American soldiers. Just as Harris failed to break the morale of the Germans between 1943 and 1945, so US strategic bombing campaigns did vast amounts of ecological damage without seriously damaging the Communist military potential. This tremendous demonstration of American power shocked the Vietnamese peasant soldiers without ever threatening to

diminish their efficiency. Instead, the United States scored an enormous 'own goal', the consequences of which are only now being fully appreciated.

Defoliants had been briefly used in warfare, by the British in the Malayan Emergency in the 1950s, but no power had ever possessed America's potential to destroy the food on which their enemy depended. From 1962, military pressure built up to begin a defoliation campaign. US Secretary of State Dean Rusk saw this as a blunder, 'The way to win the war basically is to win the people. Crop destruction runs counter to this basic rule' as it is impossible to differentiate friendly from enemy crops.

At first, defoliation was introduced carefully, to avoid harming friendly peasants, but mistakes soon proliferated as defoliant spread in the wind. By 1967 – during which year 1.7 million acres were sprayed – public disquiet was reaching epidemic proportions. The Vietcong claimed that the defoliant used by the Americans – Agent Orange – was not only poisonous but caused birth defects. Failing to research its own weapons adequately, the United States had been using chemical warfare, which was impossible to control. The health of American soldiers on the ground was also beginning to suffer. Significantly, American courts have made awards totalling over $200 million to 250,000 veterans who have suffered side effects from handling or using defoliants, or whose children have suffered genetic damage.

An American B-52 Superfortress on a bombing mission during the Vietnam War. Such aircraft were often used to carry out defoliation raids which besides their serious ecological effects also poisoned many American servicemen.

BLUE-ON-BLUE IN VIETNAM

The helicopter gunship was first used in Vietnam. However, that country's jungle terrain presented enormous difficulties for rotary bladed aircraft to be employed effectively. Observation was almost impossible for crew looking down onto the jungle's green ceiling, which also shrouded enemy missile batteries and anti-aircraft guns. The helicopter's slow speed and hovering capability made it an excellent platform for ground support, but also made it vulnerable to enemy attack. Moreover, the helicopters carried with them a special kind of danger, particularly for the ground troops they were supposed to be supporting. They frequently misidentified their targets, leading to many cases of 'friendly fire' or 'blue-on-blue', as the Americans term it. Human error is always part of the problem, but the helicopter's rotary blade and its proneness to instability in high winds often provided mechanical explanations.

On 27 August 1967 a CH-47 helicopter was offering ground support for men from the 12th US Infantry Regiment, who were in contact with Communist forces. As the helicopter flew over a company of the 2nd Battalion its door-gunner was shot and killed by enemy fire. But the gunner was in the act of firing as he was killed and his grip on the trigger tightened in death, so that he sprayed bullets onto the friendly troops below, causing numerous injuries. Even stranger was the incident when a fractured traverse rod on a door gun caused the helicopter gunner to fire into his own cockpit, wounding the pilot. During August 1969, near the town of Pleiku, a UH-1H helicopter flown by an inexperienced aircrew on their first flight responded to a command from the pilot to fire on some smoke rising above the trees. The helicopter went into action without any attempt at identifying the target and fired straight into an American unit. In 1971, another UH-1H helicopter was shot down by American infantry from the Fire Support Base Mary Ann, near Chu Lai. Indiscipline was the major cause of this disaster, in which the ground troops may have engaged the helicopter 'for a lark'. It is difficult to understand how intentional 'friendly fire' is possible, but the standard of discipline among American troops in Vietnam was not always very secure.

Helicopters were by no means alone in causing 'friendly fire' incidents. Fixed-wing aircraft frequently strafed and bombed 'friendly' troops. Confusion over marker flares was widespread. One unit of the (South) Vietnamese Civilian Irregular Defence Group marked its position in the undergrowth by using green smoke. Two B-57 fighters were called in to give ground support but one of them strafed the wrong target and managed to hit 'friendly' troops, killing four men and wounding 28. The reason for this mistake was not just poor visibility but pilot confusion.

During 1968 a Forward Air Controller, overseeing the mission of an F-4D aircraft armed with an M-117 bomb, marked a target just over 200 yards from 'friendly' troops. The target was too tight for marking, particularly as the 'friendlies' had put up no smoke for guidance and the Controller's guidance rocket went 75 yards west of the intended target. The pilot now made two errors of his own. He misinterpreted the position of the 'friendly' troops and incorrectly estimated the position of the target, which lay between the 'friendlies' and the inaccurate rocket guide. The result was that the bomb landed squarely in the middle of the US troops, killing three men and wounding twelve others.

Nobody likes to suggest that 'friendly fire' is ever intentional. Yet there can be no doubt that in Vietnam human irresponsibility played a substantial part in these tragedies. Many American servicemen were responsible for drug- or drink-related carelessness while on active service and this applied as much to pilots and air crew as to ground troops. Sometimes it would be kinder to refer to over-exuberance and youthful high spirits, as was common among some First World War pilots. Whatever the cause, Vietnam was to witness the beginnings of 'friendly fire' – or amicide - as a major cause of American battle casualties.

A PAINTED SHIP UPON A PAINTED OCEAN

Britain fought the Falklands War of 1982 blindfold. She was punished for playing blind-man's-buff by suffering more casualties in ships and – later – in men, than she need have done. Against a more active and tactically able opponent, Britain might well have lost the war, before her troops had even set foot on the Falklands.

Sending the Task Force to the South Atlantic in the full knowledge that it would face an apparently overwhelming drawback – the lack of Airborne Early Warning – and therefore would suffer unnecessary losses to Argentina's far larger air force, was a political decision of the worst kind. Prime Minister Thatcher's decision was fuelled by patriotic anger and desire for revenge coupled with an unrealistic appreciation of Britain's military strength in the 1980s. At the outset of the Falklands War 20 British Sea Harriers would be all that stood between the Task Force and well over a hundred modern Argentinian Mirage III, Dagger, Super-Etendard and Skyhawk fighter-bombers. A saturation attack on the fleet would in all likelihood have resulted in the loss of one or both of the aircraft carriers and the end of the campaign.

Without AEW (Airborne Early Warning) the British were forced to improvise - a British habit in wartime though not so much of a virtue as is sometimes claimed. As the Task Force sailed south in April 1982 many experienced officers could not believe that some arrangement had not been made with the Americans to provide early warning (it had not). It was simply an invitation to a major air power – and the Argentinians qualified as that in the context of South American warfare – to saturate the British defences. The British Task Force was, in fact, less well equipped in this department than any similar British force would have been in the previous 30 years. The general belief was that the politicians were getting themselves into a war which could go terribly wrong.

Operating basically in coastal waters the British ships, without AEW, would be susceptible to low-level attacks over the land which would mask the approach of incoming aircraft. This problem was to occur again and again, and was partly responsible for the loss of the *Sir Galahad* off Bluff Cove. The effectiveness of the Super Etendards with Exocet missiles might have been reduced if, through AEW, it had been possible to shoot down the aircraft before they fired their missiles, instead of trying to destroy the missile in flight. With a mere 20 Sea Harriers to provide early warning of air strikes there was a danger of these versatile planes being overburdened by both reconnaissance and fighting duties. As a result, warships were placed on 'picket duty', far ahead of the rest of the Task Force and acting as a first line of defence, though themselves uncov-

H.M.S. Sheffield on fire after being struck by an Exocet missile fired by an Argentinian Super-Etendard aircraft on 4 May 1982. The absence of Airborne Early Warning meant that destroyers and frigates of the Task Force had to take up dangerous advanced positions to give early warning of air attack, a policy that cost Britain both ships and lives.

ered by the main missile defences of the fleet. It was a lonely and dangerous task which led to the loss of or damage to several destroyers and frigates, notably the *Sheffield*, hit by an Exocet missile, and the *Coventry*.

For Britons watching the war on the television, one of the most terrible memories was the graphic coverage of the disaster at Bluff Cove, when the *Sir Galahad* was hit by incoming Argentinian warplanes and set ablaze. This showed the bitter reality of war against which the politicians must necessarily steel themselves if they are ever to use war as a part of their policy. But, like many disasters in wartime, the *Sir Galahad* disaster should never have happened. It was the result of a series of blunders ranging from minor decisions taken by junior officers to major strategical errors perpetrated by political and military leaders. As we have seen, the absence of AEW removed Britain's capacity to anticipate surprise air attacks. In fact, it added the element of 'surprise' to those attacks.

The loss of Britain's Chinook helicopters when the merchant carrier *Atlantic Conveyor* was sunk forced the British ground commander, Sir Jeremy Moore, to transport much of 5 Brigade by amphibious transport. Originally the two assault ships *Intrepid* and *Fearless* were supposed to carry the Scots and Welsh Guards, but the bad weather and the risk of air attack made Moore change his mind. Reluctantly, he agreed to use the civilian-manned landing ships and on 7 June units of the Welsh Guards boarded the LSL (Landing Ship Logistical) *Sir Galahad* to be transported to the Fitzroy Settlement to the west of Port Stanley. Aboard her, as well as the Welsh Guards, was 16 Field Ambulance, with all their equipment.

Nobody ashore at Fitzroy or Bluff Cove was aware that the *Sir Galahad* was on its way and there were no aerial defences to cover the disembarkation of the troops she was carrying. But the Argentinian aircraft had been notable by their absence for several days and an unfortunate air of complacency existed among some officers. The senior Guard's officer aboard *Sir Galahad* insisted that his men did not want to be landed at Fitzroy but at Bluff Cove, saving them a twelve-mile march. He therefore insisted that landing-craft be brought alongside *Sir Galahad* so that his men could be taken to his chosen destination. However, the sight of the vessel in broad daylight, anchored of the coast was too much for several of the Marine beach officers at Fitzroy. She was just asking to be bombed. They commandeered a landing-craft that was unloading ammunition from the *Sir Tristram* and was half-filled with explosives and hurried over to *Sir Galahad*, calling on the Welsh Guards to disembark immediately. But the Guards' officers refused, partly because it was against regulations to mix troops with ammunition, and partly because they wanted to land at Bluff Cove, not Fitzroy. Marine Major Southby-Tailyour, one of the officers who had commandeered the landing-craft, went ashore to convince the 5 Brigade staff that there was going to be a disaster. At first the staff officers refused to believe there could be any troops aboard *Sir Galahad*. When Southby-Tailyour convinced them, they rushed off to try to set up anti-aircraft Rapier missiles to defend the ship in case it was attacked.

Orders went out to the landing-craft to get the Welsh Guards off the *Sir Galahad*. But aboard the LSL a decision had been taken that was to ensure disaster. The Guards' officers had agreed to allow the field ambulance personnel with their equipment to take precedence over the troops and land first at Fitzroy. Meanwhile, the guardsmen, unaware of their grave danger, watched videos or leaned against the rails of the ship enjoying the peaceful scenery.

At just after 13.10 hours four aircraft streaked across the sky towards *Sir Galahad*. Ground fire from the troops ashore was subdued when someone identified them as Harriers. In fact, they were two Mirages and two Skyhawks.

Before anyone could take shelter aboard the LSL bombs were exploding on her decks and deep inside her, igniting petrol stores and white phosphorus bombs, which inflicted terrible burns on the soldiers. Air defence was now far too late. All that was left was rescue and helicopters and landing craft now rushed to the succour of the stricken *Sir Galahad*.

In wartime it is recognized that calculated risks must be taken. As we have seen, the whole war was a 'calculated risk'. But the *Sir Galahad* was not a 'calculated risk' at all, it was a blunder. Allowing a ship carrying troops to anchor just off the coast, without any aircraft cover, without airborne early warning of any kind, and even without a ring of surface-to-air missiles was unforgivably lax. The Royal Navy acknowledged its mistakes in allowing the *Sir Galahad* to sail around to Fitzroy with inadequate protection. But what they could not understand was why there were any troops still on board at the time when it was attacked. There had been a breakdown in communication between all three services, but the threat of Argentinian aircraft should still have acted as a warning to everyone about the dangers of being caught without aerial defences. The Welsh Guards' officers should have insisted on getting ashore at Fitzroy as an absolute priority. Never mind the twelve-mile march or even the medical supplies of the Field Hospital – men's lives came first. The location of the *Sir Galahad*'s anchorage was an invitation to the enemy to score an easy kill. As Admiral Woodward later commented, 'I have no doubt that they [the

Argentinian pilots] could scarcely believe their luck: "Bluff Cove – no hills, no cliffs, no escorts, no Rapier – no problem. Excelente.'"

The Fitzroy 'massacre' cost Britain more than fifty lives, with 57 men badly burned. It should never have happened. It did so because too many people were complacent. Too many junior officers made the wrong decisions or took short cuts. Above all, however, it happened because the Task Force lacked the capacity to give early warning of air attack. The troops aboard *Sir Galahad* might have done more to help themselves, it is true, but those in command of air defence should have stressed to every British soldier the limitations of their own power. It is never wise to underestimate the enemy. Those who do often pay for their errors in blood.

BRIDGING THE GULF WAR, 1991

As military technology advances, we are told, weapons become smarter. They are even more destructive than before, but it seems now they are more careful about it. They leave less mess to tidy up. One awaits with trepidation the first 'green' weapon, environmentally friendly but fatal to humans . . . As these weapons become smarter, we learn, they are less likely to make mistakes, like killing their own men instead of the enemy, or identifying civilian air raid shelters as enemy control centres, or confusing baby milk factories with nerve gas centres. And as we gulp in amazement at man's destructive ingenuity we believe what we read in the newspapers, or are told on television by war correspondents briefed by the commanders to disseminate the accepted line of how the war is progressing. For centuries it has been known that the first casualty in any war is the truth, but five years on from the Gulf War one can only respond with incredulity to learn that the Patriot missile – that prime-time television favourite – was in fact a complete dud. Rather than saving Israel and Saudi Arabia from the evil Saddam's Scud peril, it was no more effective than a firework, illuminating the night sky, reassuring millions of American and European viewers that all was well with the lads in the desert but offering less security to Israel than a stone from David's sling. Far from bringing down the majority of Iraq's Scud missiles, the latest research shows that the Patriot failed to stop a single one.

SCUDS

The failure of the Patriot missile was far less significant than the fact that it was needed at all. American intelligence knew everything there was to know about the Iraqi military machine and was aware of the Scud missile, for all its limitations. And, knowing Saddam Hussein for the ruthless killer he was, the Americans must have suspected that he would launch Scuds against Israel in an attempt to break up the coalition against him. Failing that he would use the Scuds with nerve- or biological-warheads against the Coalition troops. In fact, he did both, but we will come to that later. As a result, one might have supposed that Colin Powell and his advisers would have made the Scud threat top priority. Instead the Americans ridiculed the Scud - who thought up that name? - such a dumb weapon compared to their smart, politically correct and ethnically-named 'Tomahawk' missile. Norman Schwarzkopf publicly declared that the Scud had no military value. It was definitely of 'Cold War' vintage, and low-tech, like a flying Lada car.

DUMB WEAPONS

Can 'smart' weapons overcome the disadvantage of being launched by 'dumb humans'? And if not, do they suddenly become 'dumb' weapons? On at least two occasions during the Gulf War 'smart' weapons behaved in a way that nobody would consider smart. In the first case, Stealth bombers mistook a public air raid shelter in the Amiriya district of Baghdad for an Iraqi military bunker, killing 300 women and children. In the second case, bombs were just not 'smart' enough to tell the difference between The Baghdad Baby Milk Factory and a chemical warfare establishment, before blowing it to pieces. Later investigations disproved Washington's assertion that the factory was involved in chemical warfare. It just goes to show that you cannot trust 'smart' weapons. Or are we missing something?

DESERT BLUE-ON-BLUE

On February 26 1991, the second day of the ground war, the desert of western Iraq was covered with hundreds of Coalition tanks, as well as thousands of other armoured vehicles, heading north and east to outflank the Iraqi defences in Kuwait. Heavy Iraqi tank concentrations awaited them in fortified positions. Above them all flew swarms of American jet fighters, raptor-like, looking for their prey scuttling across the sand thousands of feet below. The problem of identification was a very real one. Yet in an age of high-tech warfare the pilots of the fighters were trained in identification and were covered by various fail-safe systems to prevent 'friendly-fire' incidents. The fact that many such incidents would occur during the Gulf War was just further proof, if it was needed, that war was no perfect science, and mechanical systems are only as good as the humans who operated them.

According to initial reports of what happened next on 26 February, around 15.00 hours and in very bad weather and poor visibility, two British Warrior Infantry Fighting Vehicles (IFVs) of 'C' Company of the Royal Regiment of Fusiliers were attacked by American A-10 tankbuster aircraft firing Maverick missiles. During the attack nine British soldiers were killed. The fog of war, or in this case the rain, the high winds and the sandstorms were reported to the grieving parents by the Colonel-in-Chief of the Fusiliers, H.R.H. the Duke of Kent, as being responsible for the tragedy. As a description of what really happened this was simply not true. In fact, if the weather was being advanced as an explanation of why an error had occurred the whole report smacked of a cover-up for, at 15.00 hours on February 26, the bad weather of the previous night had passed. The sun shone brightly, the wind had dropped and visibility was perfect. And yet the Americans had still mistakenly fired on the Warrior IFVs. The parents of nine young soldiers deserved to know why. But would they get an explanation? After all, this war had been presented to the public as a clean war, characterized by surgical precision. Blunders of this kind might undermine public confidence in the military as well as damage Anglo-American relations at a crucial moment in the war.

There are many people—soldiers, politicians and diplomats—who know what really happened to the British IFVs that February afternoon, yet so far none of them has been allowed to 'come clean'. As a result, any description of the events that took place can only make use of limited evidence. There had already been other examples of 'friendly fire' before the Warrior catastrophe, notably during the recapture of the town of Khafji, where a group of US marines in an armoured personnel carrier had been attacked and killed by American aircraft. As a result, the commanders had adopted an identification system for ground troops when seen from the air. Orange and green recognition panels were used for allied vehicles with huge inverted V markers—at least six feet in height—painted on the sides of tanks and on their turrets. The system was tested for aerial visibility and thought to be effective. Naturally, poor weather conditions could always hinder recognition, but at the outset of the fighting both General Norman Schwarzkopf and Britain's General Peter de la Billière were satisfied that friendly casualties could be minimized if not entirely eradicated.

What happened to the Fusiliers in their Warriors is difficult to piece together, as none of those who hold the full evidence want the truth to be revealed. By mid-afternoon, it would appear, and in perfect weather and good visibility, the tanks and armoured vehicles of the British 1st Armoured Division had already accomplished their first task – which was to destroy Iraqi tanks at a point code-named Objective Brass – and had headed off towards their second target, Objective Steel. Warrior IFVs accompanied the Challenger battle tanks to provide infantry back-up, clearing trenches and mopping up knots of Iraqi resistance. At the head of the 3rd Battalion of the 4th Armoured Brigade were the vehicles of 'C' Company, with 8 platoon commanded by Lieutenant Brett Duxbury in the lead. On arrival at Steel, it was found that the Iraqis had fled and no enemy fire was experienced. The four lead Warrior IFVs drew up about fifty metres from the empty Iraqi gun emplacements. While the engineers blew up the Iraqi guns, the young Fusiliers disembarked from their IFVs to relieve themselves or have a smoke, but once the charges were primed everyone was ordered back inside their vehicles in case of casualties from shrapnel. No sooner had the men returned to their vehicles than one was ripped apart by an explosion. Inside the stricken IFV shells and grenades were exploding and four men were already dead, with others grievously wounded. As Lieutenant Duxbury raced to help get the survivors out of the burning IFV, he ordered a second Warrior, Callsign 23, to close in to give further help, but as it did so it too was struck by a huge explosion, killing five of its occupants and wounding others. To British onlookers, it seemed most likely that the Iraqis were mounting a counter-attack. But, in fact, there were no enemy troops within firing distance. The IFVs had been struck by two Maverick missiles fired by either one or two American A-10 tankbuster aircraft. Some of the Fusiliers present claimed they had seen a single A-10 flying low, which gave a 'victory waggle' of its wings after scoring two hits, others claim there were two A-10s at high altitude – American reports speak of 8000 feet – while still other Fusiliers claim to have picked up the pilot's report of his error on their radio.

A-10 tankbusters were specialist aircraft, designed to provide close support for ground troops in action against enemy tanks and in the desert pilots enjoyed better visibility than on any other type of battle terrain. In fact, the desert was a perfect killing ground, as long as pilots were careful to identify their targets before they fired. In good weather conditions and where coalition units were not in direct combat with active Iraqi ones, there should have been no errors. Yet, on 26 February 1991, the pilots of possibly two A-10s made serious and costly mistakes in identification.

The A-10s involved in the 'blue-on-blue' had apparently taken off at midday on February 26 and had initially encountered the fag-end of the bad weather that the units of the British 1st Armoured Division had reported, but soon after refuelling from an air tanker they reported that the clouds were clearing and visibility was good. Once they were fuelled they contacted the air controller in one of the AWACS Boeings, whose job was to find them a target. For two hours he failed to find them one and they were growing bored and frustrated. Their adrenalin had boosted them to fight, but they simply could not find anything or anyone to fire at. They were then ordered to contact a forward air controller, who happened to be a British officer and who was handling the air-ground support in the area of the British 1st Armoured Division. At this moment something happened that may have contributed to the eventual tragedy. As well as contacting the British air controller, the A-10 pilots also got talking to an F-16 fighter pilot, who suggested they go looking for the target he had just attacked. He told them to look for a crossroads, but the desert in that area was crisscrossed with roads and they could not have been certain as to which of these the F-16 was referring. Nevertheless, the two A-10s found a suitable crossroads, complete with smoking vehicles and apparently 'juicy' targets. According to both pilots, their attack on these Iraqi targets was unsuccessful and so they both flew south – presumably even more frustrated – until they came upon a target consisting of about 50 vehicles. They claimed that the British air controller had assured them that there were no friendly vehicles within ten kilometres of their area of operations. Whatever the truth of this, their next step should have been to identify these targets by using the binoculars with which each pilot was equipped. According to the official American version the pilots claimed that they identified the vehicles below as Iraqi by using these binoculars and passing over the target twice to ensure correct identification. They were adamant that there were no coalition markings on the vehicles they attacked. There was nothing now to prevent them from attacking the vehicles below, which they were convinced were Iraqi T54/55 tanks and not the much smaller British Warrior IFVs.

How was this misidentification possible? The most obvious difference between the two vehicles is the size of the turret cannon. The 30mm cannon of the Warrior is short, stubby, and in length hardly reaches the end of the vehicle's body. In contrast the long, heavy gun of the T54/55 projects far ahead of the main body, showing itself in outline to be the main armament of a heavy battle tank. In other respects—size, outline, profile, tracks—the two vehicles are utterly dissimilar. But—above all—the Warriors were carrying brightly coloured fluorescent sheets as well as large, freshly painted V identification signs. Bearing in mind that the American pilots were, as a last resort, able to use high powered binoculars for final identification it is hard to understand how confusion was possible in such good weather conditions.

The news of the 'blue-on-blue' had serious implications for the progress of the war. The British commander, General Sir Peter de la Billière, was aware

The infamous Gulf War 'friendly fire' incident on 26 February 1991 in which two American A-10 tankbusters fired on British Warrior IFVs of the 3rd Battalion, Regiment of Fusiliers, killing nine British soldiers.

that he had a vital political as well as a military duty. Unity of purpose between the United States and Britain was absolutely essential. Any breach of Anglo-American relations could have been exploited by the Iraqis to weaken the resolve of the entire coalition and so this particular blue-on-blue, tragic and wasteful as it was, would have to be played down. Unfortunately, while de la Billière was able to smooth things over with Norman Schwarzkopf, matters were more difficult with the US air chief, Chuck Horner, who 'became deeply emotional, and could not agree that the issue needed to be left open until a formal investigation had been carried out'. He simply insisted that there was no case to answer as the fault lay entirely with the British air controller and no blame attached to the A-10 pilots. His defence of his airmen was emotional and could not be justified by the facts. In spite of the magnificent performance by the vast majority of US airmen, there had been a number of 'friendly fire' incidents involving loss of life and the responsibility for most of these rested fairly and squarely on the shoulders of some of Horner's pilots. So eager was Horner to defend his corner that he even resorted to blaming mines for the incident. It was clear that Horner intended to stand by his own men at whatever the cost. From that point until today, as de la Billière records, 'the USAF were not in line with our interpretation of events'.

There are many unanswered questions concerning this 'blue-on-blue' tragedy and neither the British nor the American authorities have been prepared to help solve them. There is an obvious conflict of evidence. Of the three men who knew the truth at the time of the incident, the British air controller and the two American pilots, the former has claimed that before being contacted by the two A-10s he had already given target grid references to American planes which had successfully attacked Iraqi armour some 20 kilometres to the east of the British Warrior APCs. He asserts that he gave the same grid references to the two American pilots involved in the blue-on-blue, something that they both deny. The British Board of Inquiry was told by the air controller that he had also issued a code word with the grid reference to reassure the American pilots that they were not being fed information by Iraqi intelligence. Curiously, the two pilots deny receiving such a code word and furthermore claim not to know its significance. This conflict of evidence is so wide that one is left with no other conclusion than that someone is lying as part of a cover-up.

Without a full knowledge of the conversation between the pilots and the air controller we cannot tell at this stage what really happened. However, even if the air controller gave neither code word nor grid reference, how could the pilots have misidentified the Warrior IFVs as T54/55 tanks and have claimed that they carried no markings? Apparently, once the A-10s had carried out their attack on the Warriors they informed the air controller of the grid reference which showed him for the first time that they had attacked a friendly force. He ordered an American reconnaissance plane to overfly the area and received the significant report that, 'fluorescent air recognition panels could be seen from 6,000 feet and the type of vehicles could be identified from 14,000 feet.' This report would seem to demolish the claims by American commanders that dust and sand could have obscured identification signs and perhaps even made the shapes of the vehicles difficult to identify. What is possible, of course, is that some of the Warrior IFVs could have become dirtied by sand or dust, and some others perhaps lost their fluorescent panels in the wind, but so many vehicles in close proximity do not all suffer identical mishaps and transform themselves in shape into T54/55 tanks. General Horner himself is on record as saying that American pilots had been instructed 'If in doubt, don't drop.' How was it possible for the two pilots to fail to identify any of the hundreds of identifying panels and signs on the Warriors or notice the many other vehicles of the 3rd Battalion of the 7th British Armoured Brigade spread out across a perfectly flat plain? The desert was swarming with British vehicles, all thoroughly equipped with coloured panels and inverted 'V's, as was apparent from television film shown only minutes after the attack.

Conclusive evidence does, of course, exist. Audio and video recordings are kept of conversations between air controllers and pilots as well as the pictures of targets as seen by the aircraft's weapons system. Thus the conflict of evidence between the two A-10 pilots and the British air controller could easily be resolved by the production of this material. The fact that it has not been produced in public indicates that a cloak of secrecy has been drawn over this particular incident. If the British Ministry of Defence has seen the videos and heard the recordings then it has become part of the American cover-up.

Certainly, the authorities in the United States have gone to some lengths to conceal details of 'friendly-fire' incidents in the Gulf War, of which there were many. At least 35 US servicemen died as a result of 'blue-on-blue' incidents and, significantly, casualty reports that use the phrase 'hit by friendly fire' have been altered at high level by a handwritten 'vehicle hit by enemy fire'.

Truth may be the first victim in wartime, so that it may offer no help to the enemy, but there is no reason why that should continue to be the case once the war has ended. In the case of the widespread illness known as 'Gulf War syndrome' many men and women who served in the Gulf must question who their real enemy was – Saddam Hussein or the secrecy of their own government.

INDEX

GENERAL